PLAYING

contemporary

SCENES

Thirty-One Famous Scenes and How to Play Them

GERALD LEE RATLIFF

MERIWETHER PUBLISHING LTD.
Colorado Springs, Colorado

Meriwether Publishing Ltd., Publisher
P.O. Box 7710
Colorado Springs, CO 80933

Editor: Theodore O. Zapel
Typesetting: Sharon E. Garlock
Cover design: Tom Myers

Library of Congress Cataloging-in-Publication Data

Ratliff, Gerald Lee.
    Playing contemporary scenes : thirty-one famous scenes and how to
play them / Gerald Lee Ratliff. -- 1st ed.
        p.   c.m.
    Includes bibliographical references.
    Summary: A collection of scenes from plays by contemporary
playwrights, divided into several age groups and accompanied by
performance hints and exercises.
    ISBN 1-56608-025-8 (pbk.)
    1. Acting--Juvenile literature. 2. Drama--20th century.
    [1. Acting.   2. Plays.]   I. Title.
PN2080.R38   1996
792'.028--dc20   96-36394
                                                                CIP
                                                                 AC

2   3   4   5   6   7   8   03   02   01   00   99

CONTENTS

"My dismal scene I needs must act alone!"

— Romeo and Juliet
William Shakespeare

*For Harvey Kelly, Larry L. Life, and Laura Woodson —
friends all! — who share the burden as well as the bounty
of the creative imagination; and happily engage its
many premises and promises.*

PHOTOGRAPHS

All photographs in this scene study book are from faculty and student productions at Montclair State College and Montana State University that are part of the Mainstage Theatre Series. I am deeply indebted to the kindness and the support of Joanne Owens, Managing Director of the Mainstage Theatre Series, for use of the theatre library and the production files in framing both the selected scenes as well as the descriptive photographs. This sourcebook would also not have been possible without the high quality performance and production approaches of the faculty and students that provided the inspiration for this publication.

PREFACE

"Everything in the labor of art amounts to one thing: the difficult should become customary, the customary easy and the easy — beautiful!

— Stanislavsky

The fundamental performance principle that brings together this sourcebook for playing contemporary scenes is not at all simple and may, at other times, appear to resist more traditional approaches to playscript interpretation and scene study. What does it mean to be an inventive, imaginative actor; and what is an appropriate blueprint for the contemporary theatre that will promote the intricacies of playing the role and playing the scene to accurately distinguish the art of performance? These are the intriguing questions that leap to mind at once — and return again periodically throughout the pages of this sourcebook — as I cast about for the most direct prefatory remarks to this volume. And they are questions that, hopefully, I may be able to answer here by way of a few observations.

An actor is a creative artist and the most essential ingredient of acting is informed imagination. It should be obvious to the conscientious actor that the wider the range of life experiences and personal examples from which to draw, the more authentic and sensitive the potential performance portrait is likely to be; and, consequently, the most inspired and inventive the creation. The initial challenge, therefore, is for the actor to discover a "method" in the madness of this mimetic art and to cultivate a performance style that has a simplicity as well as a sincerity that is truly *self* expressive.

In the introductory chapters of the sourcebook attention is given to performance "theory," especially the critical skills needed to read a playscript with a keen and discerning eye toward an informed performance. The basic principles of playing the role and playing the scene call special attention to the essential details needed for a studied investigation of the dramatic and theatrical elements inherent in "visualizing" a playscript in performance; and there is a fundamental discussion of the primary vocal and physical techniques necessary to create and sustain a believable role in performance. The guide-lines and strategies suggested in the introductory chapters lay a convenient foundation for defining the general characteristics of an imaginative, self-expressive performance approach; and point out performance possibilities that may help to translate the theory of role-playing into actual "practice." The introduc-tory chapters also anticipate the actor's potential for achieving fresh, original character interpretations that are concerned with the depiction of current events and everyday happenings.

There are four individual chapters devoted to the primary age ranges discussed in the sourcebook and they include youth and young men or women (Chapter 4, ages 13-19 years); young adult men (Chapter 5, ages 23-29 years); young adult women (Chapter 6, ages 23-29 years); and adult men or women (Chapter 7, 35 years or more). Each individual chapter recognizes the special needs of the age ranges included and the representative scenes included offer a wide spectrum of performance styles to pursue in terms of vocal and physical interpretation. There are also a number of performance clues and performance objectives suggested to help the actor achieve a viable, believable stage portrait. In addition, detailed opportunities are presented to encourage the actor in a successful search for the bodily actions and gestures that will allow the character to effectively commu-nicate meaningful emotions or thoughts; and to integrate appropriate personal traits and mannerisms that might give depth and dimension to the character portrait in performance.

There are a number of special features in the sourcebook that should suggest an imaginative framework for the actor to practice the performance demands in the rehearsal period devoted to exercises and improvisations. Chapter 8, for example, explores the basic theatrical techniques associated with the audi-tion or the "call back," and suggests an orderly system of preparation that will address any possible try-out scenario. There is also a discussion that includes an interesting perspec-tive on the actor's need to cultivate an indescribable "life spirit" in the audition process so that what is seen and heard is honest, natural, spontaneous, and familiar. Representative contempo-rary monologs — in varying age ranges — are also included as potential audition material the actor might select for perfor-mance. A brief character description is also provided to indicate the performance possibilities that may be explored in rehearsal.

The discussion of rehearsal period exercises and improvisations, in Chapter 9, is especially useful in promoting a fun, relaxed approach to contemporary performance. The exercises and improvisations each have different theoretical goals and performance expectations which must be satisfied if the actor is to enjoy a memorable and rewarding rehearsal experience! In addition, a sample rehearsal playscript of Eugene Ionesco's *The Gap* is provided to test the actor's economy and efficiency in realizing the stated performance objectives in each of the exercises and improvisations. The sample rehearsal playscript should encourage original inventions and fresh interpretations to add individuality to subsequent stage characterizations. The actor should also be sure to set aside ample rehearsal time for the exercises devoted to vocal and physical warm-ups to promote personal growth and development as well as individual artistic and creative discipline.

The scenes, revue sketches, and monologs selected for inclusion in the sourcebook include a number of historical, theatrical periods that range from the early absurd sketches of Harold Pinter to the much more contemporary dramas, comedies, and satires of such distinguished playwrights as David Mamet, Christopher Durang, Horton Foote, Wendy Wasserstein, Paula Vogel, Richard Greenberg, James McLure, Steve Martin, Larry Shue, and Mark Medoff; and "new voice" contemporary playwrights Bruce Graham, John Wooten, Ludmilla Bollow, Rich Orloff, and Jack Heifner that are sure to please. In addition, there is an exciting range of audition monologs that feature such notable playwrights as Samuel Beckett, Albert Innaurato, and Patrick Meyers; and noteworthy newcomers to the monolog tradition like Sandra Fenichel Asher, Pamela Mills, Anna Deavers Smith, and Jane Wagner. The term "contemporary" is used here to suggest those scenes, revue sketches, or monologs that appear to best exemplify the general characteristics of performance, without regard to publication date, that are discussed in Chapters 2 and 3. The chronological period, for example, may vary from the early modern (1956) that includes the work of Eugene Ionesco to the most current period of theatre performance history (1995). It is also important to point out that the basic premise of the sourcebook is concerned with fresh, original interpretations of characters that appear to be flesh-and-blood, real-life stage figures; and in that respect a number of the selections included may feature just the type of character chosen from an earlier period of theatre that might *not*, at first glance, have been anticipated. A very special mention as well to the Departments of Theatre at Montclair State University and Montana State University for supporting photographs.

Now that there has been some preview of the basic theoretical principles pursued in the sourcebook, only one more question remains to be answered. What is the most appropriate performance use of these scenes, revue sketches, and monologs? It is to, finally, encourage every beginning or experienced actor to explore individual self-expression and to come to creative grips with personal performance behavior; to work diligently through rehearsal exercises to transform personal identity into inventive and imaginative stage characterizations; and then to return again to one's simple, natural self. There is nothing more fundamental to performance — and to learning — than the *desire* to "know" and, more importantly, to "understand" that the actor is a creative artist and that the most essential ingredient of acting is disciplined rehearsal. Remember that the stature of a true artist is measured by an ability to know and to understand one's own life; and to share that knowledge and experience with others who may not be as gifted in their observations of life and living. Dare to seek the truth, and share that truth with others in your performance as an actor/artist who sees with the mind, thinks with the eye, and feels with the soul. Until this philosophical prelude to performance becomes intuitive and instinctive, the actor will never be the true master of either art or life.

Gerald Lee Ratliff

April, 1996

CHAPTER ONE

BEGINNING PERFORMANCE APPROACHES

"Do not just invent something, but make something out of reality."
— Thomas Mann

There really is no such person as a "beginning actor." We have *all* been "inventing" or "impersonating" more or less instinctively — and in some cases incessantly! — from early childhood. Our youthful and adolescent role-playing games of "let's pretend," "what if," and "make believe" have provided the basic performance ingredients essential to assume imaginary roles, script creative storylines, and voice original dialog in any contemporary theatrical playscript. Our intrigues, deceptions, and disguises have given us the primary tools to convince an audience of listeners or spectators that what "might have been" is, indeed, "what was." And our repeated improvisations, spontaneous actions, and flights of fantasy have given us the advanced training necessary to sustain theatrical images and illusions.

Any serious, mature study of acting, however, suggests that there must be more involved in this imaginative art form than mere invention; that it must involve degrees of skill as well as multiple methods of performance technique. Indeed, the successful contemporary performer's approach to acting *is* carefully orchestrated and has its most profound impact when the actor possesses a well-defined acting technique, a unique method of character creation, and an honest and believable performance blueprint that is at once both consistent and competent. "One of the worst things that can happen to a beginning actor," says the outspoken playwright David Mamet, "is to [think]...that there is no such thing as technique; that there is no need to study; that the only way to learn is through *doing*. This attitude creates in the performer a necessary interest in 'knownothingism,' which denies the very existence of both technique and aesthetics."

But contemporary playscripts vary significantly in both form and content, so how does the serious actor discover an individual, unique approach to performance with so many different performance styles and techniques available in the creation and development of a character? The one common denominator that each of us brings to our understanding of contemporary performance is our own individual, collective awareness and attentiveness to the role that drama plays in sharpening our perceptions and arousing our deeper emotions so that we may examine our own lives more objectively in order to give our creative, subjective character development more depth and dimension. By probing beneath the surface of the lives of our fictional characters we also frequently discover our own inner conflicts, hidden desires, or frustrated passions; and these provide the dramatic insight and inspiration needed to convincingly portray a role in performance.

The art of performance, however, is more than the objective examination of our *own* lives in order to promote a more inspired, individual stage characterization; it also involves an ability to project ourselves into imaginary circumstances, interior psychological states of mind, and complex vocal or physical techniques that reveal how we are "different" from one another as well. And it is the inherent difference — what the poet Alexander Pushkin calls our "creative individuality" — that most clearly distinguishes and defines our performance *aptitude* and *ability*.

First Principles

Before proceeding to a theoretical and performance blueprint for contemporary playscripts, it is necessary to point out some of the first principles you should be aware of in your initial approach to the creation and development of a three-dimensional character. *First*, you must be an "informed" actor. This implies an understanding of basic techniques used in the cultivation of the *mimetic instinct,* or the ability to imitate other human beings. Being informed suggests that you have memorable life experiences from which to sketch well-detailed character portraits; and the wider the range of your experience, the more complex the character portraits are likely to be in performance. Detailed observation, informal discussion, and attentiveness to everyday events help to inform the actor and

2

enrich the performer's ability to create the illusion of reality, while at the same time persuading the audience that what is seen and heard is both natural and familiar. Informed observation of human nature and the environment that surrounds everyday life presents vivid personalities, experiences, and circumstances that may be imaginatively integrated into the world of the playscript. The possibility of allowing the character(s) of the playscript to be shaped by the actor's observations or lived experiences brings vitality and credibility to the subsequent performance and provides a "flesh-and-blood" role model by which to relate the specific events of a scene to your own understanding as well.

Second, you must be a "disciplined" actor. This implies not only a well-defined and orderly system of initial rehearsal preparation and practice, but also intensive training in scene study, playscript interpretation, and in the use of *both* the voice and the body to help amplify and delineate the character in performance. Being disciplined suggests that you have planned the performance in detail, not relied solely upon improvisation or spontaneous impulse; and that your performance blueprint has been created within a framework of analysis and evaluation of what the character is thinking or feeling in a selected scene. A carefully planned and disciplined rehearsal period may actually enable you to begin to assume the role of your character as vocal and physical exploration and refinement begin to shape your initial character portrait. You may even discover that personal traits and behavior patterns may be integrated into the character portrait during this disciplined rehearsal period as well, creating a *person/actor* composite that adds new dimension to your characterization in subsequent performance. "Nothing is more fleeting than any traditional method of impersonation," remarked the nineteenth century English actor Sir Henry Irving, so make sure that your disciplined approach to rehearsal preparation and practice is cohesive and consistent but also flexible enough to permit some diversity in unlocking the inspirational treasure chest of your *own* imagination and individual creativity.

Third, you must be a "free-spirited" actor. This implies a creative and inventive approach to character development that gives an added hint of uninhibited abandon and risk-taking in creating a memorable role for performance. Being "free-spirited" suggests that the performer has an indescribable "life spirit" that promotes spontaneous and imaginative performance responses and reactions that not only stimulate the perception of the audience but also enliven the character portrait being drawn. The performer's own individual, distinctive personality is the primary resource that frames the initial creation of character, but the inspiration to mold and give expressive vitality to character portraits also includes an ability to integrate one's own surface "self" with the more subterranean, sublime "soul" of the character reflected in the playscript. The free-spirited actor — in the exploration and definition of the character role in scene study analysis and in rehearsal — allows the action of the playscript to be shaped by personal, complementary personality traits that are helpful and truthful in *completing* the outline of the character as roughly sketched by the playwright. Ingenious, sometimes unconventional, performance approaches to character development often highlight and underscore the meaning of the words spoken and the actions taken in a selected scene — but it is the free-spirited actor who gives creative form and substance to that meaningful expression; and draws audience attention to those significant theatrical moments in which character thoughts and actions are revealed in uninhibited abandon.

There is no question that individuality applies to every aspect of the creation of a role, but there are a number of other essential performance prerequisites to be considered in your beginning approach to the conceptualization and development of a three-dimensional character portrait which are equally important. There are the following challenges:

- To pursue what the noted contemporary critic Francis Ferguson had in mind when he coined the term *histrionic sensibility*, the mechanics of responding actively to the dramatic suggestions inherent or implied in a playscript; and the ability to visualize action through sensorial impressions.

- To communicate directly and honestly with the audience in simple and uncomplicated character portraits of authentic people, places, and events.

- To reveal the basic impulses and "inner truths" of a character without distortion or deception.

- To become inextricably bound to giving a character a sense of profound dignity and importance that provides the audience with a glimpse of human compassion and understanding.

- To reduce the amount of extraneous theatrical posing and posturing that inhibit the ability to sketch lifelike character portraits drawn from the workaday world.

- To discard convenient stereotypical stage figures in favor of vibrant characters that mirror contemporary reality in performing heroic deeds, committing errors in judgment, and in displaying basic emotional urges such as anger, frustration, jealousy, or greed.

Although there are a number of theories on the basic approach to acting, there are not, as yet, basically theoretical actors! Perhaps that is because all creative artists, as the influential French novelist André Malraux reminds us, "...say what they would like to do and do what they can." Perhaps that is also why every creative actor must envision a role according to individual talent and disposition, adopting a performance style and technique that is unique or original in its personal testimony to "self expression." Limited by theoretical approaches to acting that appear artificial, sentimental, paradoxical, or even contrived, contemporary actors are apparently more inclined to pursue individual styles and techniques that reject traditional dramatic "formulas" and performance "laws" in pursuit of more nonconventional, experimental principles where they may study and express themselves as they determine what is appropriate to realize the goals and objectives of the characters suggested in the playscript.

This pursuit of a more "individual" style and technique in creating a role that exhibits a new flavor and texture of simplicity and directness focuses immediate attention on the actor's need to make more *intellectual* performance choices in dramatizing character. As you approach the selected playscripts and monologs that follow, pay particular attention to the performance choices that you make in order to achieve the goals and objectives recommended for your consideration because you will be compelled to carry them with you on the later journey to discover an acting style and technique most effective for your own skills and talents. The significant discoveries you make in this self-exploration should provide the basic foundation, as well as information and inspiration, needed to give your creation of a role fresh insight and creative substance, completely free from

5

the rigorous demands and expectations of others. As a fellow traveling companion on the quest for a meaningful, personal performance pilgrimage, may I suggest the visionary dramatic poet and playwright Goethe, whose words of simplistic inspiration should provide a warm and welcome comfort on your journey: "Whatever you can do, or dream you can, begin it. Boldness has genius, power, and magic in it."

Theoretical Blueprint

One of the primary theoretical blueprints of basic acting involves an understanding of the relationship between *internal* and *external* perspectives on performance. Internal approaches to performance suggest that the actor "lives" the life of the character, and assumes the fundamental words, actions, and movements of the character as an integral part of his/her own persona. In this respect, internal performance approaches make no distinction between the "actor" and the "character"; indeed, the illusion of the actor's performance of the character and the character itself become indistinguishable. This approach to performance promotes effective use of sensory and emotional responses and reactions to create "self-awareness" and "self-exploration" in the development of character. Internal beliefs are a vital component in conveying the actor's own personal experiences as well. They serve as a human reservoir of everything the actor has experienced, seen, thought, or imagined; and are the primary resources the actor relies upon in giving voice and body to a character. Using these inner resources that have helped to define life actually observed and lived, the actor "internalizes" these personal experiences to give form and substance to subsequent character portraits.

External approaches to performance suggest that the actor relies upon "technique" to conceptualize and convey the life of the character; and assumes that there is a clear and present distinction between the actor as "person" and the actor as "character." Clearly, the external approach to performance is acting from the "outside" rather than from the "inside," and involves a more objective approach to character development than internal theories of characterization. The more technical theory of external development of a character suggests the actor's voice and body — rather than internal beliefs and personal experiences — are trained as the most responsible and responsive instruments in the creation of imaginary stage figures behaving in the given circumstances and performing the stated actions conceived by the playwright. External signposts are best revealed by isolating the *physical* rather than the emotional actions of a character, and the master acting theorist Stanislavsky's advice in *Creating a Role* is unequivocal: "Let each actor give an honest reply to the question of what physical action he would undertake, how he would act (*not feel*, there should for heaven's sake be no question of feeling at this point) in the circumstances given by the playwright...when these physical actions have been clearly defined, all that remains for the actor to do is to execute them."

As interesting as these performance theories might appear to be at first glance, they can honestly only point in directions and heighten awareness of the essential need for the proficiency of *both* internal belief and external technique in the conceptualization and execution of character. You need to approach these theoretical principles of basic acting as mutually compatible rather than as contradictory; and look for interesting and innovative approaches that integrate rather than isolate these theoretical performance perspectives. Remember that you are just as dependent on your internal beliefs to tell you "what" to do as you are on your external technique to tell you "how" to do it! In a way, as an actor whose primary obligation it is to conceptualize and then to communicate believable stage figures, you cannot *not* have experiences, passions, and purposes lurking beneath your character portraits or you risk a very superficial interpretation and a very uninspired performance.

In playing contemporary scenes it is important to be truthful to your own *nature* and to envision each scene or monolog as if you were examining your own *life* more intimately and objectively. There should be attention paid to the personal opinions expressed about your character, to the reliability of the character's own truthful statements, to the significant issues addressed by the character, and to the final choices made by the character. Although it may be difficult for you at first to imagine yourself as some of the characters detailed in the scenes and monologs you may be playing on stage — or in his performance book — approach each role and character portrait with the same

7

intensity, dedication, and discipline. *Analyze* the character and make notes concerning the character's physical, vocal, and mental qualities. *Define* the character and make decisions regarding specific goals and objectives. *Create* the character based upon the character's relationship to others, mood, attitude, and point of view in the individual scene as well as in the complete playscript. *Visualize* the character in terms of style of apparel, textures, and accessories. Attention to these basic details in the initial reading and rehearsal period should help punctuate your characterization and amplify your interpretation in the subsequent performance.

The actor must be "free-spirited," and this implies a creative and inventive approach to character development that gives an added hint of uninhibited abandon and risk-taking in creating a memorable role for performance.

An interesting theoretical blueprint to consider in your basic approach to acting scenes and monologs is a detailed exploration of the character's *physicality*, especially those "physical actions" that help to define a character's basic motivation or intention. The successful discovery of a character's physical life reveals the inherent reason(s) a character acts or reacts in specific instances; and helps to clarify a character's basic impulses and spontaneous outbursts. A careful analysis and assessment of the "given circumstances" of the playscript should help you identify and interpret a character's physical actions as well; and also enhance your performance ability to depict a well-defined, three-dimensional character portrait.

The given circumstances that help to define a character's attitude and action are derived from an intensive study of the playscript and usually entail an objective evaluation of the plot, dialog, setting (locale), and point of view of the character as revealed in the basic storyline. In addition to what the character may say about him/herself and what others may say about the character, the playwright indicates the overarching significance of the given circumstances by providing clues that indicate *who* the character is, *what* the character is doing, *where* the character is doing it, *when* the character is doing it, and *why* the character is doing it. These traditional journalistic "five Ws" provide an initial composite of the character; and they may be stated explicitly or implicitly depending upon the playwright's dramatic perspective or writing style. These clues furnish at one level or another — intellectual, emotional, social, or ethical for example — our perspective for viewing and understanding the actions of the character. Whether as inklings or as clearly articulated beliefs, these clues also provide an inherent "order," or sequence of events, attitudes, and incidents that help us to better recognize and reconcile the character's subsequent behavior when we witness it in the context of an individual scene or monolog.

The accuracy of discovering specific responses to the questions posed by the "five Ws" should suggest the physical actions the character would most logically execute in any of the given circumstances described — and here is your impetus to explore and to discover the performance mystery of what a character might "think" or "do" in an isolated situation. Of course, if the playwright has not provided sufficient clues to adequately inform your analysis of the given circumstances then you must rely upon the details that are provided *and* supplement the supporting materials with your own creative imagination to complete the character portrait. The answer to the question(s) "who, what, when, where, and why" that the playwright and the actor provide constitute the real-life stage figure seen and heard by the audience — and this is what gives authenticity to both the playscript and the performance.

In your beginning exploration of the given circumstances and physical actions it is important to play the role with your own voice, body, movement, and inner resources — based upon

9

either observation or lived experience — to depict the physical-ization of the character and the logical sequence of events, attitudes, and incidents that are an integral part of the character's subsequent behavior. It is also important to express your responses to the "five Ws" in plentiful and precise detail to help clearly distinguish and delineate your character from other similar characters who may share common attributes. For example, in William Shakespeare's playscript of *Hamlet* the rather vague response of the title character to the question, "Where am I?" is incomplete if the answer is an abbreviated and abrupt "in a castle." The more elaborate, invigorating actor response of "in a dark and gloomy castle isolated from gentle humanity and reeking of corruption and foreboding death" strikes a more imaginative and inspired reflection of a textual analysis of the appropriate performance blueprint to highlight and enliven the character portrait being drawn. Likewise, in the Tennessee Williams' playscript *A Streetcar Named Desire* the rather obscure response of the primary character Blanche DuBois to the question, "Who am I?" is distorted if the answer is a simplistic, one-dimensional "neurotic, scorned woman." The more perceptive and penetrating actor response of "a gentle soul burning with passion for a lost love and an unquenched desire for the poetic beauty of life" hints at a more comprehensive textual analysis and a more compelling performance blueprint to underscore and heighten the character portrait being visualized.

Your awareness of the theoretical role that the given circumstances and physical actions play in character develop-ment should be invaluable when approaching the selected scenes and monologs that follow. As you continue your study of these two necessary ingredients in "character building," strive to make the actions of the character your own so that they appear to be spontaneous and natural. Do not hesitate to extend your character development through active response to the five senses, giving added performance flavor to what is touched, heard, smelled, seen, or tasted by your character in the given circumstances and in physical actions. Use basic impulses as well to focus attention on the logical and lucid behavior of your character in the sequence of events depicted in the playscript. In this respect, your exploration will give not only "life" but also "meaning" to the character portrait for you and the audience.

Another imaginative theoretical blueprint to consider in your basic approach to acting scenes and monologs is *improvisation.* Contrary to popular misconceptions by some beginning actors, improvisation is *not* a role-playing game of inventing imaginative dialog to develop a random situation or a "warm-up" exercise designed to loosen up the performer(s) before rehearsal. In its most theoretical form, improvisation is an actor training technique in which the performer(s) is asked to explore character development in the rehearsal process executing the "actions" and the "intentions" of a character as suggested by the director. Reacting to the description provided by the director, the actor's primary goal in improvisation is to respond in voice and body as the character might in a specific situation and to perform clearly defined actions and intentions by an imaginative — but still logical and sequential — series of events that reveal internal and external intimations of character mood, attitude, and point of view suggested in selected scenes of the playscript. Improvisation in the rehearsal process also encourages the actor to explore and extend time, space, form, and content without the limiting restrictions of a traditional playscript or a conventional set of rehearsal expectations like polishing lines of dialog or reviewing blocking and movement positions.

As a rehearsal technique, improvisation may provide valuable insights for later character development and help to clarify the role that actions and intentions play in character interpretation. Without a reference to the playwright's "words" to guide the performer in the practice of character definition, improvisation demands that the actor "envision" and then "enact" an imaginary character's actions and intentions — in both voice and body — as a direct means of communicating basic truths that emerge in the imaginative rehearsal exercise.

Improvisation in rehearsal — especially when it is related to the imagined character's motivation(s) and objective(s) detailed in the formal playscript — encourages a creative, risk-free environment in which to pursue new performance dimensions. This performance approach to the rehearsal period views improvisation as an organic process, one that grows naturally and honestly from a detailed analysis of the playscript and the character rather than from an unstructured, arbitrarily imposed scenario

11

of suggested actions and intentions devised at random by the director. When viewed from this perspective, improvisation has the positive potential of:

- Revealing moment-to-moment character interaction and inter-personal relationships.

- Promoting dramatic visualization of the central action and the storyline of the playscript.

- Encouraging the actor's spontaneity and immediacy in speaking *and* listening.

- Enhancing the illusion that the actor is performing the role for "the first time."

- Experimenting with different character attitudes, moods, and points of view.

- Providing creative opportunities to engage in active and meaningful "word play."

- Discovering new layers of character subtext and subtle shades of undercurrent meaning.

- Enriching an understanding of internal/external technique.

- Reinventing imaginative stage business or production accessories.

- Generating fresh nuances in the interpretation of the playscript.

The use of improvisation — especially when focused on individual segments of the playscript that are troublesome or problematic — also helps to direct attention to the resolution of dramatic action and its relationship to characterization. Some of the exercises that might be of value in this theoretical approach to improvisation include experimentation with "role-swapping," in which the parts of two or more characters are distributed among several actors to stimulate different performance points of view or approaches to character interpretation; or pursuing character spatial relationships and interpersonal distances in improvised staging exercises that revolve around creative use of stage furniture, decor, or the setting. Character building exercises may include improvisations that encourage the actor to create "biographies" of events or actions that happened prior to the scene(s) described in the playscript; or may encourage the creation of "new" scenes that help to deepen the actor's recognition and understanding of a character's intention, motivation, or relationship to others in the more detailed scenes included in the actual playscript. There are also performance opportunities to use improvisation in the rehearsal period to experiment with movement and pantomime to more clearly define or more precisely refine a character's gestures and bodily actions. Finally, there are ample opportunities in the playscript related improvisation for the actor to create "interior monologs" that help to reveal the subconscious or submerged feelings and thoughts of a character; or to engage in "confrontation charades" that provoke discovery and resolution of the conflict context that is an essential ingredient of character development.

There are, of course, certain risks involved in relying too heavily upon improvisation in the initial discovery or later development of character, and you should be aware that — especially when executed poorly or with no sense of structured purpose — improvisation may diminish or even distort your understanding of a character's attitude, action, or motivation in a selected scene or monolog. In focusing upon the "freedom of form" encouraged by improvisation don't lose sight of the basic pattern of episodes in the playscript, the sentiments of the playwright's language, or the internal tempo and rhythms of a character's physical actions in the given circumstances during your rehearsal experimentation. Although the performance temptation to rely upon improvisation to cultivate spontaneous character responses and reactions will undoubtedly be attractive, resist an improvisational attitude that is chaotic and unfocused in favor of one that is filled with the warmth and wonder of honest invention of character action and interaction, genuine discovery of character motivation and subtext, and authentic creation of character feelings and thoughts as they are revealed to you in a detailed analysis of the playscript.

A final theoretical blueprint to consider in your basic approach to acting scenes and monologs is a brief review of *movement* and *pantomime* to enhance their potential performance impact on characterization. Both movement and pantomime are essential actor training techniques to the performer seriously interested in cultivating a vivid, responsive physical character portrait; and each has unlimited potential to help the actor understand a character's intention and motivation or to visualize a character's physical action. Experimenting with movement and pantomime in the rehearsal process may also provide the insight and imagination needed to broaden an actor's sense of character relationships and promote dramatic interaction as well.

Although there is no general agreement in actor training circles at the present time on which particular movement technique is most appropriate for character development, there is a considerable range of popular choices you may wish to consider. One very popular movement technique designed specifically for actors is the Laban style, detailed in Rudolf Laban's textbook *The Mastery of Movement*, which describes the basic approach of using physical traits and types of body alignment to enrich characterization. Oriental movement disciplines such as T'ai Chi and yoga are highly recommended movement techniques that promote the relaxation and physical conditioning necessary for expressive character development. A number of actor training programs endorse elementary instruction in acrobatics, fencing, tumbling, modern dance, shadow movement, jazz, and circus techniques — primarily juggling — as an effective approach to character movement. The more contemporary "Alexander technique," although not specifically a movement exercise, is also a very valuable rehearsal method to promote the relaxation and balanced posture critical in promoting character movement style.

No matter which particular movement technique you may choose to pursue for character development, remember that the primary role of the body in performance involves well-executed posture, physical reactions that are clearly defined, and responsive movement patterns that reflect a character's motivation and inner thought. The specific role of the body in character development is generally determined by the character's age, social position, mood, attitude, or objective in a selected scene or monolog. The visual portrait should be consistent with what the playscript suggests about the character, and the movement or physical reactions or responses should be fluid and yet clearly visible to indicate what the character is thinking or anticipating. The body alone is sometimes sufficient to suggest a character's predominant mood or attitude. It not only reveals the emotional and mental state of the character but also helps to visualize the context in which physical actions may be performed. In addition, the use of the body and movement patterns creates a dramatic sense of "telescoping" a character's motivation and relationship to other characters, the setting, the situation, or the storyline.

Taking movement classes and practicing programmed body exercises should be a daily rehearsal goal in the actors' routine if they are to become proficient in physical character development. Consistent and disciplined rehearsal in posture, movement, and physical mannerisms or transformations that might help to visualize a character provides authentic performance opportunities for the actor to expressively interpret the dramatic action of the scene or monolog. The physicalization of a character through movement and body may also help the actor isolate and identify a character's emotional or intellectual state of mind within a selected episode or sequence of events detailed in the playscript.

One of the most common faults of a beginning actor says the experimental theatre director Jerzy Grotowski in *Towards a Poor Theatre* is "...the overstraining of the voice because one forgets to speak with the body." In learning to "speak" with the body, the most obvious and natural performance approach is to cultivate a relaxed, comfortable posture. Although we may unconsciously achieve proper body alignment while lying flat on our backs on a firm surface — which eliminates excess tension and allows the weight of the body to conform to its natural and correct alignment — it requires much more concentration and self-discipline to duplicate proper body technique in a standing, upright position. It is important, however, for the actor to continually strive for a relaxed, comfortable posture because the voice and the vocal mechanism — including proper breathing techniques — are greatly influenced by body responses; and correct body alignment enhances and amplifies fluent and expressive speech.

The role of the body in conveying character intention or to suggest character motivation requires an almost musical quality for your movement and physical actions to give a sense of rhythm to character development. The need to practice muscular coordination in character development, from the tips

15

of your toes to the top of your head, is part of the rehearsal process that results in fluid and graceful character movement. The muscular coordination necessary to promote expressive movement in characterization demands total physical concentration on *centering* — which is the mutually correct spatial relationship between head, chest, and pelvis — the body so that movement in any direction may be executed with a minimum of effort or an obligatory shift of weight to initiate counter-movement. Repeated practice on centering the body should enhance natural expressiveness in subsequent movement, enrich the visual portrait of the actor, and reduce distracting physical mannerisms or personal eccentricities in an actor's bodily actions that might interfere with meaningful character development.

The primary role of the body in performance involves well-executed posture, physical reactions that are clearly defined, and responsive movement patterns that reflect a character's motivation and inner thought.

"Body awareness" should encourage you to control the anxiety and tenseness that often accompany performance, and to train your body to respond subtly to any movement that is necessary to communicate character moods, attitudes, or points of view. A simple preliminary exercise to test your own sense of body awareness is to imagine that a rope is suspended from the ceiling directly above your head. Attached to the rope is an object that barely touches the center of your chest. Practice positioning your head and body so that neither of them touches the imaginary object. When you have completed this part of the exercise, stand erect with heels together and feet at a ninety-degree angle from each other. Allow your head to fall forward as slowly as possible without bending your neck. Now relax, and allow your neck to fall slowly forward until your head rests comfortably upon your chest or slightly above your waist. Continue to relax your head and neck as you allow them to sink slowly forward until they are at your knees with your arms sliding down toward the floor. Then relax your hip muscles and allow your entire body to sink slowly toward the ankles. When you have successfully relaxed all parts of your body and are almost touching your toes with the tips of your fingers, slowly count to ten as you reverse the process and return to a standing position.

Continue this brief exploration of body awareness by allowing your head to fall slowly to the right without bending your neck. Now, bend your neck to allow your head to fall still further to the right. When you have inclined your body as far right as possible, raise your left shoulder and bend your upper body toward the right. Allow your left arm to fall across your body, while your right arm rests relaxed at its side. As your body is now moving toward the right, bend your left leg and relax your hips. All parts of your body — with the exception of your left arm — should now be on a direct angle toward the right side. Now reverse your body angle to the left, starting again with erect posture and heels together at a ninety-degree angle from each other to complete the exercise.

Hopefully, this brief exercise in body positioning will encourage you to think of correct movement in performance, especially the body as an expressive instrument that helps to convey a meaningful visual portrait of your character; and to search the playscript for physical clues that might be translated into definitive character posture, movement patterns, or physical actions that indicate character. Systematic training and routine rehearsal will, of course, tone the muscles of your body to be both supple and responsive to physical hints of characterization, but the basic fabric of character movement used sparingly and wisely can be knit, laced, and woven decoratively throughout the playscript to accessorize and embroider the mind, the body, and the spirit of a character. Just remember to "suit the movement to the physical action" and your character portraits should exhibit a well-defined use of body that conveys strength and vigor.

When discussing pantomime as an integral part of the theoretical blueprint to consider in your basic approach to acting scenes and monologs, it is important to recall that this ancient art form of communicating ideas and emotions without using spoken dialog actually preceded the first recorded instances of primitive drama. Pantomime developed as a separate art form — termed "mime" — during the Middle Ages and continues to flourish in the contemporary arena as theatrical entertainment as well as a basic actor training technique. The basic "language" of pantomime from its ancient province to its more contemporary practice is *action*, and developing an awareness of the degree of subtlety and suggestion necessary to "silently communicate" action in pantomime requires a well-trained, flexible body that is capable of expressing a broad range of emotional feelings and intellectual thoughts.

There are primarily four types of actions needed to script and to perform an effective and imaginative pantomime in the rehearsal process. These include:

• *Character action,* which describes and details individual traits and habits of selected characters.

• *Instinctive action*, which is spontaneous, inventive, or inspired and grows out of character actions.

• *Descriptive action*, which is studied gesture and movement that helps to visualize and physicalize the character being created in a pantomime.

• *Dramatic action*, which is the "story" being told in the individual episodes of the pantomime.

Developing character in pantomime involves placing a well-defined figure in a specific situation or environment and then suggesting relevant actions and intentions that reveal apparent changes in mood or attitude as well as in intention or motivation. Like the beginning actor, the mime's first performance responsibility is to "score" or to "notate" commonplace observations and to be alert for potential character portraits so that a scenario — or general plot outline — of the situation, the setting, and the potential character is documented and preserved for performance exploration.

In observing and recording potential characters for performance exploration, the mime pays particular attention to scripting physical actions and mental details that may be translated into both *gesture* and *movement* to create the illustration and the illusion necessary for character development. When delineating the physical actions and the mental details of potential characters for performance the mime is influenced by distinctive posture, gesture, and movement that has been part of the initial observation process. The "mimetic instinct," so essential for the actor, also applies to the mime artist and pantomime skills are enhanced by a self-controlled and orderly system of preparation, rehearsal, and execution that develops precision in hand gestures and movement to convey significant character intentions and motivations.

Perhaps a convenient starting point to consider when integrating basic pantomime techniques into the acting rehearsal process is the injunction offered by the playwright Anton Chekhov, who said that "...when a [performer] spends the least possible number of movements over some definite action, that is *grace*." The economy of movement recommended by Chekhov is also appropriate for the use of pantomime in the rehearsal period: use it economically and efficiently to help visualize character portraits. This is especially true in responding to the physical actions of the character suggested in the playscript, where it is essential that you concentrate on direct and vigorous movement or physical action that reinforces the mood and attitude of the character being treated. In these instances, encourage your body to speak for the action described and rely upon pantomime skills of descriptive accuracy and precision to "spell out" the suggested size, shape, weight, and texture of objects mentioned in the selected scene or monolog.

Pantomime in the rehearsal period can be an effective

performance tool extending an actor's personal, descriptive use of physical gestures to reinforce a character's action, attitude, or mood as well. Meaningful physical gestures that define and clarify character actions suggested in the playscript — a raised eyebrow, a quick toss of the head, or a crisp snap of the fingers — highlight individual character traits and lend added dimension to characterization. Pantomime in the rehearsal period also encourages the actor to think of the individual parts of the body — feet, legs, arms, hands, chest, neck, and face — in isolation, and then to combine the most appropriate parts of the body to complete a character thought, convey a character mood, communicate a character attitude, conceptualize a character point of view, or to crystalize a character action. This is an especially valuable approach in the rehearsal process, particularly in its focus upon the importance of the actor's *face* in subsequent performance. The actor's ability to use "facial gestures" to communicate subtle changes in mood or attitude and to define physical actions invites three-dimensional characterization!

The theoretical blueprint that has been presented for your review encourages individual performance choices to be made when engaged in the rehearsal process. A number of the detailed strategies surveyed in acting technique and character development should be useful in your personal approach to the selected scenes and monologs that follow. Increasing familiarity with the basic principles of internal/external acting perspectives, physical actions, given circumstances, improvisation, movement, and pantomime will no doubt result in your own imaginative strategies for rehearsal gamesmanship that enriches character development. Creative expression and originality alike are the primary ingredients in determining the particular approach you will select in discovering the meaning and the feeling evoked in a selected scene or monolog. You are encouraged to use your imagination in pursuit of the ideal "theatrical mind" needed to visualize playscripts and to give life and meaning to dramatic characters; but you are also reminded of the concentration, the discipline, and the preparation that is needed to insure performance success. As the talented director Michael Chekhov reminds us all, "The technique of acting can never be properly understood without practicing it."

Performance Blueprint

Although a more comprehensive performance blueprint on "playing the role" and "playing the scene" will follow in Chapter 2 and Chapter 3, this discussion of the beginning performance blueprint is concerned with some basic acting assumptions and traditional role-playing assertions that, hopefully, will inform and inspire your later scene study and character portraits. One of the first guidelines to inform your beginning performance blueprint is that a playscript is primarily a literary work that is designed for *visual* as well as for *oral* interpretation and presentation. In this sense, the playscript should be viewed as a vehicle for self-expression — within the careful context of an ensemble of actors, director, playwright, and other creative artists like the lighting, set, and costume designers, of course — in which the creation of character, the exploration of feelings or thoughts, and the discovery of theme or author point of view are of vital importance in the performance blueprint.

In analyzing the structure of the playscript, in examining a character's motivation or intention, in deciding upon possible interpretation or probable character portrayal approaches, and in visualizing descriptive or decorative scenic images to bring the playscript to life on the stage there is one single objective for all involved in the creative process: *truth* and *honesty*. The beginning performance blueprint, therefore, must always take into account innumerable production elements and differing dramatic perspectives if the actor is to achieve a truthful and honest character portrait. In addition to these imposing restrictions placed on self-expression, there are frequently additional limitations related to acting technique, stage experience, or intuitive imagination that may at first inhibit an actor from achieving memorable characterization without understanding the need for a disciplined and focused performance technique.

It is also valuable to point out that the actor's performance goal of giving visual and oral life and meaning to the character described by the playwright is also a *shared* experience in the intellectual participation and emotional involvement of an "audience" that ultimately makes rehearsal meaningful and performance rewarding. The actor does not merely "play to the

21

audience" as if the spectators were casual observers who are irrelevant witnesses to the performance, but actively interacts with the audience to cement a fierce and dynamic partnership of mutual recognition and understanding. The performance paradox for the actor, of course, is the need to deny the existence of the audience in order to remain immersed "in character," and yet constantly having to affirm the audience's existence in order to promote the reciprocal recognition and mutual understanding needed to enhance the character portrayal, performance, and production.

There are a number of other beginning performance perspectives that should be addressed in this preliminary discussion so that the later, more detailed blueprints related to "playing the role" and "playing the scene" that follow might make a more profound impression of your scene study and character building skills. These beginning performance perspectives are fundamental "truths" that will help to distinguish the communicative, focused stage actor from the chaotic, unfocused stage apprentice. The communicative, focused stage actor learns early in the beginning performance blueprint to:

• Listen to what is being said on stage and react to what has been heard.

• Direct audience attention to a specific character thought, emotion, or physical action with active "word play" and expressive, subtle movement.

• Appreciate sensorial experiences and sensory recall to express the scenic truth of character moods and emotions.

• Pay careful attention to the vocal attributes responsible for meaningful character interpretations and make a personal checklist of the properties of vocal sound that are most appropriate for conducting and amplifying a potential character's voice.

• Understand that correct production of sound is the first step toward "vocal characterization" and that the preciseness with which speech sounds are voiced enables you to form the sounds, syllables, and words necessary to communicate effectively with the audience.

• Cultivate a rehearsal technique that observes the basic principles of discipline and dedication to achieve concentration and clarity in your performance studies and skills.

Remember, also, that the performance time spent on the stage is always the "living present," a fleeting moment in the eternal life of a literary character. As an actor you are sharing the meaning of only a limited number of imaginary events and incidents in the dramatized storyline — although you are responsible, of course, for the performance representation of *all* the essential events and incidents that may have taken place in the character's "untold" life before the opening scene or between the scenes that follow in the playscript. Make sure that you have an emphatic indentification and response to both the character and the playscript to lend honesty and believability to your beginning performance blueprint. This final performance perspective may mean the difference between achieving an imaginative, inspired character portrait and a stale, pedestrian one. Recall the advice of the novelist Thomas Mann that introduced this chapter's discussion of beginning performance approaches and take a solemn vow "...not to just invent something" in your character portraits but, rather, to "...make something out of reality."

Additional Dimensions

The eighteenth-century comedy of manners playwright, Oliver Goldsmith, offers a very intriguing caricature of a beginning actor that is worthy of your contemporary concern when we speak of the "additional dimensions" of performance: "On the stage he was natural, simple, affecting: 'twas only that when he was off he was acting." The significance of the deeper undertones of Goldsmith's humorous observation is an apparent reminder that the actor has a "dual personality," the *player* and the *person*; and there needs to be a clear distinction between the two in performance and in public. In your beginning performance approaches — no matter what circumstances you may find yourself in at the moment — it is important to keep this perspective in mind, clearly separating your "character" life from your "personal" life. This does not imply, however, that you should absent yourself from the reality of everyday life, but only that you avoid immature "theatrical antics" that frequently call attention to themselves at the expense of the credibility of the serious actor.

It is also important for the actor in beginning performance approaches to cultivate a "professional" attitude throughout the rehearsal and production process. Although the maxim of "hurry up and wait" may still be an apt description of the typical rehearsal process, it is essential to respect your rehearsal time and to exhibit concentration and self-discipline in your rehearsal technique. The professional motto of Actors' Equity Association, "All for one and one for all," communicates the significance of the cooperative nature of working in mutual harmony as an ensemble; and in rehearsal the beginning actor must focus primary performance attention on one single, collective objective: the "group effort" to find complete and meaningful expression of the playscript.

The infectious atmosphere of imagination and creativity that characterizes a rigorous rehearsal period demands that an actor be prepared and punctual; and that an attitude of generosity and genuine concern for other actors be demonstrated at all times. The serious actor at rehearsal exhibits a conscious spirit of cooperation and professional responsibility to other actors and to the production, while at the same time avoiding disruptive behavior that leads to aggressive, arbitrary, and argumentative incidents that may provoke negative responses from other actors or the production staff. The rehearsal period should provide a useful framework for exploration of an actor's creative initiative in character development, for understanding the dramatic sequence of the action and character relationships in the playscript, and for clearly defining performance technique that is honest and consistent with the ensemble approach to the artistic integrity of the production. It is a time, says the critic Alberto Moravia, when "inspiration sometimes comes and sometimes doesn't...but [I] wait and work for it *every day.*"

As you now prepare to investigate the basic performance principles inherent in "playing the role" and in "playing the scene," only one more question remains to be answered. It is not only a convenient summary of the discussion of this chapter but also, perhaps, a working performance credo for all of your future scene study and role-playing experiences. What is the most appropriate beginning performance approach? The answer, quite simply, is to recognize the significant relationship of the following words to the total meaning of performance: *action* and *reaction*. These are the key words that should inform you in the interpretation of the playscript and in the creation of the character. They are the key words that — when pursued with imagination and intelligence — unlock the mystery of the playscript's thematic intent and reveal the character's true identity.

Recommended Reading

The following textbooks and recommended readings are intended for the actor who may like to review some of the basic principles related to beginning performance theories and techniques. The recommended readings provide useful information related to dramatic theory, theatre history, and performance studies as well as valuable reference and resource materials that identify acting styles, rehearsal practices, theatre games, and alternative performance blueprints. There is also an effort made here to direct the actor toward more practical supporting materials related to basic stage movement, improvisation, and scene study that may enrich the beginning performance blueprint.

Barton, Robert. *Acting: On Stage and Off*. New York: Holt, Rinehart and Winston, 1989.

Bates, Brian. *Way of the Actor*. New York: Random House, 1988.

Brockett, Oscar. *History of the Theatre*. 5th edition. Boston: Allyn & Bacon, 1987.

Callow, Simon. *Being an Actor*. New York: Grove Press, 1984.

Cohen, Robert. *Acting Professionally*. Mountain View, California: Mayfield Publishing Company, 1990.

Colyer, Carlton. *The Art of Acting*. Colorado Springs, Colorado: Meriwether Publishing Ltd., 1989.

Crannell, Kenneth. *Voice and Articulation*, 2nd. edition. Belmont, California: Wadsworth, 1991.

Finchley, Joan. *Audition!* Englewood Cliffs, New Jersey: Prentice-Hall, 1984.

Hagen, Uta. *A Challenge for the Actor*. New York: Charles Scribner's Sons, 1991.

Hornby, Richard. *The End of Acting: A Radical View*. New York: Applause Theatre Books, 1995.

King, Nancy. *A Movement Approach to Acting*. Englewood Cliffs, New Jersey: Prentice-Hall, 1981.

McTigue, Mary. *Acting Like a Pro*. Whitehall, Virginia: Betterway Publications, 1992.

Poggi, Jack. *The Monolog Workshop: From Search to Discovery in Audition and Performance*. New York: Applause Theatre Books, 1995.

Schechner, Richard. *Performance Theory*, revised edition. New York: Routledge, 1988.

Spolin, Viola. *Improvisation for the Theatre*. Evanston, Illinois: Northwestern University, 1985.

Worthen, W. B. *Modern Drama and the Rhetoric of Theatre*. Berkeley, California: University of California Press, 1992.

CHAPTER TWO

PLAYING THE ROLE

> *"...there are those precious few [actors] whose high gift it is to act themselves, to adapt their spirits to the spirits of the parts they are playing, to possess and then to be possessed by the characters they project, and to give them the benefit of their beauty and their intelligence, their sympathy and their virtuosity, their poetry and their inner radiance, their imagination and their glamour."*
>
> — John Mason Brown

The actor, by nature of the "mimetic instinct" inherent in imagination and invention, is a creative artist who attempts to faithfully capture the unique traits and mannerisms of a character suggested in a playscript with as much authenticity and accuracy as possible, weaving a rich tapestry of texture and technique in playing the role with keen and discerning individuality and insight. That is not to say, however, that the actor merely "copies" what has been observed or discovered in a critical analysis of the playscript and then submits that interpretation of the character to an audience for comparison with the original source of inspiration. To take this approach to playing the role would undoubtedly lead to a static, uninspired performance that could not accurately reflect either the dramatic vision of the playscript or the considerable skill of the performer.

Dynamic role-playing is an essential ingredient in interpretation and performance if the actor is to learn the technical skills of believable stage characterization and to give life and meaning to the fictitious character being portrayed. Character does not leap from the printed page full-blown in its descriptive suggestion of intent or motivation; it emerges in infinitely subtle and frequently disguised performance clues pointing the way to particularly striking elements of character development that enrich role-playing opportunities. The unique contribution of the actor is to seize these role-playing opportunities provided by the playscript and to fill in the playwright's tentative, incomplete character outline with as much imaginative and inventive "self-expression" as possible to embody a character of substantial form and content. The noted director David Magarshack, writing in *Stanislavsky on the Art of the Stage*, captures the spirit of the role-playing experience in his perceptive "marriage and family" performance analogy to explain why the same role may be portrayed quite differently, and yet effectively, by a number of actors. In this comparison of marriage and family to role-playing Magarshack suggests that character may have the same father (playwright) but a different mother (multiple actors) playing the same role.

"Every artistic stage character is a unique individual creation, like everything else in nature. In the process of its creation there is a 'he,' that is the 'husband,' namely the author of the play, and a 'she,' that is the 'wife,' namely the actor or the actress. Then there is the 'child,' or the created part. There are in this process, besides, the moments of the first acquaintance between 'him' and 'her,' their first friendship, their falling in love, their quarrels and differences, their reconciliations, and their union."

The significance of the performance analogy suggested here for the actor is not only that no two performers play the same role with an identical interpretation, but also that no two performers sketch the same character portrait with identical information provided by the playwright in the given circumstances of the playscript. Common performance sense tells us, therefore, that effective role-playing techniques are a mutual harmony of "author" and "actor"; and that the performer most capable of the happy marriage of *script* and *self* has, indeed, realized the potential role-playing opportunities inherent in a selected scene or monolog. The essential truth and honesty of the role — the "inner core" of characterization — is also immeasurably enhanced in this character identification approach to interpretation without diminishing the contribution or the creativity of either the playwright or the performer.

Playing the role *is* an art that requires discipline as well as dedication in the critical analysis of the playscript, the perceptive interpretation of actions and words, the conceptualization of intentions or motivations, and the creation of intriguing character portraits that speak across time and space. The actor must allow the role to "penetrate" the performance declares the theorist Jerzy Grotowski, and yield willingly to the *character's point of view* in order to achieve the "egocentricity," or self-centeredness, of the character's emotional, intellectual, physical, or psychological state of being in a selected scene or monolog. To accomplish this performance technique, it is important in playing the role to think of a character as a *subject*, rather than as an *object* in the action of the playscript; and to engage in performance actions or reactions that place the character — even a minor supporting character — in the center of the playscript's imaginative universe.

As you review the scene from Eugene O'Neill's *Long Day's Journey Into Night* in Chapter 5, for example, the characters Edmund and Jamie engage in a number of egocentric games to establish themselves as active subjects rather than as passive objects in the action that unfolds between the brothers. Recognizing the basic motivation and intention of their behavior in this selected scene should give you role-playing opportunities to more clearly understand each character's personality; and to explore creative performance approaches that visualize each character's personal response to the awkward situation in which they find themselves in this imaginative universe of their own making. In playing the role primarily from the character's point of view, you may also discover a very special relationship between two brothers who are living life secondhand, with little genuine affection for each other or for their family, and consumed with personal conflicts, problems, and sorrows that inhibit the natural bond of brotherly love and the vast sweep of a compassionate human spirit from consoling each other in their private, nightmare relationship.

Remember that the basic approach to playing the role is made explicit in performance when there is a simple and honest attempt made to portray character accurately and authentically by providing depth, dimension, integrity, and believability. Surface details, common actions, and incidental events all contribute to the dramatic backdrop against which the "inner truth" of a character is made to be known — and in which the characters can speak more directly and sincerely about the true meaning of their own lives. So, let the characters speak freely and openly when you are playing the role, and encourage each character to become a *transparent* medium through which the soul of the playscript and the performance is revealed in all of its theatrical grandeur.

First Principles

One of the principles in playing the role is to read the playscript with a critical eye to grasp the creative performance suggestions that are implied in the dialog and stage directions; and then to translate them into an imaginative performance blueprint that features concrete character actions and movements. In *reading for meaning*, the root ideas and inspirations for character development are generally revealed in an objective analysis of the playwright's stylistic writing technique, structure, language, theme, and point of view as expressed by the figurative characters. Understanding the basic principles of dramatic criticism should give the actor the critical skills necessary to read a playscript with discerning insight; and should also provide the literary skills of interpretation needed to visualize the dramatic and theatrical elements of the playscript.

The more knowledge the actor has about the playwright, the playscript, and the production the more perceptive will be the interpretation of the action, the dialog, and the character. Such an approach, however, demands an inquisitive and penetrating mind that is capable of capturing and cataloguing a flurry of vivid incidents, speeches, and images. These dramatic impressions which emerge in the reading of a playscript are part of a related sequence of actions or events which have been carefully crafted by the playwright in a particular structural arrangement — the literary construction of the playscript — to illuminate a specific point of view; and the actor must unravel the playwright's sequence of actions or events in order to give creative license to an imaginative interpretation of the character.

At first, it is well to read the playscript with appreciation to determine the degree of association and familiarity needed to dramatize the character descriptions. Read the playscript as you might read a novel or a short story, initially sorting out the characters and allowing the "story" to tell itself in the narrative, the dialog, and the action. If possible, try to read the playscript in one sitting, sensing the momentum of the inevitable build to a climax and the detailed character relationships. Pay attention to the description of the setting and the scenic design, or other theatrical production elements that might help you visualize the action and the situation described in the playscript.

The second reading of the playscript should be more analytical and critical than the first, and should concentrate on clarity and comprehension. Re-evaluate the primary scenes of a character's interaction with others and visualize potential performance reactions and responses. Rethink your initial interpretation of the playwright's point of view and then isolate and identify those specific character actions, quotations from the dialog, or other supporting examples that help you to reinforce or refine your interpretation. The more objective second reading of the playscript should suggest adjustments that must now be made in both interpretation and playing the role. Initial, perhaps preconceived, notions of character cannot be served with honesty or believability after a more perceptive review and understanding of the given circumstances is provided by the playwright and your own detailed analysis.

Continued reading of the playscript should help you polish and refine your interpretation, especially in terms of maximum identification of distinctive character actions, attitudes, and moods. When accompanied by basic skills in critical analysis and dramatic criticism, continued or frequent rereading of the playscript should also provide abundant inspiration in playing the role to:

• Encourage the theatrical voice and body of the character.

• Reveal the movement necessary to visualize the character.

• Clarify the physical actions that help to define the character.

• Sharpen the stage behavior that gives life and vitality to the character.

Because characters have only the limited time and existence the playwright provides for them in the playscript, frequent rereading of each speech and each scene is often the only appropriate way to clearly define a fleeting dramatic impression of memorable characterization in playing the role.

A second principle in playing the role is to clearly understand the preliminary "process" of character building in terms of its imaginative challenge. A comparison might be drawn

33

between character building and architectural design. Both the actor and the architect plan a foundation — whether of imagination or concrete — that will support the proposed structure; and both calculate the dimensions, size, and scope of the blueprint that will give character, and the physical complex, its inner strength and outer beauty. For the actor, however, the imaginative challenge is to design a stage figure whose solid foundation (playscript) will not only reinforce a visual image (character) but also support a structure that is not bound by a conventional code of traditional building regulations or restrictions (performance).

The two most important steps involved in the preliminary process of character-building are *assuming the role* and *relating the role*. In assuming the role the actor must first have a so-called mental symbol that helps to clearly define the suggested character; and that is why careful analysis of the playscript is essential to understanding the character's primary motivation. The mental symbol indicates the character's desire, what actions the character is willing to commit to achieve the desire, and the fateful price that must be paid by the character for the desire. For example, in Eugene Ionesco's sample performance playscript *The Gap* that is included in Chapter 9, the Academician desires the respect and recognition that is traditionally bestowed upon a scholar, is willing to engage in deception and fraud to assume the role of the scholar, and must pay the fateful price of public humiliation and disgrace for his desire when it is revealed that he has no undergraduate academic degree or scholarly credentials to recommend himself in the role he has been ficticiously playing during his academic career.

Isolating the character's primary motivation should clarify the actor's mental symbol of the scene or monolog and stimulate the action and reaction that follows in the performance. Stanislavsky emphasized the importance of giving the character's primary motivation and desire a "name" as part of the process of creating a character; and as an essential ingredient in promoting the actions inherent in playing the role. Writing in *An Actor Prepares,* Stanislavsky recalls his experience in directing Molière's comedy of manners playscript *The Imaginary Invalid.* The actor playing the title character, Argan, must assume the role of a hypochondriac who is obsessed with a host of imaginary ailments or afflictions and, as Stanislavsky observes, the preliminary process of character building in assuming the role is, indeed, an imaginative challenge:

"Our first approach was elementary...we chose the theme 'I wish to be sick.' But...the more evident it became that we were turning a jolly, satisfying comedy into a pathological tragedy...we soon saw the error of our ways and changed to: 'I wish to be thought sick.' Then the whole comic side came to the fore and the ground was prepared to show up the way in which the charlatans...exploited the stupid Argan, which was what Molière meant to do."

In giving the character's primary motivation and desire a specific name, the actor is better equipped to express the mental symbol that has informed an interpretation of the selected scene or monolog, but is also better prepared to assume the role and pursue, hopefully to achieve, the character's basic desire through the actions suggested in the playscript. Without this attention to character building, especially when it is enhanced with an interesting subtext, the actor's performance is merely a charade. It is important, therefore, to assume the role armed with a strong sense of the character's motivation or desire and ample ammunition that targets a character's inner/outer actions and reactions as well.

In relating to the role the actor must give significance to the circumstances, the images, and the objects that are a part of the character's imagined life. The responses a character might exhibit to specific circumstances, images, or objects promote awareness of attitude, focus attention on objectives, and intensify the emotional or intellectual content of the scene or monolog. In Arthur Miller's domestic tragedy *Death of a Salesman*, for example, the actor relating the role must give significance to the imagined circumstances, images, and objects inherent in Willy Loman's action of trying to plant a small "garden" in the backyard of his modest dwelling. As the character kneels to scratch a patch of dirt from the asphalt surface of the pavement that blankets the backyard, the actor must transform the packet of seeds, the stage directions of the character clawing at the earth, and the description of the dark, foreboding apartment buildings hovering over the space into a meaningful performance relationship that heightens the emotional or intellectual moment being experienced at this moment in time by both the character and the actor.

In giving significant meaning to circumstances, images, or objects the actor "personalizes" the action being performed and directs attention to the dramatic *function* that each of these elements reinforces in relating to the role. By discovering the precise response the character has to each of these elements the actor is able to establish a more personal connection between the "things" that represent the character and the "things" that are an extension of the character. Relating to the role, therefore, requires that the actor pursue an *illustrative* approach to character building, giving a life and meaning to circumstances, images, and objects associated with the character as well. This approach to actively relating to the role may also enable the audience to understand otherwise unintelligible character dialog, movement, or action and subsequently reveal the truth of a character's inner motivation.

Sergei Eisenstein, the innovative film director who subscribes to the cinematic style of "inner technique" in character development, encourages his film actors to relate to the role by "...[compelling] the appropriate consciousness and the appropriate feeling to *take possession*" of their imagination in the character building process. The basic elements of this process as Eisenstein describes them in *The Film Sense* are certainly worthy of the stage actor's review and consideration here as a potential performance technique in relating to the role.

"What we actually do is to compel our imagination to depict for us a number of concrete pictures or situations appropriate to our theme. The aggregation of the pictures so imagined evokes in us the required emotion, the feeling, the understanding and actual experience that we are seeking."

As you begin to explore performance approaches to relating to the role, remember to make a personal and specific link with the circumstances, images, objects, and the character so that you may enrich your performance opportunities. Creative imagination and originality will still have a major impact on your approach to relating to the role, but you will also need to make use of descriptive mental symbols and frequent rereading of the playscript before attempting to give vocal or physical expression to the character. Once you have established the identification and the relationship between circumstances, images, objects,

36

and the character, relating to the role should be an effortless performance approach to intensify the emotional or intellectual context of the scene or the monolog.

Theoretical Blueprint

The theoretical blueprint for playing the role is much less "technical" than it is "tactical" — and offers practical advice for achieving distinctive goals and objectives to fulfill the performance needs of a selected scene or monolog. Understanding basic theoretical techniques and conventions will certainly give credibility to playing the role, but there must also be a tactical blueprint for integrating theory into actual performance practice. Being knowledgeable of theoretical approaches to playing the role encourages the actor to incorporate a number of traditional performance techniques and conventions into playing the role and promotes the authenticity and the texture of a well-defined character portrait. The suggestions that follow indicate a systematic approach to playing the role and ask the actor to rely upon keen observation, studied investigation, and imagination in weaving sources of potential performance material into the rehearsal process. It is important, therefore, to have a very broad, expansive vision of the dimensions of the playscript and yet a very narrow, responsive view of the smallest character detail and trait in playing the role.

When used properly, *stage business* opens up an entirely new world of imagination and invention in character building. Stage business may help to advance the storyline of the playscript, provide an additional dimension to the development of character, or clarify the meaning of a scene or monolog. Although stage business is not generally related to the basic movement of the playscript, it can suggest a tempo or rhythm to the action and reaction of a character if there is subtle repetition of the activity to punctuate individual lines of dialog. The most common uses of stage business involve the handling of small props, like cigarettes, handkerchiefs, glasses, or pens; relating to small pieces of furniture, like chairs, tables, appliances, or sofas; adjusting articles of clothing, like pants, skirts, ties, or scarves; or exhibiting habits and mannerisms, like scratching the head, cracking the knuckles, rubbing the chin, or coughing to clear the throat.

Effective stage business establishes a sense of familiarity and intimacy in playing the role when it is used to indicate the mood or attitude of the character. For example, Blanche DuBois's "heavy trunk" of glass trinkets, bundles of old love letters, and faded gowns in Tennessee Williams' *A Streetcar Named Desire* helps the audience to understand the burden and the weight of frustration and despair that the character must be experiencing as she carefully pulls each item from its dusty tray or drawer and sadly clings to them in her speech of recollection about past "glories" and "happiness" of days spent at her lost southern mansion of Belle Reve. Stage business in this selected scene is a dramatic, visual clue of the character's historical past as well as an ironic vision of the desolate present tense in which the scene is being played.

Although hints of stage business are generally found in the dialog of the playscript or in the actions of the character, there is also ample evidence of potential stage business to be discovered in what other stage figures might say about the character, in the stage setting of the production, in the playwright's narrative illustration of the character, or in the physical description of the character. The stage setting, especially long, low tables and sofas, are excellent "framing" devices for stage business when they center the action and the angle of the scene, and enter very obviously into visual composition by directing attention to the actions a character performs in certain situations. For example, a character who sits in a particular chair smoking a cigarette or softly humming a familiar tune aloud when contemplating a major decision might suggest that this stage business is a basic ingredient of the deliberation process and an essential performance approach to reflect the character's mood or attitude under certain stressful moments in the scene. Or a character who routinely clinches the fist, knots the belt, or rubs the hand through the hair when faced with a threatening situation might suggest that this stage business is a necessary part of playing the role to reflect the character's apprehension, indecision, or insecurity.

Stage business, then, permits a clarification and definition of the actions and thoughts of the character at the same time the actor is revealing the motivation and intention of the character. The actor must be attentive to the apparent *meaning* of the stage

When used properly, "stage business" may help to advance the storyline of the playscript, provide an additional dimension to the development of character, or clarify the meaning of a scene or monolog.

business and its use by the character or any obvious contradictions might distort the playwright's thematic point of view, and also delay the audience's understanding of the character's subsequent actions or reactions. Careful selection and refinement of stage business is essential when playing the role to clearly identify significant character moods or attitudes in a simple and direct manner; or to encourage an immediate recognition and response from the audience. And while stage business should be simplistic in both design and execution, it should suggest a complexity in its expression of a character's motivation and intention or emotional and intellectual disposition at any given moment in the scene. The potential dramatic impact of stage business on playing the role is a highly imaginative performance approach that visually conveys the mysterious truth about the life that lies just beneath the surface of the character.

In addition to stage business as an influential element in playing the role, the theatrical principle of *focus* makes an important statement as well in the rehearsal and performance process. Focus in an intense concentration on the dramatic "situation" rather than on the theatrical "concept" of the performance or the production; and involves a conscious absorption of the character's situation in terms of primary motivation, intention, and objective in a selected scene or monolog. Focus is a conscious approach to playing the role that tries to reduce awareness of distracting theatrical mechanics like the theatre auditorium, scenery, lights, spectators, or the text of the playscript itself. Focus also includes directing attention to points of interest or importance in a character's situation with what Stanislavsky terms "...complete concentration of all physical and inner nature, the participation of all physical and inner faculties."

There are a number of approaches to concentrated focus in playing the role and the most beneficial to a meaningful performance include those that direct attention to the following:

• Execution of stage business.

• Interpretation of dialog.

• Position of stage properties.

• Or participation in the physical actions of the character.

Focus involves active concentration on the emotional, intellectual, or psychological state of the character *in* the situation as it may affect subsequent actions and reactions. The theoretical principle of focus further demands that the actor be a good "listener" on stage as well, exhibiting an intense concentration on what is said by other characters and responding with an alertness that suggests not having heard before the moment of the exchange of dialog. Used in this performance approach to playing the role, focus is a powerful device for intensifying the shifting actions, attitudes, or moods inherent in character relationships; and provides the dramatic effect necessary to achieve what the actor and theorist William Gillette aptly called the "illusion of the first time":

> "Each successive audience before which the [performance] is given must feel — not think or reason about, but *feel* — that it is witnessing, not one of a thousand weary repetitions, but a life episode that is being lived just across the magic barrier of the footlights. That is to say, the whole must have that indescribable life-spirit or effect which produces the Illusion of the First Time."

This is, perhaps, the most famous expression of the theoretical concept of the intense concentration on the dramatic situation rather than on the theatrical concept of the performance or the production in basic acting. Hopefully, with experience and focused attention on detail this theoretical approach to acting scenes and monologs will become intuitive, an almost unconscious element in the rehearsal period and in subsequent performances.

Remember, also, that focus involves "looking out" and "looking in." In "looking out," the actor must be muscularly free of tension in order to respond to what has been seen or heard; and the concentrated focus needed to achieve relaxation in playing the role means a total involvement of the voice, breathing techniques, and physical body working together to sketch a successful character portrait that is vivid and full of vitality. The total physical concentration necessary for good relaxation technique in playing the role also suggests that the bones of the body are in proper alignment and that, although at ease and apparently comfortable, the actor's posture is alert in anticipation of the character action or reaction to follow.

When "looking in," the actor's focus must be attentive to the degree of internal concentration needed to execute the actions and reactions of the character. The focus on internal concentration is related to expressing intentions and motivations as well as influencing and affecting the actions and reactions of other characters in a selected scene. There is much more of the thinking process in "looking in," a perceptive understanding of the character's purpose in the situation and how each line of dialog spoken serves the character's objective. The total internal concentration necessary for meaningful execution of actions and reactions further suggests that the actor's focus must be directed toward keeping the character's thoughts fresh and the dialog crisp.

The theoretical concept of performance *style* in playing the role should be a primary concern of the actor in contemporary scenes as well. Although the critic Michel St. Denis assures us that, essentially, "...there is no difference between classical and realistic acting. It's only that they do not take place on the same level," there still remain certain fundamentally different views that govern the actor's playing the role in comedy, tragedy, farce, melodrama, or even the musical. The style of performance may be influenced by the historical period (classical Greek or Shakespearean), the genre (romantic comedy or domestic tragedy), or the production approach (absurdism or surrealism). Style may be influenced by the technical demands of *representation*, in which the actor attempts to represent stage action as if it were happening in real life and makes *no* conscious effort to have direct contact with the audience so as not to destroy the "illusion" of reality that is being portrayed on stage. Style may also be influenced by the technical demands of *presentation*, in which the actor makes *no* attempt to present stage action as if it were lifelike, and not only calls attention to the theatrical conventions with which the playscript is being performed — like direct address to the audience, asides, or movement into the auditorium — but also presents the playscript, the performance, and the supporting technical or production devices directly to the audience, even inviting the audience on stage occasionally to more directly participate in the action!

The notion of style when playing the role in the historical period, in the genre, or in a majority of the production theory approaches may be more easily explained as a "nonrealistic" view of presentation in which the actors are often frankly theatrical and audience-centered, with manners and methods of acting that now appear dated and distracting in comparison to contemporary theatre performance practices. In the classical Greek performance style, for example, actors had to develop an enormous range of vocal quality to effectively voice the declamatory speeches of the poetic dialog and to cultivate a lyrical quality in the voice that would permit the singing of choral odes or recitatives written as solo or as duet accompaniment to the character's dialog; and classical Greek actors wore *cothurni,* elevated thick-soled boots similar to those worn today by Chinese actors, as well as *onkus,* a high headdress, as part of their stylistic approach to visual suggestion of character. The eighteenth-century comedy of manners style of playing the role was frequently characterized by much buffoonery and witty repartee that ridiculed social customs and moral issues of the times. The playscripts featured stock comic characters like the "rake," "fop," or "sentimental fool," and the actors wore elaborate costumes that mirrored the current fashion; exhibited exquisite grace and elegance in their artificial posing or posturing, and often took extended pauses following a particularly well-delivered speech, or while waiting to receive audience adulation and applause before returning to the scene.

Even the theoretical styles of the more recent production approaches to absurdism and surrealism fail to provide a convenient performance blueprint for the actor in playing the role in contemporary scenes or monologs. In absurdism, for example, actors execute extremely fast or unduly slow movement to emphasize the urgency or the futility of a given moment, and often voice mechanical speech like that of a computer or robot to suggest the apparent loss of individuality and humanity depicted in the playscript. Similarly, playing the role in absurdism demands an exhaustive background of sound effects, unusual hand props, slides, projections, or symbolic placards, and signs to assist the actor in conveying the words and actions of the characters. Playing the role in surrealism, in contrast, places the actor in an unfamiliar relationship with unrecognizable objects in order to explore the subconscious world of grotesque dreams and nightmares, using symbols, signs, and images to communicate significant character points of view. There is also a frequent use of symbolic actor poses or tableaux, like Michelangelo's "Pièta" figure, to suggest the myth and magic that is needed to visualize our daily lives if we are to confront the inexplicable, mysterious forces that guide our tomorrows.

While it is very important to be aware of the historical influence of style on playing the role in a period, genre, or production approach to the playscript — each of which requires a different preparation and a different perspective in character building — it is much more important for the modern actor to discover an acting style that is more representative of the scenes and monologs currently being performed in the contemporary theatre. Perhaps a convenient starting place is an assessment of the theatrical point of view that appears to define contemporary theatre practice, and a review of contemporary acting approaches to playscripts that feature a more "here and now" performance emphasis upon personal behavior and individual mannerism in playing the role.

Performance Blueprint

The contemporary performance blueprint for playing the

role is indebted to robust characters that add a new flavor and texture of directness and simplicity in interpretation and performance. These intriguing contemporary characters are much more "like us today"; they are common men, women, and young adults who express universal human qualities while at odds with present-day social mores, customs, or laws. Contemporary characters may also be seen as "misfits," dejected or often depraved outlaws who suffer from emotional and psychological dilemmas that have resulted in their loss of human dignity or in their extended periods of silence and withdrawal from society. The loss of one's basic humanity — perhaps the result of an unfortunate but commonplace incident like losing a job, hearing tragic news, having insufficient funds, or being forced by necessity to perform degrading tasks — invariably forces the characters to explore the outer limits of human suffering with courage and fierce determination in spite of the fact that there is no apparent practical means of escape.

This rather pedestrian and pessimistic character world view — although profoundly personal and tragic — requires that the actor pay special attention to the "atmosphere" that results from the playwright's detailed description of imagery, setting, and staging in playing the role to better understand the effect that behavior, heredity, or manners may have had on conditioning a character's action, attitude, or mood. This studied investigation may provide inventive, reality-based performance approaches to playing the role as well as essential interpretation hints needed to understand the emotional or psychological dilemma being dramatized in the playscript. An analysis of the character's intention or motivation *in* the atmosphere — especially in relationship to other characters in the scene — should reveal specific bodily actions, personal traits or mannerisms, intrinsic behavior patterns, and gestures that allow the character to communicate basic ideas, thoughts, and emotions in performance.

In playing the role it is important to reinforce the detailed analysis by accurately charting the vocal and physical changes that appear to take place in the character during the scene or monolog being performed; and to visualize the character as objectively as a scientist might record an experiment or a television commentator might describe an event or conduct an informative interview. The more objective you are in playing the role in the contemporary theatre, the more likely you are to achieve an honest and authentic "flesh-and-blood" character portrait that speaks directly to a modern audience. But this approach to playing the role requires the constant perseverance of the "mind" or "emotion." This is the same performance principle that the famous theatre theoretician Diderot, writing in *The Paradox of Acting*, encouraged nineteenth-century actors to embrace when attempting to create more "realistic" and "reasoned" characters for an audience with a long and colorful history of wishing to see stage figures similar to themselves portrayed on the stage.

"...the [actor] should remain master of himself. He should be able to see what he is doing, to judge of his effects, and to control himself. The actor ought never to let his part 'run away' with him. If you have no more consciousness where you are and what you are doing — you have ceased to be an actor: you have become a *madman*."

Of course, the contemporary actor cannot also appear to be "unconscious" in playing the role, becoming only an unfeeling or unresponsive observer to the character's comic or tragic plight. There must still be an awareness and a sensitivity to the current events and present-day life situations or predicaments of commonplace characters that the actor translates into an honest and believable performance blueprint as it might be found to exist in the natural, everyday world of the contemporary audience as well.

A good starting point to consider in playing the contemporary scenes and monologs is to view performance from a more subtle and suggestive perspective than that of previous historical periods that associated traditional role-playing with "theatrical" characterization based upon a particularized "system" or "method" of acting technique. The "here and now" actor may wish to explore alternative acting principles that feature nontraditional approaches to playing the role to more accurately reflect contemporary practice. The actor may:

• Speak in a more conversational, personal tone of voice to suggest intimacy or quiet urgency.

- Slur syllables, mispronounce names or swallow the endings of words to suggest more conventional speech patterns.

- Utter inarticulate grunts, groans, or growls to suggest nonverbal character responses or reactions.

- Punctuate dialog with forceful gestures or bodily actions to call attention to significant character statements or sentiments.

- Display incongruous facial expressions, poor posture, or awkward movement to underscore raw and "unskilled" stage habits.

- Reduce selected dialog exchanges to muttering, stuttering, or vocal hesitation to communicate an "untrained" stage voice.

- Or practice economy in subtle actions and reactions to others in the scene to suggest the private and personal nature of a single, solitary character pursuing individual goals and objectives.

This more contemporary view on playing the role, however, should not exclude traditional principles of ensemble performance, interpreting the playscript truthfully, or yielding freely to the vocal and physical demands of the character within the context of a collaborative production point of view. You must still play the role in partnership and relationship to other characters in the scene and to the playscript as a whole. The important fact to remember is that while your contemporary acting approach is still detailed and studied — analysis of the playscript, character building based upon intention and motivation, and interpretation determined by character actions and reactions — the object now is to "conceal" the basic acting technique and the obvious mechanics of the creation so that the living performance appears to be spontaneous self-expression. This performance approach to playing the role speaks directly, and with more immediacy, to an audience of contemporaries who easily recognize and identify both the character and the situation in their own similar lives, or in the personalities and predicaments of their casual acquaintances or intimate friends. This "seeing ourselves in the lives of others" recognition and identification is the essence of authentic role-playing in contemporary theatre, and is the true measure by which you should judge a character's actions, intentions, and emotions when playing the role in life's actual events as they are revealed in the playscript.

Contemporary theatre practice also appears to be returning in some respects to what Henrik Ibsen, the realistic playwright of the early nineteenth century often referred to as the "Father of Modern Drama," might have called a *photographic* representation of life in playing the role. The photographic approach to playing the role attempts to frame specific visual character portraits of authentic people as if they had been "snapped" by a camera or "shot" on a camcorder. This more documentary approach to visualizing stage figures suggests that the actor playing the role capture the action or the dialog of a character as an exact transcription of everyday activity and speech that addresses the needs of the plot or the situation without calling undue attention to himself. In the attempt to freeze an image of the "present tense" in both the interpretation and the perfor mance, the actor must assume that an invisible "fourth wall" exists between the playing space and the audience; and that all action and dialog will be directed to the other actors within the playing space as the audience "eavesdrops" on the scene to witness the real-life resemblance of stage characters to themselves.

But when playing the role in contemporary scenes you must keep in mind that the basic principles of performance — the "mimetic instinct" of imitation discussed in some detail in Chapter 1 — are still at work, and the stage actions or dialog being presented are but a "picture" of reality, not reality itself. As the Russian playwright Anton Chekhov reminds us, "Life on the stage should be as it really is, and the people, too, should be as they are." If you are to be consistent in the performance approach to playing the role in contemporary theatre it is necessary to *note, record,* and *translate* your initial impressions and photographic images with clarity and simplicity so that the character's action and situation reveals itself naturally as the "negative" of your camera snapshot is developed and enlarged in a candid interpretation and performance.

The more intimate and introspective nature of contemporary drama also suggests that in playing the role you must avoid exaggeration and superficiality in voice and body; maintain normal spatial relationships with other characters; and establish visual contact as one might expect to find in everyday "nontheatrical" settings or environments. Stage business or the use of theatrical props and set pieces must be minimized with an eye to

47

subtlety; and careful pacing of dialog or transitions indicating a shift in character mood or attitude must feature greater awareness of the tempo and emphasis that is to be found in everyday speech and pausing patterns. There should also be special efforts taken to focus your photographic camera or recorder on only those necessary impressions and images that are *absolutely essential* to suggest an interpretation of the character; and that any personal performance additions like distinctive mannerisms, habits, or personality traits be included only if they are complementary in helping to complete the character portrait initially revealed in an analysis of the playscript. In this respect, please recall the stern observation of the outspoken critic and playwright George Bernard Shaw, who warned that "...the one thing not forgivable in an actor is *being* the part instead of *playing* it."

Contemporary theatre practice appears to be returning to "photographic" representation of life in playing the role, which attempts to frame specific visual character portraits of authentic people as if they have been "snapped" by a camera or "shot" on a camcorder.

The final ingredient to consider in playing the role in contemporary theatre is perhaps the one most frequently ignored by actors: the *individual* nature of the audience. Each present-day member of the audience brings to a viewing of a playscript — no doubt influenced by the visual elements of film and television — individual, personal expectations of awareness and attentiveness to the seemingly simple and natural approach to acting that is reflected in other forms of popular entertainment. The power and passion that motivate "action film" characters to perform either heroic or rash deeds and the less demanding, more subdued tone of characters in a "situation comedy" or a prime-time television "drama series" promises relatively brief lighthearted or emotional episodes of a limited time and duration that depict average men, women, and young adults in nonthreatening life situations has surely contributed to the current audience expectation that contemporary acting is conversational, behavioral, and informal, featuring characters who think, speak, and "act" much like the audience members themselves.

Therefore, in playing the role you should remember that the audience may be accustomed to viewing small or insignificant character "souls" rather than the more cosmic, eternal mysteries of human destiny being displayed on the stage in a live performance; and that initially the audience may be inclined to eye the entertainment of the performance rather than hear the provocative ideas and thoughts expressed in the playscript. Your approach to playing the role should address these audience expectations and advance strategies to awaken the viewer's interest in the character, the action, and the situation being portrayed in the scene. The best performance strategy is to present "derived" character observations of life that are recognizable, person-to-person actions and interactions without trying to "duplicate" life in its intricate detail. Remember, also, that your performance in playing the role and the anticipated audience response are both related to the basic human communication process of what we say, what we do, and what we feel: an honest, open exchange of ideas, actions, and images presented in a direct, simple, and sincere manner that transforms the "unfamiliar" into the more "familiar" to express common truths recognized by all.

Additional Dimensions

The contemporary approach to playing the role that encourages stage figures to be shaped by the actor's personal observations and lived experiences provides a valuable performance blueprint to relate the action and the events of the playscript to the modern audience. So be aware of the simple actions and surface details that provide the backdrop against which you will play the role in the scenes and monologs that follow, rehearsing in as economical and believable a manner as possible to achieve a more selective and sensitive character portrait that is truly contemporary. So be spontaneous, encouraging your characters to live moment-to-moment in their day-to-day lives and also to be responsive to what is happening *in* the moment of their theatrical lives.

The "performance sense" you develop in observation and in the rehearsal process should provide you with the additional dimensions needed to play the role in contemporary theatre. You should discover, for example, that what emerges in both observation and rehearsal is the "spirit" of the character you are performing, the sensibilities and the sensitivities of the character you are performing, and the actions and the mannerisms of the character you are performing *now* — not the exact duplicate of the role model you may have observed in real life at another point in time. With intelligence and inventiveness, you should achieve a greater intensity of the "now" experience in performance by virtue of your more narrow, focused attention on modest detail and moderate elaboration of the character to address simple, universal truths that are more easily recognized by an audience. This appears to be the same noble vision Robert Edmond Jones, the noted scenic designer and critic, describes in *The Dramatic Imagination* in this manner:

> "All that has ever been is in this moment; all that will be is in this moment. Both are meeting in one living flame, in this unique instant of time. This is drama, this is theatre — to be aware of the *Now*."

The most appropriate guideline for achieving the "now" when playing the role in contemporary theatre is the degree to which you can personally relate to your character's situation, and the depth and dimension with which you can voice your character's feelings, thoughts, and emotions with honesty and authenticity, and no more. In a truly individual sense, *you* are taking responsibility for your character — and your creative impulses must be channeled to discover *belief, form*, and *shape* in the eventual life of the character you are creating in rehearsal and re-creating in performance. The more you can visualize your *self* and your own *life* in the character, the more contemporary — and human — your performance on stage is likely to read to an audience who knows you like a book, because you are one of them!

Recommended Reading

The following textbooks and recommended readings are intended for the actor who may wish to explore the basic performance principles involved in playing the role or in alternative approaches to creating a believable character. The suggested readings may also provide practical information related to performance approaches to film and to "internal" acting approaches or character building. A serious application of the performance principles suggested in these recommended readings should provide a solid theoretical foundation for the actor who wishes to create an imaginative blueprint for playing the role with spontaneity and style.

Barton, Robert. *Styles for Actors*. Mountain View, California: Mayfield Publishing Company, 1988.

Benedetti, Robert. *The Actor at Work*. Englewood Cliffs, New Jersey: Prentice-Hall, 1986.

Caine, Michael. *Acting in Film*. New York: Applause Theatre Books, 1990.

Carnicle, Sharon Marie. *The Theatrical Instinct.* New York: Praeger Press, 1995.

Carnovsky, Morris. *The Actor's Eye*. New York: Performing Arts Journal Publications, 1984.

Cohen, Robert. *Acting One*. Mountain View, California: Mayfield Publishing Company, 1984.

Crawford, Jerry. *Acting in Person and Style,* 3rd edition. Dubuque, Iowa: William C. Brown Company, 1983.

Felnagle, Richard. *Beginning Acting: The Illusion of Natural Behavior.* Englewood Cliffs, New Jersey: Prentice-Hall, 1987.

Gordon, Mel. *The Stanislavsky Technique.* New York: Applause Theatre Books, 1987.

McGaw, Charles and Larry Clark. *Acting Is Believing: a Basic Method,* 5th edition. New York: Holt, Rineholt and Winston, 1987.

Moore, Sonia. *Stanislavsky Revealed: The Actor's Complete Guide to Spontaneity on Stage*. New York: Applause Theatre Books, 1995.

Owen, Mack. *The Stages of Acting.* New York: Harper-Collins Publishers, 1993.

Skinner, Edith. *Speak With Distinction,* revised edition. New York: Applause Theatre Books, 1995.

Whelan, Jeremy. *Instant Acting.* Boston: Baker's, Ltd., 1995.

Wirth, Jeff. *Interactive Acting.* Boston: Baker's, Ltd., 1995.

Yakim, Moni and Muriel Broadman. *Creating a Character: A Physical Approach to Acting.* New York: Applause Theatre Books, 1995.

CHAPTER THREE

PLAYING THE SCENE

"The poet's eye, in a fine frenzy rolling,
Doth glance from heaven to earth, from earth to heaven;
And, as imagination bodies forth the forms of things unknown,
The poet's pen turns them to shapes, and gives to airy nothing
A local habitation and a name."

> *A Midsummer Night's Dream*
> — William Shakespeare

Playing the scene is the basic foundation of the contemporary approach to acting. Although each actor has a major role to play in making an individual performance contribution to the scene, the overall effectiveness of each performer's interpretation only suggests the dramatic impact of the scene itself and the playscript as a whole. Understanding the playwright's unique approach to composition, content, characterization, and theatrical conventions in a selected scene permits the actor to capture specific visual images of people, places, or events that communicate directly and honestly without deception or distortion; and provides the ultimate performance blueprint to enrich the playwright's point of view (theme) in terms of both the *character* and the *situation*. In his own inventive frenzy the actor, like Shakespeare's poet figure in *A Midsummer Night's Dream*, must translate the "forms of things unknown" revealed in the playwright's imagination and give "to airy nothing a local habitation and a name" when playing the scene.

In considering the application of these basic principles to contemporary playscripts, the actor must cultivate a broad perspective on playing the scene. Although there may be no conscious attempt by the playwright to disguise the point of view, it sometimes may appear to be concealed in the changing character action and dialog of the scene. Some playwrights, like Edward Albee and Harold Pinter, appear to concern themselves primarily with intellectual issues and attempt to delve into the subconscious mind of the character to reveal hidden desires or motivations; but their characters also frequently engage in childish "word games" and immature emotional conflicts with other characters that may appear to disguise or even distort the theme. Other playwrights, like Eugene O'Neill and Tennessee Williams, appear to concern themselves primarily with autobiographical issues and attempt to capture the spirit of past events in drawing dramatic comparisons between what "is" and what "was"; but their characters also just as frequently resort to brutish behavior or crude actions in their relationship with other characters that may appear to confuse or even conceal the theme.

In playing the scene, therefore, it is important to remember that contemporary playwrights appear to work within their own unique writing abilities, interests, and technical skills; and yet still confront issues or address topics in a scene that may not appear — at first glance — to be an integral part of the action or the character but still capture the obvious comic or tragic sense of life as we all know it and live it in the contemporary world. In playing the scene the actor may expect to discover a more direct and frank treatment of action, character, or issues than in previous historical periods that were more concerned with social customs of the day or in patterns of behavior observed in the society of the times.

Like the contemporary actor in performance, the playwright from a modern perspective appears to be pursuing playscripts that are more credible, more closely related to actual experience, and more representative of the observed facts of life. This is the trumpet call that Émile Zola, the nineteenth-century novelist and playwright commonly known as the "Father of Naturalism," had sounded for his own generation of artists in *The Experimental Novel:*

> "I am waiting for them to rid us of fictitious characters, of conventional symbols of vice and virtue, which possess no value as human data. I am waiting for the surroundings to determine the characters, and for the characters to act according to the logic of the facts. I am waiting, finally, for this evolution to take place on the stage."

Although some modern theatre critics and scholars might argue that Zola's naturalistic vision of the ideal playscript has already been achieved to some measure in both principle and practice, contemporary playwrights — especially David Mamet and Sam Shepard — appear to be even more intent on realizing Zola's dramatic vision in their treatment of character that has a:

- Narrow focus on situation.
- Greater intensity in actions and emotions.
- More obvious attention on cause-and-effect relationships.
- Concern for the influence of environmental surroundings.
- Factual approach to observed human nature.
- Scrupulous fidelity to detail in character and in situation.

In playing the scene, the actor should be attentive to the playwright's conscious arrangement of each episode and its specific purpose in the overall structure of the playscript. Each scene should logically and organically evolve from what has preceded it; and it is in the pattern of structure that actions and characters — usually in conflict with the actions of other characters — provide clues to playing the scene to the point of the final expression and resolution of the playwright's point of view. A generalized conception of the scene, a rather tentative version of what is happening to the character in the situation and in the environment, is essential if the actor is to play the scene for its fundamental truth; and to clearly identify and understand an interpretation of character that reinforces the playwright's point of view in the scene.

First Principles

One of the first principles of playing the scene is that the actor's eye must be trained — in the same manner that the musician's ear must be tuned — to visualize the actions and the events described by the playwright as *sequential;* paying special attention to subtle nuances of meaning suggested in the interpersonal relationships of the characters that have been established in an extended sequence of scenes or related events. This is especially important in dealing with scenes or monologs in a playscript that are being performed independently as audition material featuring two or three characters or as longer, individual speeches featuring only one character. In order to clearly visualize the sequential nature of a playscript, the actor should begin an analysis of the scene by gaining an understanding of the "chronological" order of character actions and events; and then place those actions in an appropriate historical time frame in which they appear to have happened in the real or imagined history of the complete playscript.

Even though it may be difficult at first to determine the chronological order of character actions and events, a solid performance knowledge related to the exact time sequence in which actions and events occur should provide the actor with ample evidence of changing character moods or attitudes; and should also help to explain changing character intentions or motivations. This is an especially valuable performance principle in playing the scene when it helps to indicate the "cause-and-effect" relationship of character actions and reactions. For example, in Henrik Ibsen's social drama *A Doll's House* the heroine, Nora, finds herself in a rather uncompromising marriage to Torvold Helmer, who treats her as a "childish plaything" in the actions and events detailed in most of the playscript. An analysis of the chronological order of the playscript, however, reveals a historical time frame in which past and present tense actions and events in Nora's life suggest a consistent pattern of similar treatment that views the character as a frail, bird-like creature incapable of independent thought. Confined to a "doll's house" by a domineering father, Nora now finds her dreams of freedom and independence frustrated and thwarted by her husband. The cause-and-effect of this pattern of chronological actions and events on the character is an essential ingredient in understanding Nora's later assertion of independence — from past as well as present actions and events — as she gradually assumes a more forceful, dynamic attitude and finally exits her marriage in a flourish, abandoning both her husband and her small children in order to seek her own identity in the world.

A second principle the actor should be aware of in playing the scene is the fundamental role that *dramaturgy* has in shaping the dramatic perspective of the playscript. Dramaturgy is related to the artistic craftsmanship of the playwright in the arrangement, the structure, and the expression of actions and events in the playscript. Each playwright's dramatic vision is a reflection of a unique "system of codes" that initially shape the written playscript and communicate the author's individual point of view. When the actor is successful in "breaking the code" of the playwright's arrangement, structure, and expression of actions and events in the playscript the potential for a more informed and inventive performance of individual scenes or monologs is greatly enhanced.

In addition to the more traditional elements of dramaturgy that were discussed in Chapter 2 as part of dramatic criticism and playscript analysis, here are some less common approaches to understanding artistic craftsmanship that may provide clues to deciphering a playwright's system of codes that may stimulate imaginative performance hints in playing the scene. Begin by reviewing the introduction to the playscript, familiarizing yourself with any critical commentary or author comments that may precede the printed text. Of particular value should be any discussion of the playwright's life, historical incidents, or dramatic techniques which may have influenced the author's point of view in the depiction of character actions or events. For example, a perceptive reading of Eugene O'Neill's treatment of the family, the sea, or women is dependent upon prior knowledge of his relationship with a cold, stern father, an alcoholic brother, and a drug-addicted mother. Likewise, a precise understanding of Christopher Durang's social and spiritual frustrations or personal traumas that are subsequently revealed in comic parodies or satires in his playscripts demand prior knowledge of the Roman Catholic church as it may have influenced his artistic — and comic — vision.

Be attentive to the title of the playscript or any suggestive caption or slogan that is used to introduce a selected scene. Titles, captions, and slogans often suggest the playwright's dramatic perspective or may indicate the thematic approach necessary for an understanding of the individual elements of the playscript. For example, Albert Innaurato's suggestive title *The Transformation of Benno Blimpie* indicates that the actions and events of the playscript will be concerned with a longed-for wish or craving that will have to be satisfied as part of the culmination of the character's change of appearance or form. Playscript titles that rely upon imagery, like Pamela Mills' *Scene of Shipwreck*, James McLure's *Laundry and Bourbon*, or Eugene Ionesco's *Bald Soprano*, also provide initial dramatic perspectives that may be related to the playwright's point of view and may provide perceptive performances clues as well.

In addition, the actor may wish to review the listing of character names as part of the preliminary analysis of the playscript. Character names often suggest the playwright's basic approach to character definition and may reveal distinctive features or suggestive allusions that stimulate the actor to reinforce or amplify an interpretation of the character when playing the scene. For example, Arnold Powell's symbolic use of character names like "Everymom," "Alldad," and "Baby" in *The Death of Everymom* should suggest that the playscript is a modern parable or allegory related to the playwright's point of view on family, social, and spiritual or moral relationships. Likewise, Harold Pinter's use of the nondescriptive title character in *The Applicant* calls attention to the impersonal nature of the interview situation and may evoke imaginative performance approaches that result in unmistakable personal identity and sensitivity when playing the scene.

The basic dramaturgical approach to understanding the playwright's dramatic perspective should also include careful attention to the playwright's choice of *words,* specific use of *imagery,* and *descriptive* or *figurative language* that give meaning to the action and the situation. The actor's ability to translate metaphors, similes, or dramatic devices such as stream-of-consciousness dialog, action "flashbacks," or introspective interior monologs into imaginative performance opportunities may also result in inventive, stimulating interpretation principles when playing the scene as well. For example, in Jean Genet's *The Balcony* the playwright's choice of words is built upon the role-playing games that permit each character to indulge private illusions as each acts out a favorite sexual fantasy; and in Samuel Beckett's *Act Without Words* the specific use of inanimate objects and fragmentary images that appear mysteriously from an open space above the playing area all contribute to the playwright's apparent dramatic perspective of the character's psychological despair in the situation being described in the scene. Likewise, Imamu Amiri Baraka's descriptive *and* figurative language in *The Dutchman* not only directs attention to the social issue of racial prejudice but also gives immediate meaning to the action and the situation that shapes the playwright's transparent dramatic point of view.

A final principle to consider in playing the scene is its *structure.* Dramatic critics and scholars generally refer to structure in a discussion of the entire playscript rather than in one isolated scene. They tend to think of the basic structural elements as "exposition" (background information needed to understand action, character, and situation); "rising action" (character actions and situations that intensify audience interest); "complication" (obstacles or barriers that provoke conflict and prevent characters from realizing goals or objectives); "climax" (resolution of the conflict and solution of the obstacles or barriers); and "denouement" (French term for "unknotting," of the tying together of all loose ends of the storyline [plot] following the climax so that there are no uncompleted actions or unclarified situations). To be sure, the structural analysis of a playscript in these terms will undoubtedly give shape, form, and meaning to an overall dramatic perspective of the complete playscript; but the same critical principles applied to an individual scene or monolog may also provide valuable performance clues as well.

The structural approach to playing the scene suggests that the actor view each individual scene logically and independently as one complete unit of the playscript; and secure the exposition or background information needed to understand character actions and situations from the words, imagery, and descriptive or figurative language suggested in the scene itself. By isolating the rising action and complication in each independent scene, the actor may more easily detail the events or incidents that propel the character's action and situation toward a scenic climax; and by building each independent scene to its own climax it should, hopefully, follow that the resolution and denouement can more easily summarize the character actions and events that have transpired but also complete and clarify the specific situation detailed in the scene.

Remember, however, that this is primarily a rehearsal or audition technique that is intended to focus attention on the character's actions and the situation in an individual scene; it is *not* representative of the action, the situation, or the ultimate development of the character in the complete playscript itself. As a rehearsal or audition technique, this approach to playing the scene should, nevertheless, help the actor:

- Build suspense and heighten the climactic character moments inherent in the scene.
- Provide an imaginative performance framework that gives the

scene a single, complete goal or objective with a beginning, a middle, and an end.

• Focus attention on the intentions or motivations of a character on a particular issue or in pursuit of a particular plan of action.

• Explore the consequences and implications of individual character actions in isolated and detached situations.

• Highlight the significance of psychological or emotional aspects of character actions or reactions within a specific frame of reference.

• Promote immediate audience identification and intellectual or emotional response to the character and to the situation.

During the rehearsal period — especially in preparation for auditions — practice economy and efficiency in playing the scene. Clearly define the tidbits of character action and reaction that are indicated in the playscript for that individual episode and concentrate on a *single* performance objective and a *selective* character portrait most appropriate to the scene at hand, rather than striving for a representative character portrait that is detailed in the complete playscript. The actor cannot include all of the information related to a character's actions and situations in the limited time and space of a selected scene or an audition monolog, so practice economy and efficiency in applying complete knowledge of the playscript to that informative moment in the scene or monolog where the character is revealed in a concise, limited series of actions or in a single, specific situation.

Theoretical Blueprint

It is a tempting theoretical blueprint for the actor to think that playing the scene is primarily an act of dramatizing an individual character's actions and the situations in relationship to other characters in the scene, or to think that the "whole character" is created at one time in either the rehearsal period or in actually playing the scene. But the more accurate theoretical blueprint for both the rehearsal period and for playing the scene is a continuing exploration of the various impressions of *each* character in the scene to achieve the resolution of the actions and the situations described by the playwright. Thinking of characters as something distinctly "separate" from the holistic nature of the playscript can easily lead to confusion and contradiction in playing the scene and distort the playwright's dramatic perspective or thematic point of view. There are, however, some selected theoretical principles that feature the actor as an individual character but from the more complex view of the other characters in the scene. Remember that characters are inextricably entwined in each scene, and it is only through their action, intention, and motivation that they distinguish themselves as individuals from the other characters in the scene. The following theoretical perspectives may help to clarify the relationship between characters and also define the basic need for continued exploration of character impressions in both the rehearsal process and in playing the scene.

A good theoretical starting point is to discover, one by one, what Stanislavsky termed the *units of action* in a scene. The units of action are a catalog of the character's multiple goals and objectives in the particular situation being described by the playwright. They culminate in a *super–objective*, or the character's overarching emotional or intellectual desire in the particular situation. Although generally thought of in terms of defining character in the complete playscript, isolating these primary motivating forces that drive the character to accomplish fundamental goals and objectives may also provide specific performance clues for playing the individual scene as well. The choice of the super objective is a psychological one for the most part. The actor, that is, carefully reviews the units of action, determines the primary intention, and makes performance choices that clarify or amplify the character's efforts to accomplish the stated goals and objectives.

For example, the actor playing the title character in Eugene Ionesco's *The Leader* determines after a detailed analysis of the units of action and the obvious intention that an appropriate super-objective might be to play the scene with a performance approach that suggests, "even though this is absurd, I must not appear to be foolish or incompetent." This is a most appropriate interpretation of the title character in *The Leader*, which presents an unseen "role model" authority figure who is idolized by the unsuspecting public for his assumed charisma and wisdom. It is only revealed later in his eventual appearance on stage in the playscript that "the Leader" has no head! The use of this particular super-objective makes a significant political and this particular super-objective makes a significant political and philosophical statement regarding the nature of those who would blindly follow a headless leader; and also provides an inventive performance approach to playing the satire and humor of the scene.

The value of this theoretical approach to using units of action and the super-objective in playing the *individual* scene is to focus immediate attention on the character's intention or motivation; and to explore imaginative performance solutions to realize the character's primary desire as an integral part of the overall balance of the scene, rather than as an independent series of actions or reactions to other characters in the scene. Continued exploration of units of action and the super-objective in the rehearsal process should also lessen the number of interpretation "adjustments" or "alterations" that are inevitably made in later playing the role in performance. The theoretical appeal of this approach to playing the role is that it affords the actor an opportunity to extend the scope and depth of imaginative character building and is also a convenient means of enlarging one's perspective and perception of the complete playscript.

One of the most interesting theoretical principles you might wish to consider in playing the scene is to experiment with the *William James-Carl George Lang* notion that "physiological responses follow physical actions." The implications of this performance concept in which emotions are viewed as being provoked as a direct result of active physical activity — which, incidentally, reverses the traditional belief that emotions spark physical responses — has been treated primarily in theatre rehearsal games or improvisations in which the actor is given a descriptive performance clue like, "You are alone and frightened," and is then expected to exhibit a physical response like "crying," "trembling," or "running away." When applied to playing the scene, this theoretical principle suggests that if the actor can "simulate" the physical activity that results in the desired emotional response there is no need to rely upon invention, inspiration, or emotion memory to enrich the performance.

The ability to reproduce the precise motor activity that generates a desired emotion is an invaluable performance tool for the actor if it can be achieved with subtlety and without loss of authentic and honest emotion, and is an additional dimension in exploring character in the rehearsal period. Using the James-Lang theory in your approach to playing the scene should encourage a wide variety of psychological responses that extend your emotional range and refine your performance technique in playing scenes that call for sudden outbursts or subdued weeping. For example, the James-Lang implication that sadness is the physical act of the cry or that happiness is the physical act of the laugh has a special performance appeal for the actor who may be unduly inhibited or initially incapable of expressing emotional responses or reactions suggested in the scene. It may also be an unusually helpful performance approach for the beginning actor with limited stage experience or a very narrow life experience that has not provided significant emotional memories to relate to playing the scene.

Of particular interest to you in the rehearsal process should be controlling your bodily actions so that the emerging emotions do not appear to be exaggerated or "larger than life." A good rule of performance thumb is to experiment with the James-Lang notion in moderation; and then only when it is essential to capture those fleeting emotions that cannot be grasped with certainty or with clarity. The primary theoretical objective that physiological responses follow physical actions must continue to be an emphasis upon *honest* emotional intensity and intimacy, as well as upon *authentic* emotional responses and reactions when playing the scene.

When the actor has clearly identified the action, the character, and the situation in a selected episode of the playscript, the theoretical question that arises next is the definition and the role of the actor as *image-maker* in playing the scene. Although the playwright will undoubtedly provide a multitude of literary images that help to give form and substance to the narrative description of the action, the character, and the situation it is the actor who must give shape, size, and dimension to images in the performance, and to help clarify or amplify the playwright's dramatic perspective and point of view. "Playing the image" is the actor's creative ability to incorporate past experiences, memories, and responses into a meaningful interpretation of the character's action and dialog in the playscript. If the image is vague or even distorted, the actor's performance in the scene may appear to be lackluster, dull, or vacant; and without clear, vivid performance imagery the audience only "hears" the printed words or only "sees" the scripted events of the character's literary life detailed by the playwright. "A rose is a rose is a rose," the poet Gertrude Stein might say if the actor is unable to enrich the image with personal associations, emotions, or memories that give it expressive distinction or dimension that is imaginative and sensitive.

One of the first theoretical steps in playing the image is to determine a "self-image" for the character in the scene — especially in terms of height, weight, age, physicality, and posture. With a distinct, vivid self-image of the character in mind, the actor is in a much more informed position to define the action, the character, and the situation that is described in the scene. A clearly defined self-image should also promote a more perceptive understanding of the character's intention or motivation as well as dramatic function in the scene. As an "image-maker," the actor's creative genius lies in the capacity to translate literary allusions into poignant word pictures and scenic landscapes that arouse the imagination and interest of the audience, while simultaneously communicating a "shared" understanding of what the allusion or image means to both the actor and the audience. Peter Brook, the visionary director, describes the inherent performance value of shared communication of imagery between actor and audience in *The Empty Space* in this manner:

> "The exchange of impressions through images is our basic language; at the moment when one man expresses an image at that same instant the other man meets him in belief. The shared association in the language — if the association evokes nothing in the second person, if there is no instance of shared illusion, there is no exchange."

There are a number of creative approaches the actor might consider in playing the scene to achieve vivid sensory imagery. Once the role of imagery in the scene has been discussed and defined by the participating actors, the collecting of possible sources of imagery that could enrich playing the scene might include:

• Paintings, historical portraits, or photographs that suggest a mental picture of the action, the character, or the situation described in the scene.

- Magazines, novels, short stories, or other works of literature that suggest similar action, character, or situation described in the scene.

- Visual, graphic, or plastic arts that are analogous to the action, character, or situation described in the scene.

- Biographies, autobiographies, or memoirs that capture comparable emotional, intellectual, or psychological action, character, or situation described in the scene.

- Popular music lyrics, recordings, or tapes that recall familiar action, character, or situation described in the scene.

The rehearsal period is an excellent performance laboratory to experiment with imagery in playing the scene. It provides you a "risk-free" playing space in which to discover the dominant image that best conveys the action, character, and situation of the scene. Your imagination, however, must still provide the basic mechanism that sets the image in motion; and once an effective image has been discovered, your imagination must continue to refine and refresh the image so that it remains vibrant in its ability to visualize the action, the character, and the situation when you are playing the scene in performance. Once you have discovered your own effective performance image to communicate the self-image of your character — and reinforce the playwright's own point of view — strive continuously to maintain the honesty and the validity of that image at every rehearsal and in every performance.

A final theoretical principle to consider in playing the scene is the actor's ability to visualize the *body image* in performance that expresses the primary characteristics of action, character, and situation in a few, selectively chosen gestures, body positions, or movements. Although a great deal of attention is generally paid to the actor's vocal image in playing the scene, the body image appears quite often neglected in comparison. An expressive body image in performance is one that clearly defines or amplifies the character portrait in terms of stance, posture, and gesture. The actor can reveal significant intentions and motivations simply by the manner in which a character sits, walks, stands, or gestures in the scene. In using a body image when playing the scene, it is essential that the actor analyze and understand that character movement should be

As an "image-maker," the actor's creative genius lies in the capacity to translate literary allusions into poignant word pictures and scenic landscapes that arouse the imagination and interest of the audience.

part of a well-conceived and well-executed movement pattern for the complete playscript as well as for the dramatic context of the individual scene. Looking at the body image in terms of an introductory biology lesson that dissects movement into its individual, separate elements and pinpoints the spine of the structure as well as the basic framework of the fragment parts can be a dynamic theoretical principle in playing the scene, especially if the actor can discover a meaningful and sustained pattern of character movement in the playscript, and then select individual elements of that movement pattern to create a striking body image within the context of an action or an event in a representative scene. Detailed analysis of the selected scene in terms of character building should encourage spontaneous body images. Thoughtful selection of distinctive features of the spontaneous body images that freely emerge in rehearsal should prompt inventive and imaginative physical expression of the character as well.

Although the body image alone is not sufficient to create

the total portrait of a well-defined character, it may indicate the mental state of the character and assist the audience in visualizing the emotional state in which the character speaks the dialog or performs the action in the scene. To a great extent, successful actors are those who are most in tune with their character body image, practice a variety of character postures, explore physical mannerisms and gestures, or cultivate demanding physical transformations when playing the scene. In addition, the well-conceived and well-executed body image in an interpretation of the role "externalizes" the character relationship to the storyline and to the other characters in the scene.

When using the body image in playing the scene it is important to take into consideration the chronological as well as the mental age of the character. It is also important to be aware of the character's emotional, intellectual, and psychological state of being as described in the selected scene. Using the playscript and your own informed perceptions of how a character body image might be effective in playing the scene, it is important to chart a "personality profile" to underscore prominent or potential movement "phrases." For example, the character is viewed with a movement phrase like "a withered tree" or "a flowering bud" that might help to define the movement and make the expressive intention clearly visible. The primary characteristics of a typical personality profile might include:

- Peculiar behavioral patterns of the character.
- Physical condition of the character.
- Physical self-image and personal appearance attitude of the character.
- Submerged intentions and motivations of the character
- "Internal" conflicts and contradictions of the character.
- The bodily actions, gestures, or physical mannerisms of the character.

Remember that your use of a body image in playing the role *and* in playing the scene are similar: external reflection of internal characterization. In searching for the most appropriate body image when playing the scene, detail the opportunities suggested for movement with the other actors; search for the bodily actions and gestures that best communicate the character emotions and thoughts; and integrate appropriate physical mannerisms that help the audience visualize the character in performance. The body image gives shape and form to the character, and the character gives substance and meaning to the body image, while *both* enrich an honest and authentic character portrait in playing the scene.

Performance Blueprint

It is a rather traditional theatre anecdote to pose the question, "How do you get an elephant out of the theatre?" And to treasure the witty response, "You can't, it's in his blood!" There is a great measure of comic truth in this thinly veiled allusion of the "dumb-struck" elephant and the equally "star-struck" actor that plays an important role in the modern theatre, and offers an interesting perspective on the contemporary performance blueprint. It is, in fact, the difficulty of clearly discerning a compelling definition of the contemporary approach to playing the scene. The open-air, carnival spectacle of "big-top" star personality actors, "side-show" avant-garde actors, and circus "barkers" or "ringmasters" like the theorists Stanislavsky, Grotowski, Brecht, and Artaud have had a profound influence on modern acting styles and have been instrumental in shaping contemporary theatre practices.

Nevertheless, in spite of these obvious influences there have been relatively few abrupt departures from the basic principles of realistic acting in the contemporary theatre — with the notable exception of Joseph Chaikin and Peter Feldman's *Open Theatre* "transformation acting" approach that asks the actor to assume multiple roles in full view of the audience — that rely upon the actor's personal observation, lifelike situations, individually developed performance methods, and playscript interpretation skills to convincingly play the scene. Perhaps that is why it is so difficult to accurately define a "contemporary" acting style or to adequately detail even the most popular, custom-built contemporary performance blueprints currently in practice.

In your own rational efforts to resolve the imposing mystery of a contemporary acting style, and in your own creative pursuit of a personal, compatible performance blueprint that addresses the complex needs of playing the scene in contemporary theatre, it may be beneficial to consider a timely suggestion from the dramatic critic Joseph Wood Krutch. Although Krutch was writing in *The Idea of a Theatre* to describe his initial theory of literary criticism, his analysis of the *purpose*, the *passion*, and the *perception* of dramatic rhythm in the structure of drama appears to be an excellent model for the contemporary performance blueprint in playing the scene as well. It also remains a most perceptive analysis tool to determine a character's basic motivation.

In his analysis of dramatic rhythm in the structure of drama, Krutch defines "purpose" as the primary intent or motive; "passion" as the complementary feelings of pain or pleasure that result as a consequence of the intentions or motive; and "perception" as the meaningful insight or view of the situation that has been gained as a direct result of the consequences. When applying Krutch's dramatic criticism model to the actor's performance blueprint, the potential for purpose, passion, and perception to give added depth and dimension to playing the scene is intriguing. For example, if you approach the scene with a decided purpose of expressly revealing the character's intention or motivation, your performance should be subtle and simple in its single-mindedness, with no elaborate concealment or disguise of specific goals and objectives. If you approach the scene with a concentrated passion for voicing the character's feelings of pain or pleasure, your performance should be free of irritating vocal gymnastics or false sentiments, with no distracting or conflicting flights of emotional indecision or hesitation. If you approach the scene with an understanding perception of sharing the character's insight or view, your performance should be mentally and emotionally alert and responsive, with no self-indulgent theatrics and theatrical posing.

The "3-P" performance blueprint for the contemporary theatre in playing the scene encourages you to achieve a measure of personal dignity and professional satisfaction in the performance. It also asks you to play the scene with courage, fierce determination, and independence. At the same time, the "3-P" performance blueprint affords an opportunity for you to play the scene in a rehearsal setting where you can be truthful to your own nature or follow your own performance instincts in pursuit of a more practical and yet personal acting style. This is the "flesh-and-blood" approach to playing the scene in contemporary theatre. It is one that is consistent and yet courageous in its search for inventive, incisive character portraits that mirror reality as it is *lived*, while, at the same time, speaking directly and sincerely about the *truth* of the character's life.

In your approach to playing the scene in rehearsal, it is important to convey an attitude of objectivity and sensitivity, a conversational tone of delivery, and a natural sense of movement that suggests concentrated energy and focus on attention to detail. You should direct action and dialog to the other actors in the scene to reinforce the intimate nature of character relationships, and look for potential opportunities to interact and exchange interpersonal reactions whenever possible. Remember that your primary performance goal in playing the scene is to illustrate the "appearance" of action, character, and situation rather than the actual events themselves. The emphasis upon the appearance of reality also demands a more clearly directed attention on character behavior, mood, and attitude in playing the scene in order to highlight the more familiar, everyday view of life experiences as they are commonly seen with the human eye or felt by the human heart.

Knowing your character's specific goals and objectives in the scene and the concrete physical actions that help to communicate them will give you a performance blueprint frame of mind to play the scene in a consistent and convincing manner. Finding an expressive, forceful performance *verb* that propels your character into the immediate action of the scene may also help to underline the spontaneity and energy of the character's spoken dialog and physical actions. For example, the creative use of a character performance verb like "to live or to die," "to run or to hide," or to "accept or not to accept" in playing a scene in Sam Shepard's *The Curse of the Starving Class* not only provides exquisite playscript analysis and documentation of the playwright's dramatic perspective on decaying social morals and values but also suggests an imaginative performative blueprint to reveal the character's primary objective in a selected scene. Your analysis of the playscript and perceptive interpretation of the character's actions and dialog should provide a number of performance verbs to explore in the rehearsal period; and selective use of expressive, forceful performance verbs should help you communicate character subtext and the inherent meaning of the scene in the context of the complete playscript.

The analogy between performance verbs and corresponding character subtext is an especially important principle in playing the scene in contemporary theatre. Modern playwrights, discarding stereotypical, one-dimensional stage figures that had predominated the playing space in other historical periods of the theatre, appear to be much more concerned with presenting characters whose interior motives and psychological neuroses speak more directly to our own capacity for knowing and understanding life as it is being lived today. The tone of this new approach to drama that reveals "hidden" facts regarding a character's action, attitude, or motivation in behavioral or psychological terms needs active performance verbs to point the way toward final resolution and ultimate expression of the character as well as the playwright's point of view in playing the scene.

Finding an expressive, forceful performance verb that propels your character into the immediate action of the scene may also help to underline the spontaneity and energy of the character's spoken dialog and physical actions.

Perhaps the most significant principle in the performance blueprint for contemporary theatre is that it encourages the actor to make "choices" in playing the scene. Although the playscript provides numerous road signs and signposts that may direct the actor's traffic through the scene — dialog, situation, character, locale, stage directions — the pathway to an effective character portrait is a long and perilous journey traveled along winding, often uncharted roads, that may not always reach the performance destination. It is important, therefore, to be well prepared for the journey and to make appropriate choices that avoid detours or roadblocks in planning your performance blueprint.

As you anticipate your own performance road map that leads to the scenes that follow, pay particular attention to those choices which:

- Generate interesting and inventive stage business to help clarify the subtext of the character's action and dialog.

- Reveal moment-to-moment character interaction and interpersonal relationships with other characters.

- Create challenging improvisational opportunities that lead to discovery and demonstration of character intention and motivation.

- Promote visually explicit movement patterns or pictorial compositions that underline character mood and attitude.

- Highlight the "inner" and the "outer" character in terms of vocal and physical presentation.

- Encourage a natural and conversational tone of expression to give depth and dimension to character thoughts, ideas, or emotions.

- Communicate a sensitivity to the action, the character, and the situation detailed in the selected scene.

Your performance choices should provide a deeper insight into the special meaning that observation, association, and imagination have in playing the scene; and fresh, inventive theatrical images should emerge to promote your own self-expression and self-confidence in both the rehearsal period and in the final performance of the scene.

What remains for you in playing the scene is to blend theoretical principles and personal performance principles into an artistic expression that accurately reflects and reinforces the dramatic perspective and point of view of the playwright, while at the same time revealing the heart and soul of the character. Your identification and understanding of the actions and thoughts expressed in the scene should enhance the authenticity of the character portrait being drawn as well. Although you cannot hope to duplicate every element of characterization as it is suggested in the scene, careful selection and attention to significant details which help you visualize the character for yourself and for the audience should provide an artistic and creative interpretation and performance of the scene; one that you can take pride in and the audience can appreciate and applaud. And it is playing the scene with these basic principles in mind that allows you to experience the personal measure of achievement and self-satisfaction that comes — according to Polonius in William Shakespeare's *Hamlet* — when you embrace a performance blueprint that encourages you to follow your own instincts and to trust your own inventions:

"To thine own self be true
And it must follow as the night the day
Thou canst not then be false to any man."

Additional Dimensions

As you review the primary principles of playing the scene in the rehearsal period and in subsequent performance settings, it may appear that the process is extremely detailed and complex — perhaps more than it should be if your expectation is merely "saying" the words and "doing" the actions described by the playwright. But that is because playing the scene comprises a series of distinct, separate skills related to playscript interpretation, critical analysis, improvisation and imagination, vocal or physical preparation, movement patterns, and character building techniques that are often only *fused* or *integrated* in the actual performance of the scene itself. No matter how you choose to approach scene study or the playing of the scene, however, the additional dimensions of your investigation should always consider the preliminary elements described here as well as your own discoveries as they are revealed in the rehearsal period. Each scene remains a unique, unpredictable challenge for the actor to unravel the mystery of the playwright's dramatic perspective and point of view in the complete playscript as well as in the individual, representative scene.

With experience and the practical knowledge gained through extensive analysis and rehearsal, you should be able to advance a consistent performance blueprint that operates in a logical, systematic order and with a personal, specialized technique or method that is most appropriate for your own performance needs or skills. The creative process that you devise or discover in your individual approach to playing the scene is never complete, and is always limited by the information supplied by the playwright, so it is especially important to formulate a performance blueprint that is uniform and unified in its ability to promote the "look" and the "feel" of the character you are playing in the scene.

Remember that the rehearsal period is an opportunity for you to re-evaluate the initial analysis of the scene and to anticipate new performance insights that might be suggested by the other actors in the scene. It is a time to be open and flexible in your interpretation of the character, and to test that interpretation against the understanding of the other characters/actors in the scene. The rehearsal period is also an opportunity for you to fill in the blanks left unanswered in the scene — especially if the scene indicates very little or perhaps nothing to seize upon in connecting the dots of your character's specific intention or motivation. The important point to remember is that any re-evaluation or revision of the performance blueprint in rehearsal must serve to clarify the action, the character, or the situation; it should never contradict or confuse the basic information indicated in the complete playscript or suggested in the selected scene.

As you develop your own performance technique of acting in the contemporary theatre, pay special attention to the fundamental purpose of scene study and playing the scene: it is not an end in itself, but only an essential means to cultivate an imaginative self-expression in performance. Think of your performance as a personal "self-portrait," a finely etched oral and visual picture of self-confidence, poise, and accomplishment. Consider every scene as an occasion to develop interpretation skills that lead to meaningful communication between you and your scene partners as well as with the audience. It is also important to actively participate in performance opportunities that give you the first-hand experience necessary to meet the changing artistic challenges of the contemporary theatre.

Finally, as an artist you must constantly strive to increase the range and depth of your creative self-expression in playing the scene. You must give energy and enthusiasm to your basic instincts and individual nature in the pursuit of what the psychologist David Perkins calls the "...artist's drive to wrest order, simplicity, meaning, richness, or powerful expression from what is seemingly chaos." With these thoughts in mind, approach each of the following scenes, revue sketches and monologs with confidence and creativity as you demonstrate to *yourself* what you have learned from this extended discussion of contemporary theatre performance principles and practices. When you have achieved artistic as well as critical success in your personal performance blueprint, you are ready to "get your act together" and should be well on the road to exciting and stimulating theatrical adventures in scene study and in playing the scene. Happy journey!

Recommended Reading

The following textbooks are intended for the actor who may like a more detailed review of contemporary theatre in terms of performance principles and practices. The recommended readings provide a more immediate discussion and evaluation of the contemporary theatre in terms of acting style, playscript interpretation, and the more avant-garde ensemble approaches to performance. The valuable insights and observations provided in these additional readings should promote a more mature understanding of the contemporary performance principles at work in this very special period of our theatre history.

Belt, Lynda. *The Acting Primer*. Boston: Baker's, Ltd., 1993.

Berry, Cicely. *The Actor and the Text,* revised edition. New York: Applause Theatre Books, 1995.

Brebner, Ann. *Setting Free the Actor*. San Francisco, California: Mercury House, 1990.

Brook, Peter. *The Shifting Point*. New York: Harper & Row, 1987.

Chaikin, Joseph. *The Presence of the Actor*, 5th edition. New York: Atheneum, 1984.

Craig, David. *A Performer Prepares,* revised edition. New York: Applause Theatre Books, 1995.

Downs, David. *The Actor's Eye: Seeing and Being Seen.* New York: Applause Theatre Books, 1995.

Harrop, John and Sabin Epstein. *Acting With Style.* New York: Prentice-Hall, 1990.

Hornby, Richard. *Script Into Performance*. New York: Applause Theatre Books, 1995.

Issacharoff, Michael and Robin Jones. *Performing Texts.* Philadelphia, Pennsylvania: University of Pennsylvania Press, 1988.

Marowitz, Charles. *Directing the Action.* New York: Applause Theatre Books, 1995.

Meisner, Sanford and Dennis Longwell. *On Acting.* New York: Vintage Books, 1987.

Parilla, Catherine. *A Theory for Reading Dramatic Texts.* New York: Praegar Press, 1995.

Richardson, Don. *Acting Without Agony.* Boston: Baker's Ltd., 1995.

Wells, Lynne K. *The Articulate Voice.* Scottsdale, Arizona: Gorsuch-Scarisbrick, 1989.

CHAPTER FOUR

SCENES FOR YOUTH AND YOUNG MEN AND WOMEN
(With Adults)

> *"Why, I can smile and murder whiles I smile,*
> *And cry 'Content' to that which grieves my heart,*
> *And wet my cheeks with artificial tears,*
> *And frame my face to all occasions."*
> > *Henry VI, Part III*
> > — William Shakespeare

In playing scenes that feature youth and young men or women but may also include supporting roles for adults, it is important that the actors create an illusion of spontaneous and natural reactions and responses appropriate for the primary age range (13 19 years) of each featured character. There should be no attempt in playing the role to appear "childish" or "juvenile"; and a distinctly personal, familiar approach to speaking and moving is needed to convey the emotions and thoughts of these youthful, adolescent characters who are genuinely engaged in realistic episodes or relationships with adults who live their lives much like other ordinary people. These selected scenes are primarily concerned with actual events or carefully drawn sketches based upon commonplace observation, and provide the actors with actual flesh-and-blood role models that should help to more easily relate the events of the scene to each performer's own understanding of the character situation and subsequent action in the episode.

The performance demands in playing scenes featuring youth and young men or women rely upon creative invention and lively imagination in the interpretation of the selected role(s). There are ample opportunities to invest the performance with personal traits such as comic flair, physique, mannerisms, and distinctive vocal quality to give added dimension and uniqueness to the character portrait. The performance point to remember, however, is that personal traits should be complementary and included only if they are essential to complete the character portrait being drawn. A detailed analysis of the selected scene should provide the actors with important clues to the relationship of each character and help to clearly define the role that personal traits and mannerisms might play in characterization. All of the selected scenes involve a significant relationship of some depth and dimension and will need carefully chosen personal traits or mannerisms to express the mood and the attitude that is being suggested. It is important to approach each selected scene with sensitivity, concentrating on a conversational tone of delivery and a natural, relaxed sense of "open communication" that suggests active involvement and participation in the unfolding events and actions.

Because of the contemporary emphasis upon intimacy and naturalness in performance, actors playing roles especially written for youth and young men and women may need to make some inevitable adjustments in their approach to role-playing. This contemporary emphasis upon intimacy and naturalness in character performance should immediately suggest subtlety and the need to "tone down" stage business as well as the need to avoid stage movement that might appear exaggerated or unnatural. A good beginning performance principle needed to achieve the intimacy and simplicity of contemporary drama is to consciously approach scene playing from a "nontheatrical" perspective, perhaps imagining that the characters and the situations in the selected scene have the same relationship as one might expect to find in everyday life or in more traditional settings like a home, office, school, or restaurant. The "nontheatrical" perspective in performance encourages the actor to sharpen skills in personal observation and to avoid artifice and superficiality in role-playing by concentrating on subtlety and nuance in voice and movement to suggest character relationships that are authentic and believable.

The emphasis upon intimacy and naturalness in contemporary performance, however, does *not* suggest that the actor's vocal skills are diminished or devalued in playing scenes for youth or young men and women. The primary performance goal remains "natural speech" and there must be intense concentration on volume, projection, articulation, and clarity of pronunciation that promotes audience listening and understanding of character dialog. Speaking distinctly through

In playing scenes that feature youth and young men or women but may also include supporting roles for adults, there should be no attempt to appear "childish" or "juvenile" when engaged in realistic episodes or relationships with adults.

effective diaphragmatic breathing techniques and practicing vocal relaxation exercises regularly should free the voice from undue strain and tension; while at the same time continued relaxation exercises as a regular part of the rehearsal process should promote a conversational performance tone that is appropriate for the everyday speech intonations and patterns needed for voicing dialog in contemporary scenes.

The distinguished actor Raymond Massey, reflecting his own performance technique in the essay "Acting" published in *The Theatre Handbook*, reminds beginning students that "good actors, like good plays, are made of flesh and blood, not bundles of tricks." These words of caution are a good indication of the responsibility an actor has to be truthful and honest in playing contemporary scenes. Avoid the "bundles of tricks" and the insatiable urge to call attention to oneself in performance — either through miscalculated mischief like caricature and conceit or misdirected method like over-emphasis and over-exaggeration. And do not confuse cliché, repetitive stage business or aimless and wandering movement with inventive and original character interpretations that are viable, vibrant portraits of memorable and believable stage figures. Learn to appraise your work critically and objectively, with an eye toward visualizing the character as a living, breathing human being whose desires, feelings, and moods or attitudes are no more distinct or different than your own might be in a similar situation; and with an ear toward voicing the character as a thinking, feeling human being whose dreams, fears, and simple pleasures are no more unique or unusual than your own might be under the given circumstances. When you are able to approach characterization from this perspective your performance will undoubtedly have a spark of the intuition and intensity that kindles the imagination and fires the interpretation of unique character portraits.

In approaching the selected scenes that follow, be mindful of the "youthful innocence" that is part of the complex depiction of the characters and the "personal issues" that each faces in the adult world. There is a minimum of overt action in the scenes that helps to define the characters, but a wealth of narrative and dialog that reveals the "inner truth" of the character's secret dreams and private lives. Play each scene with an emphasis upon the special relationship established by the characters and use movement sparingly as you concentrate on a performance that communicates the basic ingredients of each character's mood or attitude in the given circumstances. Be sure that your interpretation gives depth and dimension to the action being described and that each character's personality as well as idiosyncrasy is highlighted individually. And don't forget to pay special attention to the apparent emotional struggle taking place within each character as they struggle to express the anxiety and turmoil that reveals itself in their agitated fears and frustrations as well as in their conflicting relationships with older adults in the scene. Finally, be aware of the fierce sense of independence and plaintive urgency voiced by the characters as they share intimate confidences and confessions related to their personal aspirations and dreams or reflect on the meaning of their lives.

Scenes for youth and young men or women pay special attention to the apparent emotional turmoil taking place within each character as they struggle to express the anxiety and apprehension that reveals itself in their agitated fears and frustrations as well as in their conflicting relationships with older adults.

The scenes with comic overtones or elements of fantasy need to be approached with sensitivity and a touch of compassionate understanding so that the spirit of humor or "make-believe" does not demote the characters to farcical one-dimensional, cardboard stereotypes, or reduce the seriousness of the situation in which the characters imagine themselves to be at the critical moment in the scene. This must be done subtly and with a sense of restraint and good fun so that there is still an honesty and humor in the interpretation that does not detract from the character's personal sense of anguish, happiness, or frustration. It is essential that the actors isolate the "cause" of the comic spirit as the key to understanding the role that humor plays in the selected scene to reveal the character's point of view; and to also use the humor to punctuate the almost absurd, unreal actions of the character in the given situation. This performance approach should promote a keen sense of jesting and playful jousting that often distinguish youth and young men or women just beginning to assert their individual self-image and independent personal values in the more adult world.

from *Moon Over the Brewery* ©
by Bruce Graham

This contemporary scene is set in the Waslyk home and front yard, somewhere in the coal regions of Pennsylvania. Amanda Waslyk, age thirteen, enters the front yard carrying a briefcase. She is a very serious, mature young lady with a sense of obvious direction and purpose. She is quickly followed by Randolph, an incredibly handsome man of indeterminate age who wears a perfectly tailored white suit. A touching, gentle comedy that mixes "fantasy" and "reality" in a child's imagination, this playscript is ideal for youth in terms of its tender, fragile character development and the possibilities for enterprising invention.

Amanda, it appears, has "created" her imaginary friend Randolph to help compensate for the loss of her father, and her caustic remarks and antic behavior are greatly encouraged by her secret companion. Randolph, who appears only to Amanda, is a free-spirited, mischievous sprite who delights in comic misadventure and suggestive, biting humor to provoke Amanda as well as her mother, Miriam. The scene that follows is typical of the "games" these childish characters play, and suggests the comic mayhem which ensues when these two wayward friends devise imaginative strategies to drive away Miriam's already dwindling list of potential suitors.

In playing the scene, the actors should indicate the comfortable and friendly relationship that Amanda and her imaginary friend Randolph enjoy; but there is also a biting undercurrent to this intimate, sharing bond that must be clearly visible just beneath the surface of their actions and dialog. There is very little inhibition expressed in the character's sharing of personal emotions or thoughts, and the basically innocent exchanges should reinforce the honesty and truthfulness that the characters share in common. In addition, there is an atmosphere of playful comradeship that lends an air of infectious fun to the special relationship established by the characters as they share intimate thoughts and emotions.

These are very inspired and inventive characters, and the actors will need to be authentic and sensitive to the performance portrait suggested by the dialog. Randolph, especially, needs to be visualized as a flesh-and-blood character rather than as a distant, fleeting creation of Amanda's vivid imagination. The charm of the scene is the sudden "surprise" that becomes evident when we realize that Randolph is a fantasy character, surprisingly resourceful and outrageously witty in his sharp, yet warm and caring compassion for Amanda. It is also important to feature Amanda's own inner conflicts and frustration as she tries to come to terms with the reality of her mother's incomplete, unmarried lifestyle; and the increasing dependence that Amanda exhibits in her companionship with her imaginary friend Randolph should be treated with sensitive awareness and understanding. Finally, the scene encourages spontaneous impulses and vivid personalities to capture the spirit of this genuine, passionate relationship; and it is essential that the actors allow the action of the scene to be shaped by an unfailing warmth and humor that is antic, hopeful, and always sincere for these two kindred spirits.

1 **AMANDA:** *(Whispering urgently)* **Go away! It's not funny**
2 **anymore.** *(At the house, cautiously)* **Mother? You home?**
3 *(No answer. She turns Off-stage, this time speaking in a*
4 *normal voice.)* **Stop following me.** *(RANDOLPH strolls*
5 *into view. He is of indeterminate age and wears a*
6 *perfectly tailored white suit which could be slightly out*
7 *of date, but it looks good on him — who cares.*
8 *RANDOLPH is incredibly handsome. Cary Grant would*
9 *be ideal in casting, but we understand he's unavailable.)*
10 **RANDOLPH: Women have such egos. You naturally**
11 **assume I'm following you.**
12 **AMANDA: You are.**
13 **RANDOLPH: Perhaps I'm just out for a stroll.**
14 **AMANDA: Up here?**
15 **RANDOLPH: The strip mine is lovely in the spring.**
16 **AMANDA: Go away.**
17 **RANDOLPH: You've missed me.**
18 **AMANDA: You wish.**
19 **RANDOLPH: You have.**
20 **AMANDA: You are so conceited, you know that?**
21 **RANDOLPH: I've never had time for fake modesty.**
22 **AMANDA: Go away.** *(She heads for the front door.)*
23 **RANDOLPH: Don't you even want to know where I've**
24 **been?**
25 **AMANDA: No.**
26 **RANDOLPH: Yes you do. You're dying for a good story.**
27 **AMANDA: I'm serious – go away. You always get me in**
28 **trouble.**
29 **RANDOLPH: You need me.**
30 **AMANDA: What for?**
31 **RANDOLPH: You know.** *(A beat)*
32 **AMANDA: I don't need you and I don't want you here. And**
33 **don't ever come to school again.**
34 **RANDOLPH:** *(Advancing on her)* **Who was that little toad**

1   with whom you were having such a serious conversa-
2   tion at the bus stop?
3   AMANDA: He's not a toad.
4   RANDOLPH: Peter, that's his name, isn't it?
5   AMANDA: I hate it when you play games like this –
6   RANDOLPH: Does Peter have a skin condition?
7   AMANDA: He has a pimple –
8   RANDOLPH: Substandard personal hygiene?
9   AMANDA: All boys have them once in awhile.
10   RANDOLPH: I never did.
11   AMANDA: Well, you're perfect.
12   RANDOLPH: After all these years you finally admit it. I
13   should go away more often. *(She heads for the door, but*
14   *he blocks her way.)*
15   AMANDA: Get out of my way.
16   RANDOLPH: So what were you and the Elephant Man
17   talking about?
18   AMANDA: None of your business. *(She moves around him to*
19   *the porch.)* Good-bye, Randolph.
20   RANDOLPH: You need me. *(She turns to protest, but he*
21   *beats her to it.)* Somebody was here last night.
22   AMANDA: *(Without conviction)* No there wasn't.
23   RANDOLPH: Then why was I called away from such a
24   fabulous party?
25   AMANDA: Nobody's stopping you. Go back to your party.
26   RANDOLPH: Didn't you hear someone laughing? Right
27   around midnight?
28   AMANDA: That was the TV.
29   RANDOLPH: Don't lie to me, m'love. I know you too well.
30   *(He moves closely to her.)* Mother had that smile this
31   morning. *(He takes out a cigarette case.)*
32   AMANDA: What smile?
33   RANDOLPH: You know. That Scarlett O'Hara-the-morn-
34   ing-after-Rhett-Butler-carried-her-up-the-stairs-smile.

1   **Cigarette?** *(She shakes her head "no." He takes out a ciga-*
2   *rette holder and proceeds to light up.)* **Now think. When**
3   **was the last time Mother had anything resembling**
4   **that smile? Four years ago. The ceramic tile salesman**
5   **with a penchant for country music. If it wasn't for me**
6   **we'd still be listening to songs about trucks.**
7   AMANDA: I got rid of him – not you.
8   RANDOLPH: You're an amateur –
9   AMANDA: No I'm not –
10 RANDOLPH: Me – I'm the one who did it. I'm the person
11   who saved you from having to ride in a car with large
12   green dice hanging from the mirror.
13 AMANDA: *(Extending her hand)* It's been a pleasure,
14   Randolph. Stop back again in four years. *(Again, he*
15   *blocks her way.)*
16 RANDOLPH: What were you and this Peter talking about?
17 AMANDA: You're so smart, you tell me.
18 RANDOLPH: He was making some sort of indecent pro-
19   posal, wasn't he?
20 AMANDA: He's thirteen.
21 RANDOLPH: That's when they start –
22 AMANDA: You're jealous, aren't you?
23 RANDOLPH: *(How absurd.)* Please...
24 AMANDA: You are.
25 RANDOLPH: Of him? He's this big. *(He indicates a very*
26   *short person.)*
27 AMANDA: No he's not. *(RANDOLPH arches his eyebrows.)*
28   He's still growing.
29 RANDOLPH: He's a dwarf –
30 AMANDA: Get out of my way –
31 RANDOLPH: I adore you – *(This stops her.)*
32 AMANDA: I know. *(She stares at him a moment.)* I'm taking
33   French now.
34 RANDOLPH: Really?

1   **AMANDA: Know how you say "I adore you" in French?**

2   *(Shakes his head.)* **Je t'adore.**

3   **RANDOLPH: Je t'adore.** *(Silence)* **Tell me you've missed me.**

4   **AMANDA:** *(Quietly)* **Once in awhile.**

5   **RANDOLPH: Because I've missed you –**

6   **AMANDA: Now go away, please. She'll be home soon.** *(He*

7   *gets out of her way. She opens the door and enters the*

8   *house.)*

9   **RANDOLPH: So this is how it ends, hmmm? Being aban-**

10   **doned for a midget with a growth on his face?**

11   *(AMANDA looks at him a second, then laughs.)*

12   **AMANDA: You're a terrible martyr.** *(Silence)*

13   **RANDOLPH: I'm around whenever you need help getting**

14   **rid of the midnight laughter.** *(The phone rings.)* **All you**

15   **have to do is whistle. You do know how to whistle,**

16   **don't you?**

17   **AMANDA: Get an original line, OK, Randolph?**

18   **RANDOLPH: You're right. It's better when Bacall says it.**

19   *(He blows her a kiss.)* **I'm around.** *(She crosses the living*

20   *room and answers the phone. RANDOLPH moves out of*

21   *her view, but remains on the porch.)*

22   **AMANDA: Hello, Mrs. Simpers...I just knew it was you...no,**

23   **I told you I wouldn't know anything until after**

24   **four...the latest offer still stands at thirteen hundred**

25   **dollars...I can't tell you who the other bidder is...** *(She*

26   *plops into a chair, taking off her shoes.)* **No, Mother's not**

27   **home yet...it wouldn't make any difference...my**

28   **mother never talks business...that's why she had**

29   **me...OK, get back to me with a figure.** *(She hangs up,*

30   *smiles. She enjoyed that. She crosses to the kitchen –*

31   *stops – sees a note hanging on the door, takes it down*

32   *and reads it. She lets out a little sigh of disgust.)*

33   **RANDOLPH:** *(From the porch)* **I said whistle, not sigh.** *(She*

34   *moves right to him, not surprised that he's still there.)*

1   **AMANDA:** *(Indicating the note)* **Someone's coming for**
2   **dinner.**
3   **RANDOLPH: Really?**
4   **AMANDA:** *(Nodding)* **She wants me to set the floor.**
5   **RANDOLPH:** *(Reading over her shoulder)* **Who's the honored**
6   **guest?**
7   **AMANDA: Doesn't say.**
8   **RANDOLPH: Care to venture a guess, old sport? The**
9   **midnight laughter perhaps.**
10   **AMANDA: Who knows.**
11   **RANDOLPH: My, he moves fast.**
12   **AMANDA: We don't know for sure –**
13   **RANDOLPH: Things are kind of reversed though, aren't**
14   **they? Isn't it customary to dine together first and**
15   **then spend the night?**
16   **AMANDA:** *(Sharp)* **Randolph!**
17   **RANDOLPH:** *(Chastised)* **That was uncalled for.**
18   **AMANDA: You always find the dirt in things.**
19   **RANDOLPH: Everyone needs a hobby.**
20   **AMANDA: It was the TV...I heard the TV.**
21   **RANDOLPH: Whatever you say** *– (AMANDA begins to clear a*
22   *place on the floor.)*
23   **AMANDA:** *(Convincing herself)* **If someone was here why**
24   **didn't I see something this morning? We always knew**
25   **when Morty stayed.**
26   **RANDOLPH: Perhaps this one doesn't use Aqua Velva.**
27   *(She begins to move a stack of canvasses.)*
28   **AMANDA: It's just a dinner – that's all.**
29   **RANDOLPH:** *(Looking at the canvasses)* **Doesn't she ever get**
30   **tired of moonscapes?**
31   **AMANDA: Why should she?**
32   **RANDOLPH: Kind of limits your use of color.** *(He crosses to*
33   *the easel.)* **This the new one?**
34   **AMANDA: Yes.**

1   **RANDOLPH: May I?** *(She moves to the easel, lifting the cover*
2   *from the painting.)* **What part of town is that?**
3   **AMANDA: I don't know.** *(She looks closer.)* **Looks like she's**
4   **facing...Beertown. See? That's the brewery.**
5   **RANDOLPH: Beertown. She's slumming.** *(She observes it.)*
6   **AMANDA: I like it.** *(She covers it back up and resumes*
7   *clearing the area.)*
8   **RANDOLPH: I really don't enjoy being a pest, but we**
9   **should start plotting some sort of strategy.**
10   **AMANDA: What for?**
11   **RANDOLPH: Our dinner guest. It's been a few years –**
12   **we're out of practice.**
13   **AMANDA: Stop it –**
14   **RANDOLPH: We're a team here, old sport. And when it**
15   **comes to intruders we're batting a thousand. Now, I**
16   **suggest ground glass in the ice cream –**
17   **AMANDA: We don't even know he's the one coming for**
18   **dinner –**
19   **RANDOLPH: Ahh-hahh! You admit there was a "he" here.**
20   *(She starts to answer back – stops.)*
21   **AMANDA: I've got paint on my hands.** *(She heads for the*
22   *stairs; he steps in front of her.)*
23   **RANDOLPH: How many have there been, anyway?**
24   **AMANDA: I don't know –**
25   **RANDOLPH: There was that one when you were very**
26   **little. You know...the prince of polyester...what was**
27   **his name?**
28   **AMANDA: Bill.**
29   **RANDOLPH: Right, Bill. How could I forget such an exotic**
30   **name. Then there was Steve –**
31   **AMANDA: You're in my way again –**
32   **RANDOLPH: Remember Steve? The truck driver who**
33   **lived to spit. Delightful chap, as long as you kept him**
34   **outside.**

1 AMANDA: Randolph...

2 RANDOLPH: And Morty, the country music fan. A lover of

3 women who sing through their noses –

4 AMANDA: You're getting on my nerves –

5 RANDOLPH: That's three. And all of them...gone. With my

6 help, of course.

7 AMANDA: *(Holding out her hands)* **Out of my way or I smear**

8 **this all over your suit.** *(RANDOLPH gets out of her way;*

9 *she exits up the stairs.)*

10 RANDOLPH: We're three-zero, old sport. And you know I

11 hate to lose. *(The quilt catches his eye.)* **My God, that is**

12 **beautiful.**

13 AMANDA: *(Off)* **What?**

14 RANDOLPH: *(He moves to pick it up.)* **This quilt.**

15 AMANDA: *(Off)* **Don't touch it. That's my ticket to New**

16 **York. I'm getting ten percent for that and I've got to**

17 **get her up to thirteen hundred dollars.**

18 RANDOLPH: My God, who has that kind of money around

19 here?

20 AMANDA: Guess.

21 RANDOLPH: Mrs. Simpers.

22 AMANDA: That's right.

23 RANDOLPH: She is a vile woman –

24 AMANDA: But her checks are just fine. And as soon as I get

25 her up to thirteen hundred dollars, I'll take my

26 percentage and pay for the school trip.

27 RANDOLPH: I really don't like the idea of something this

28 lovely wrapped around someone like her. It's too big of

29 a contradiction. *(AMANDA enters to the top of the stairs.*

30 *She stands a moment, then walks down, looking grim.)*

31 AMANDA: **Guess what I just found on the edge of the tub.**

32 *(He shrugs; she holds out a man's wristwatch.)*

33 RANDOLPH: **A Timex.**

34 AMANDA: **Do you believe that?**

1   **RANDOLPH:** Not even a top-of-the-line Timex –

2   **AMANDA:** How could she do this? Here I am, willing to

3   give her the benefit of the doubt, and...and she snuck

4   a man in here. She's never done anything like that

5   before –

6   **RANDOLPH:** As far as we know –

7   **AMANDA:** I mean, she always brought them home so we

8   could go through the whole charade of meeting them

9   and everything. But...I mean...to sneak a man in here

10   so that she could... *(She looks over at him. Simultan-*

11   *eously, they do an identical "ecchhhh..." sound, indicating*

12   *their displeasure.)*

13   **RANDOLPH:** I think it's time you sat your mother down

14   and had a very stern talk with her.

15   **AMANDA:** It's so dishonest. I mean, I know she's a little

16   goofy sometimes, but she's always honest.

17   **RANDOLPH:** I think we may have a problem here. *(He*

18   *moves away from her; she follows.)*

19   **AMANDA:** What?

20   **RANDOLPH:** Let's face it: when it comes to men your

21   mother is not exactly a gourmet. She's more into fast

22   food.

23   **AMANDA:** Get to the point –

24   **RANDOLPH:** Look at her résumé, m'love. It's a long line of

25   losers and slobs.

26   **AMANDA:** *(Sharply)* Except my father.

27   **RANDOLPH:** *(Softening)* Of course. An intelligent, sensi-

28   tive man. And a good dresser. But let's face it, Amanda,

29   he was a fluke.

30   **AMANDA:** So.

31   **RANDOLPH:** So if she went to all the trouble to introduce

32   us to the three stooges...why would she feel compelled

33   to sneak this one in? *(AMANDA sits, allowing this to*

34   *sink in. From Off-stage, WARREN ZIMMERMAN enters. He*

1   *wears a summer mailman's uniform, complete with*
2   *shorts and knee socks.)*
3   **AMANDA: My God...you're probably right.** *(WARREN looks*
4   *up at the house.)*
5   **RANDOLPH: Don't be surprised if our dinner guest turns**
6   **out to be a leper in a bowling shirt.**
7
8
9
10
11
12
13
14
15
16
17
18
19
20
21
22
23
24
25
26
27
28
29
30
31
32
33
34

from *Blind Date* ©
by Horton Foote

The setting for this scene by the Academy Award-winning playwright is the generously furnished living room of Robert and Dolores Henry, in the small town of Harrison, Texas, in 1929. "Aunt" Dolores, a former high school beauty queen and now a shrew to her henpecked, weak-willed husband Robert, is busily schooling her visiting niece, Sarah Nancy, on the art of dating. It has taken some time for "Aunt" Dolores to locate a desirable suitor for her rather out-spoken, unconventional niece, and the "blind date" is expected at any moment. The well-meaning aunt takes this opportunity to prepare a fundamental, introductory lecture — based upon her own past experiences and recollections — to instruct Sarah Nancy in the art of "conversation" that is needed for these initial, exploratory dating encounters.

Sarah Nancy, bookish and rebellious, is not easily persuaded. Her attitude, critical and skeptical, is very distressing for "Aunt" Dolores, who must use all of her communication skills to convince Sarah Nancy to play the game of polite conversation and innocent flirtation that the occasion demands — at least as far as "Aunt" Dolores is concerned, or can easily recall from her own dating memory! The scene is a genuinely funny commentary on the courting behavior once popular in "Aunt" Dolores's circle of young ladies; and also on the more progressive opinions of dating expressed by Sarah Nancy's independent generation of thinkers. In spite of their obviously different social points of view on the subject, however, there is an attitude of compassion, tender caring, and tolerance that prevails and brightens the scene with touching adolescent desperation and adult comic sensitivity.

In playing the scene, there are moments when the well-meaning, fluttery "Aunt" Dolores wistfully remembers her own gentlemen callers; and when willful Sarah Nancy simply refuses to give serious thought to what she considers a ludicrous proposition. The atmosphere may be charged with tension and frustration, or there may be quiet moments that suggest a sharing and understanding that is meaningful and wonderfully insightful for both characters. In addition, the spirit of anticipation and excitement for the impending arrival of the "blind date" should propel each character's action and reaction in the spoken lines of the dialog.

It is very important in this scene for the actors to be truthful to their own nature and to clearly define each character's basic motivation or intention in the given circumstances. Resist the urge to play "Aunt" Dolores as a troublesome, meddling fool; and do not allow Sarah Nancy to become too bold or strident in her self-conscious, independent attitude and viewpoint. Attention to these basic details should help to clarify each character's natural impulses and spontaneous outbursts in the scene. There are sufficient clues revealed in the dialog to encourage the actors to use their own creative imagination in completing the character portraits suggested; but any imaginative inventions must appear to be authentic in order to focus attention on the obvious differences in each character's age, point of view, and mood or attitude in this scene. As a rehearsal technique, improvisation of this scene — especially in physical actions and interactions — may provide additional performance clues for character development and help to communicate the moment-to-moment interpersonal relationship and individual perspectives of "Aunt" Dolores and Sarah Nancy as they each respond honestly and truthfully in the scene.

1   **DOLORES: Now where were we? Oh, yes. I was going over**
2   **my list of things to talk about.** *(DOLORES picks up her*
3   *list and begins reading.)* **One: Who is going to win the**
4   **football game next Friday? Two: Do you think we have**
5   **had enough rain for the cotton yet? Three: I hear you**
6   **were a football player in high school. What position**
7   **did you play? Do you miss football? Four: I hear you are**
8   **an insurance salesman. What kind of insurance do you**
9   **sell? Five: What is the best car on the market today, do**
10   **you think? Six: What church do you belong to? Seven:**
11   **Do you enjoy dancing? Eight: Do you enjoy bridge?** *(She*
12   *puts the list down.)* **All right, that will do for a start.**
13   **Now, let's practice. I'll be Felix. Now. Hello, Sarah**
14   **Nancy.** *(A pause. SARAH NANCY looks at her like she*
15   *thinks she's crazy.)* **Now, what do you say, Sarah Nancy?**
16 **SARAH NANCY: About what?**
17 **DOLORES: About what? About what you say when**
18   **someone says hello to you, Sarah Nancy. Now, let's**
19   **start again. Hello, Sarah Nancy.**
20 **SARAH NANCY: Hello.**
21 **DOLORES: Honey, don't just say hello and above all don't**
22   **scowl and say hello. Smile. Hello, how very nice to see**
23   **you. Let me feel your warmth. Now, will you**
24   **remember that? Of course you will. All right, let's**
25   **start on your questions. Begin with your first ques-**
26   **tion.** *(A pause)* **I'm waiting, honey.**
27 **SARAH NANCY: I forget.**
28 **DOLORES: Well, don't be discouraged. I'll go over the list**
29   **carefully and slowly again. One: Who is going to win**
30   **the football game next Friday? Two: Do you think we**
31   **have enough rain for the cotton yet? Three: I hear you**
32   **were a football player in high school. What position**
33   **did you play? Do you miss football? Four: I hear you**
34   **are an insurance salesman. What kind of insurance**

1   do you sell? Five: What is the best car on the market
2   today, do you think? Six: What church do you belong
3   to? Seven: Do you enjoy dancing? Eight: Do you enjoy
4   bridge? Now, we won't be rigid about the questions,
5   of course. You can ask the last question first if you
6   want to.
7   SARAH NANCY: What's the last question again?
8   DOLORES: Do you enjoy bridge?
9   SARAH NANCY: I hate bridge.
10   DOLORES: Well, then, sweetness, just substitute another
11   question. Say, do you enjoy dancing?
12   SARAH NANCY: I hate dancing.
13   DOLORES: Now, you don't hate dancing. You couldn't hate
14   dancing. It is in your blood. Your mother and daddy
15   are both beautiful dancers. You just need to practice
16   is all. Now...
17   SARAH NANCY: Why didn't you get me a date with Arch
18   Leon? I think he's the cute one.
19   DOLORES: He's going steady, honey. I explained that.
20   SARAH NANCY: Who is he going steady with?
21   DOLORES: Alberta Jackson.
22   SARAH NANCY: Is she cute?
23   DOLORES: I think she's right cute, a little common
24   looking and acting for my taste.
25   SARAH NANCY: He sure is cute.
26   DOLORES: Well, Felix Robertson is a lovely boy.
27   SARAH NANCY: I think he's about as cute as a warthog.
28   DOLORES: Sarah Nancy.
29   SARAH NANCY: I think he looks just like a warthog.
30   DOLORES: Sarah Nancy, precious...
31   SARAH NANCY: That's the question I'd like to ask him.
32   How is the hog pen, warthog?
33   DOLORES: Precious, precious.
34   SARAH NANCY: Anyway, they are all stupid.

1   DOLORES: Who, honey?
2   SARAH NANCY: Boys.
3   DOLORES: Precious, darling.
4   SARAH NANCY: Dumb and stupid. *(She starts away.)*
5   DOLORES: Sarah Nancy, where in the world are you
6   going?
7   SARAH NANCY: I'm going to bed.
8   DOLORES: Sarah Nancy, what is possessing you to say a
9   thing like that? You're just trying to tease me.
10   SARAH NANCY: Oh, no, I'm not. *(She starts away.)*
11   DOLORES: Sarah Nancy, you can't go to bed. You have a
12   young man coming to call on you at any moment. You
13   have to be gracious...
14   SARAH NANCY: I don't feel like being gracious. I'm sleepy.
15   I'm going to bed.
16   DOLORES: Sarah Nancy, you can't. Do you want to put me
17   in my grave? The son of one of your mother's dearest
18   friends will be here at any moment to call on you, and
19   you cannot be so rude as to go to bed and refuse to
20   receive him. Sarah Nancy, I beg you. I implore you.
21   SARAH NANCY: Oh, all right. *(She sits down.)* Ask me some
22   questions.
23   DOLORES: No, dear. You ask me some questions.
24   SARAH NANCY: What church do you attend?
25   DOLORES: That's lovely. That's a lovely question to begin
26   with. Now I'll answer as Felix will. Methodist.
27   SARAH NANCY: That's a dumb church.
28   DOLORES: Sarah Nancy.
29   SARAH NANCY: I think it's a dumb church. It's got no style.
30   We used to be Methodist but we left for the Episcopal.
31   They don't rant and rave in the Episcopal church.
32   DOLORES: And they don't rant and rave in the Methodist
33   church either, honey. Not here. Not in Harrison.
34   SARAH NANCY: Last time I was here they did.

1   DOLORES: Well, things have changed. Anyway, you're not
2   supposed to comment when he answers the ques-
3   tions, you're just supposed to sit back and listen to the
4   answers as if you're fascinated and find it all very
5   interesting.
6   SARAH NANCY: Why?
7   DOLORES: Because that's how you entertain young men,
8   graciously. You make them feel you are interested in
9   whatever they have to say.
10 SARAH NANCY: Suppose I'm not.
11 DOLORES: Well, it is not important if you are or not, you
12   are supposed to make them think you are.
13
14
15
16
17
18
19
20
21
22
23
24
25
26
27
28
29
30
31
32
33
34

from *When You Comin' Back, Red Ryder?* ©
by Mark Medoff

Winner of the off-off-Broadway Obie Award and the Outer Critics Circle Award, this gripping and incisive drama features two outstanding young roles that are compelling and dynamic in their depth and dimension. The scene is set at an all-night diner in a sleepy, remote New Mexico small town. It is c. 6:05 a.m. and nineteen-year-old Stephen Ryder — who prefers to be called by his nickname "Red" — has just finished working the "graveyard" shift at the greasy spoon roadside diner. He sits impatiently reading a newspaper, waiting for his equally youthful replacement, Angel, to arrive and replace him. There is a foreboding hint of gloom and danger lurking in the air as the scene begins; and later in the playscript the sleepy diner abruptly erupts into a battlefield of insults, angry confrontations, and senseless violence.

Stephen, who proudly displays his tattoo "Born Dead" for all to see, is an exciting, irresistible stage figure with his slick hair combed straight back and his shirt unbuttoned half-way to the waist. Angel, slightly overweight and rather plain, is a stark character contrast to the robust and brooding "Red" Ryder. Although the ages may be similar, there are remarkable differences in each character's view of their small town and the world at large. The strained relationship between this young man and woman is further complicated by the fact that Angel cares very deeply for Stephen; but Stephen, on the other hand, is so consumed by an unknown, uncontrollable anger and bitterness that he cannot comprehend Angel's feelings of compassion and genuine caring.

In playing the scene, it is important that the actors establish the impending sense of violence and pent-up rage that might be unleashed at any given moment, and that the tempo of the scene has good rhythm between momentary calm and unpredictable confrontation and chaos. There may be an initial tendency for the actor playing "Red" Ryder to grossly exaggerate the brooding, rebellious nature of the character, or for the actor playing the more sensitive, would-be suitor, Angel, to be unnaturally subdued or submissive. Both of these performance approaches should be resisted so that a deeper sense of each character's personal sense of searing pain and suffering might emerge with quiet dignity and heroic courage as they cautiously reveal innermost dreams, fears, and guarded secrets.

Some attention should also be paid to each character's spontaneous responses and reactions; and the actors should not rely too heavily upon stereotypical physical or vocal actions to convey the tension and frustration that is inherent in each character's uneasy exchanges of dialog or interaction. Experimenting with movement to suggest intense moments of "distance" or "difference" in attitude or mood may provide the insight and imagination needed to broaden the actors' sense of character relationships in this scene — and may promote more inventive, dramatic interaction as well. In addition, the visual portrait of the characters should be clearly defined as well to indicate what each is "thinking" or "anticipating"; and there are ample performance clues in this scene, especially for the actors, to create a dynamic and dramatic sense of "telescoping" each character's motivation or intention in terms of attitude, mood, or point of view in the given circumstances.

1   Angel: I'm sorry I'm late. My mom and me, our daily fight
2   was a little off schedule today. *(STEPHEN loudly shuf-*
3   *fles the paper and sucks his teeth.)* **I said I'm sorry,**
4   **Stephen. God. I'm only six minutes late.**
5   STEPHEN: Only six minutes, huh? I got six minutes to just
6   hang around this joint when my shift's up, right? This
7   is really the kinda dump I'm gonna hang around in in
8   my spare time, ain't it?
9   ANGEL: Stephen, that's a paper cup you got your coffee in.
10   *(STEPHEN is entrenched behind his newspaper.)*
11   STEPHEN: Clark can afford it, believe me.
12   ANGEL: That's not the point, Stephen.
13   STEPHEN: Oh no? You're gonna tell me the point though,
14   right? Hold it – lemme get a pencil.
15   ANGEL: The point is that if you're drinkin' your coffee
16   here, you're supposed to use a glass cup, and if it's to
17   go, you're supposed to get charged fifteen instead of
18   ten and ya get one of those five-cent paper cups to
19   take it with you. That's the point, Stephen.
20   STEPHEN: Yeah, well, I'm takin' it with me, so where's the
21   problem? *(STEPHEN has taken the last cigarette from a*
22   *pack, slipped the coupon into his shirt pocket and crum-*
23   *pled the pack. He basketball shoots it across the service*
24   *area.)*
25   ANGEL: Stephen. *(She retrieves the pack and begins her*
26   *morning routine: filling salt and pepper shakers, the*
27   *sugar dispensers, setting out place mats, and cleaning up*
28   *the mess STEPHEN evidently leaves for her each*
29   *morning. STEPHEN reaches over and underneath the*
30   *counter and pulls up a half-empty carton of Raleighs and*
31   *slides out a fresh pack. He returns the carton and slaps*
32   *the new pack down on the counter.)* **What're ya gonna**
33   **get with your cigarette coupons, Stephen?** *(STEPHEN*
34   *reads his paper, smokes, sips his coffee.)* **Stephen?**

1   *(STEPHEN lowers the newspaper.)*
2   STEPHEN: How many times I gotta tell ya to don't call me
3   Stephen.
4   ANGEL: I don't like callin' ya Red. It's stupid – callin'
5   somebody with brown hair Red.
6   STEPHEN: It's my name, ain't it? I don't like Stephen. I
7   like Red. When I was a kid I had red hair.
8   ANGEL: But ya don't now. Now ya got brown hair.
9   STEPHEN: *(Exasperated)* But *then* I did, and then's when
10   counts.
11 ANGEL: Who says *then's* when counts?
12 STEPHEN: The person that's doin' the *countin'!* Namely
13   yours truly! I don't call you...Caroline or...*Madge*, do I?
14 ANGEL: Because those aren't my names. My name's Angel,
15   so –
16 STEPHEN: Yeah, well ya don't look like no angel to me.
17 ANGEL: I can't help that, Stephen. At least I was named my
18   name at birth. Nobody asked me if I'd mind bein'
19   named Angel, but at least –
20 STEPHEN: You could change it, couldn't ya?
21 ANGEL: What for? To what?
22 STEPHEN: *(Thinking a moment, setting her up)* To Mabel.
23 ANGEL: How come Mabel?
24 STEPHEN: Yeah...Mabel.
25 ANGEL: How come? You like Mabel?
26 STEPHEN: I hate Mabel. *(STEPHEN stares at her, sucks his*
27   *teeth.)*
28 ANGEL: Look, Stephen, if you're in such a big hurry to get
29   outta here, how come you're just sittin' around
30   cleaning your teeth?
31 STEPHEN: Hey, look, I'll be gone in a minute. I mean if it's
32   too much to ask if I have a cigarette and a cup of
33   coffee in peace, for chrissake, just say so. A person's
34   supposed to unwind for two minutes a day, in case

1   **you ain't read the latest medical report. If it's too**
2   **much to ask to just lemme sit here in** *peace* **for two**
3   **minutes, then say so. I wouldn't wanna take up a stool**
4   **somebody was waitin' for or anything.** *(Looking*
5   *around him)* **Christ, will ya look at the waitin' line to**
6   **get on this stool.**
7   ANGEL: *(Pause)* **Did you notice what's playing at the films?**
8   STEPHEN: **Buncha crap, whudduya think?**
9   ANGEL: *(Pause)* **I saw ya circle somethin' in the gift book**
10   **the other mornin'.**
11   STEPHEN: **What** *gift* **book?**
12   ANGEL: **The Raleigh** *coupon* **gift book.**
13   STEPHEN: **Hey – com'ere.** *(ANGEL advances close to him.*
14   *He snatches the pencil from behind her ear and draws a*
15   *circle on the newspaper.)* **There. Now I just drew a**
16   **circle on the newspaper. That mean I'm gonna get me**
17   **that car?**
18   ANGEL: **Come on, Stephen, tell me. What're ya gonna get?**
19   STEP[HEN: *(Mumbling irascibly)* **Backpack.**
20   ANGEL: **What?**
21   STEPHEN: **Whuddya got, home fries in your ears?**
22   ANGEL: **Just that I didn't hear what you said is all.**
23   STEPHEN: *Backpack.*
24   ANGEL: **Who's gettin' a backpack?**
25   STEPHEN: **The guy down the enda the counter. Chingado**
26   **the Chicano. He's hitchin' to Guatemala.**
27   ANGEL: **You're getting a backpack? How come?**
28   STEPHEN: **Whuddo people usually get a backpack for?**
29   ANGEL: **Ya gonna go campin'?**
30   STEPHEN: **No, I ain't gonna go** *campin'.* **I'm gonna go**
31   **gettin' the hell outta this lousy little town is where**
32   **I'm gonna go** *campin'.*
33   ANGEL: **When? I mean...when?**
34   STEPHEN: **When? Just as soon as I get somethin' taken**

1   care of.

2   ANGEL: When will that be?

3   STEPHEN: When will that be? When I get it taken care of –

4   when d'ya think. Lemme have a donut.

5   ANGEL: *(Getting him a donut)* Where ya gonna go?

6   STEPHEN: Where am I gonna go? I'm gonna go hitchin'

7   that way *(Pointing left)* or I'm gonna go hitchin' that

8   way *(Pointing right)* and when I get to some place that

9   don't still smella Turdville here, I'm gonna get me a

10   decent job and I'm gonna make me some bread. *(He*

11   *picks up the donut and bites into it.)*

12   ANGEL: Rye or whole wheat, Stephen?

13   STEPHEN: This is some donut. I think they glued the

14   crumbs together with Elmer's.

15   ANGEL: Rye or whole wheat, Stephen?

16   STEPHEN: *(With his mouth full)* Believe me, that ain't funny.

17   ANGEL: Don't talk with your mouth full.

18   STEPHEN: Christ, my coffee's cold. How d'ya like that? *(He*

19   *looks at her. She pours him a fresh cup of coffee in a mug.*

20   *She sets it down by him. He looks at it for a minute, then*

21   *pours the coffee from the mug into his paper cup.)* I told

22   ya, I'm leavin' in less'n two minutes.

23   ANGEL: That's right, I forgot.

24   STEPHEN: Yeah, yeah.

25   ANGEL: You better let your hair grow and get some

26   different clothes if you're gonna hitch somewhere,

27   Stephen. You're outta style. Nobody's gonna pick up a

28   boy dressed like you with his hair like yours. And

29   with a tattoo on his arm that says "Born Dead."

30   People wear tattoos now that say "Love" and "Peace,"

31   Stephen, not "Born Dead."

32   STEPHEN: Love and peace, my Aunt Fanny's butt! And

33   who says I want *them* to pick me up, for chrissake?"

34   You think I'm dyin' for a case of the clap, or what? I

1	got a coupla hundred truck drivers come through
2	here in the middle of the night that said they'd all
3	gimme a ride anytime anywhere they was goin'. You
4	think I'm gonna lower myself to ride with those other
5	morons – you're outta your mind.
6	ANGEL: Two hundred truck drivers? Uh-uh. I'm sorry, I
7	have to call you on that one, Stephen. If it wasn't for
8	Lyle's station and his motel, Lyle be our *only* customer.
9	STEPHEN: You know, right? 'Cause you're here all night
10	while I'm home sacked out on my rear, so you know
11	how many truck drivers still stop in here, now ain't
12	that right?
13	ANGEL: In the three weeks since the by-pass opened,
14	Stephen, you know exactly how many customers you
15	had in the nights? You wanna know exactly how
16	many, Stephen?
17	STEPHEN: No, Christ, I don't wanna know how many. I
18	wanna have two minutes of peace to read my damn
19	newspaper – if that's not askin' too much!
20	
21	
22	
23	
24	
25	
26	
27	
28	
29	
30	
31	
32	
33	
34	

from *For Whom the Southern Belle Tolls* ©
by Christopher Durang

This biting, wild parody of Tennessee Williams' *The Glass Menagerie* is alternately funny, outrageous, and shocking in its satire. The playwright's brilliant and inventive comedy owes much to the Williams' original in terms of the situation and the given circumstances, which are well-known to seasoned theatre veterans — but the ironic twists, role reversals, and madcap point of view are vintage Durang: comic absurdities full of sharp, penetrating dialog and an unrestrained merriment and mayhem that is reminiscent of psychological and emotional truths best left unspoken.

To fully participate in the parody of the playwright's comic vision, it would be wise for the actors to first read the original Williams' source of inspiration. *The Glass Menagerie* is a classic American drama of profound charm, beauty, and tenderness that depicts the tragic remnants of Southern gentility as seen in the disillusioned lives of Amanda Wingfield, her son Tom, and her daughter Laura. The scene in the original drama — that is here parodied by Durang — is an emotional, somewhat pathetic, moment where Tom invites a young man of his acquaintance to dinner to meet his family. Tom's mother, Amanda, immediately seizes this opportunity to promote Laura, her eighteen- or so year-old crippled daughter, as a prime candidate for marriage to the equally young man. Jim, the caller, is a nice, competitive young man who wins Laura's immediate affection and friendship — only to later reveal that he is already engaged to be married. The bittersweet encounter inevitably is doomed to failure and the lives of Amanda and Laura collapse into despair and resignation.

Durang's scene, however, massages the original plot for all the hilarity that is possible in parody. Here, Tom brings home a factory coworker (Ginny) as a possible romantic suitor for his difficult brother (Lawrence). In addition to the sex-role reversal, the parody also portrays the sensitive young Lawrence as a "hypochondriac" with psychosomatic ailments and a pronounced limp; and Ginny as "one of the guys," a hard-working and fast-talking kind of girl who, unfortunately, is also hard of hearing! Surprisingly, this "odd couple" senses an immediate attraction and manages to flower in spite of the most insane and unexpected obstacles.

In playing the scene, the actors will need a performance blueprint that is designed for *visual* as well as *oral* interpretation. The audience should be familiar with the Tennessee Williams' original version of the scene, so the potential laughter should arise from a visual and oral performance that respects the initial Williams' interpretation but *adds* inventive business, bodily actions, and reactions that are not anticipated by the audience. The special problems inherent in the parody scene that relies on sex-role reversal and physical or vocal impairments as a part of the characterization must be handled with restraint and subtlety rather than as gross overstatements of farcical movement or excessively loud volume. There should be no "theatrical antics" here to call attention to themselves, but a touch of sensitivity and selectivity so that the spirit of humor and hilarity emerges with spontaneity and the characters appear to be more than farcical, one-dimensional stereotypes.

Remember that in deciding upon possible interpretation or probable character portrayal approaches — even in scenes of parody — there is still only one single objective in the creative process: truth and honesty. Be disciplined and focused in your comic performance technique so that the use of humor to punctuate even the most absurd, unreal actions of the characters in the given circumstances appear authentic because they are treated with a simplicity that suggests a keen sense of jesting or playful good times. This performance approach should faithfully capture the unique traits and mannerisms of the characters suggested in the scene, and also provoke riotous comic responses from the audience with a minimum of effort.

1   *(Slight silence at the beginning)*

2   **GINNY:** Hi!

3   **LAWRENCE:** Hi. *(Pause)* I'd gone to bed.

4   **GINNY:** I never eat bread. It's too fattening. I have to watch
5   my figure if I want to get ahead in the world. Why are
6   you wearing that nightshirt?

7   **LAWRENCE:** I'd gone to bed. I wasn't feeling well. My leg
8   hurts, and I have a headache, and I have palpitations
9   of the heart.

10 **GINNY:** I don't know. Hum a few bars, and I'll see. *(LAW-*
11   *RENCE looks at her oddly, decides to ignore her*
12   *mishearing.)*

13 **LAWRENCE:** We've met before, you know.

14 **GINNY:** *(Not able to hear him)* Uh huh.

15 **LAWRENCE:** We were in high school together. You were
16   voted Girl Most Likely to Succeed. We sat next to one
17   another in glee club.

18 **GINNY:** I'm sorry, I really can't hear you. You're talking
19   too softly.

20 **LAWRENCE:** *(Louder)* You used to call me BLUE ROSES.

21 **GINNY:** Blue roses? Oh yes, I remember, sort of. Why did I
22   do that?

23 **LAWRENCE:** I had been absent from school for several
24   months, and when I came back, you asked me where
25   I'd been, and I said I'd been sick with viral pneu-
26   monia, but you thought I said "blue roses."

27 **GINNY:** I didn't get much of that, but I remember you now.
28   You used to make a spectacle of yourself every day in
29   glee club, clumping up the aisle with this great noisy
30   leg brace on your leg. God, you made a racket.

31 **LAWRENCE:** I was always so afraid people were looking at
32   me, and pointing. But then eventually Mama
33   wouldn't let me wear the leg brace anymore. She gave
34   it to the Salvation Army.

1   **GINNY: I've never been in the army. How long were you in**
2   **for?**
3   **LAWRENCE: I've never been in the army. I have asthma.**
4   **GINNY: You do? May I see?**
5   **LAWRENCE:** *(Confused)* **See it?**
6   **GINNY: Well, sure, unless you don't want to.**
7   **LAWRENCE: Maybe you want to see my collection of glass**
8   **cocktail stirrers.** *(He limps to the table that contains his*
9   *cherished collection of glass cocktail stirrers. GINNY*
10   *follows him amiably, but has no idea what he's talking*
11   *about.)* **I call this one Stringbean, because it's long**
12   **and thin.**
13   **GINNY: Thank you.** *(Puts it in her glass and stirs it.)*
14   **LAWRENCE:** *(Fairly appalled)* **They're not for use.** *(Takes it*
15   *back from her.)* **They're a collection.**
16   **GINNY: Well I guess I stirred it enough.**
17   **LAWRENCE: They're my favorite thing in the world.** *(Holds*
18   *up another one.)* **I call this one Q-tip, because I real-**
19   **ized it looks like a Q-tip, except it's made out of glass**
20   **and doesn't have little cotton swabs at the end of it.**
21   *(GINNY looks blank.)* **Q-TIP.**
22   **GINNY: Really?** *(Takes it and puts it in her ear.)*
23   **LAWRENCE: No! Don't put it in your ear.** *(Takes it back.)*
24   **Now it's disgusting.**
25   **GINNY: Well, I didn't think it was a Q-tip, but that's what**
26   **you said it was.**
27   **LAWRENCE: I call it that. I think I'm going to throw it out**
28   **now.** *(Holds up another one.)* **I call this one Pinocchio**
29   **because if you hold it perpendicular to your nose it**
30   **makes your nose look long.** *(Holds it to his nose.)*
31   **GINNY: Uh huh.**
32   **LAWRENCE: And I call this one Henry Kissinger, because**
33   **he wears glasses and it's made of glass.**
34   **GINNY: Uh huh.** *(Takes it and stirs her drink again.)*

1   **LAWRENCE:** They're just for looking, not for stirring. *(Calls*
2   *Off-stage.)* **She's making a mess with my collection.**
3   **GINNY:** You know what I take your trouble to be, Lawrence?
4   **LAWRENCE:** Mama says I'm retarded.
5   **GINNY:** I know you're tired. I figured that's why you put on
6   the nightshirt, but this won't take long. I judge you to
7   be lacking in self-confidence. Am I right?
8   **LAWRENCE:** Well, I am afraid of people and things, and I
9   have a lot of ailments.
10   **GINNY:** But that makes you special, Lawrence.
11   **LAWRENCE:** What does?
12   **GINNY:** I don't know. Whatever you said. And that's why
13   you should present yourself with more confidence.
14   Throw back your shoulders and say, HI! HOW YA
15   DOIN'? Now you try it.
16   **LAWRENCE:** *(Unenthusiastically, softly)* **Hello. How are you?**
17   **GINNY:** *(Looking at watch, in response to his supposed ques-*
18   *tion)* **I don't know, it's about 8:30, but this won't take**
19   **long and then you can go to bed. All right, now try it.**
20   *(Booming)* **HI! HOW YA DOIN'?**
21   **LAWRENCE:** Hi. How ya doin'?
22   **GINNY:** Now swagger a bit. *(Kinda butch)* **HI. HOW YA**
23   **DOIN'?**
24   **LAWRENCE:** *(Imitates her fairly successfully.)* **HI. HOW**
25   **YA DOIN'?**
26   **GINNY:** Good, Lawrence. That's much better. Again. HI!
27   HOW YA DOIN'?
28   **LAWRENCE:** HI! HOW YA DOIN'?
29   **GINNY:** THE BRAVES PLAYED A HELLUVA GAME,
30   DON'TCHA THINK?
31   **LAWRENCE:** THE BRAVES PLAYED A HELLUVA GAME,
32   DON'TCHA THINK?
33   **GINNY:** HI, MRS. WINGVALLEY. YOUR SON LAWRENCE
34   AND I ARE GETTING ON JUST FINE, AREN'T WE,

from *WASP* ©
by Steve Martin

Here is the newest success of the delightfully wacky comedian and playwright Steve Martin, co-author and film star of *The Jerk* (1979), directed by Carl Reiner, and *Roxanne* (1987), which won for him the "Best Actor Award" from the Los Angeles Film Critics Association and the "Best Screenplay Award" from the Writer's Guild of America. Martin's whimsy and warm-hearted humor is characteristic of both his acting and his writing; but he also deftly combines biting and clever satire with a mad pursuit of sight gags and pratfalls that are alternately funny and touchingly poignant in offering comic, stinging critical social commentary on life in contemporary America. In addition, there is a genuine comic spirit in his writing that bears the unmistakable imprint of farcical intrigue and serious "spoof," especially when he manages to underscore very bittersweet as well as very serious impressions about intimate family relationships.

This selected scene is set in the Son's bedroom in a typical 1950s house. A very awkward conversation between Dad and Son on, "What do you plan to do with your life?" serves as the comic anchor for individual viewpoints related to paternal comaraderie, responsibility, and resignation in the face of an uncertain adolescent present and an unimaginable adult future. There are transparent struggles with aspirations, beliefs, and conflicts in the comic dialog; as well as a spirit of resolute hope that propels Dad through the struggle to express himself and to encourage his Son to be happy and successful in his later adult life. There is also a highly imaginative element of fantasy in the scene which blends domestic humor with moments of the Son's probing intensity and inquisitiveness as he consults with a spirited "Male Voice" to seek guidance in discovering his future direction in life.

In playing the roles, the actors should approach the scene from a "nontheatrical" perspective; perhaps imagining that the characters and the given circumstances are rather traditional ones that might be found in everyday, commonplace conversations between a concerned parent and an inquisitive younger child. This approach should encourage the actors to avoid the potential exaggeration of artifice and superficiality inherent in these decidedly theatrical, quirky characters in favor of a more subtle, restrained performance that is sure to inspire a satiric and wildly comic interpretation of the contemporary "family" relationship being suggested by the playwright. Be sure, also, that the apparent "nonsense gibberish" spoken by the Dad character is voiced in a believable, natural tone that is reminiscent of everyday, conversational speech or the subtlety and nuance of the father's apparent inability to communicate with his teenage Son may become distracting and unintelligible.

Don't forget to pay special attention to the "Male Voice" that reveals the Son character's secret dreams and private desires as they share intimate confidences. The comic overtones of fantasy and make-believe in the almost surrealistic use of the "Male Voice" is a primary ingredient in understanding the Son's imagined "self-image" in the scene, and is essential in pointing out the final moral statement of the playwright. It might be an inventive performance blueprint to tape the "Male Voice" as a well-known, recognizable adult public figure who has, perhaps, had an influence on the Son character or kindled his imagination as a potential father figure. It might also be an imaginative performance approach to have the "Male Voice" played by the Dad actor as well, perhaps to suggest the "duality" of the father figure as fantasized by the adolescent Son. Either approach should promote an immediate sense of playful jesting and brittle satire that might undeniably add a wry sense of social commentary to the playwright's point of view; and also add comic dimensions to the ironic climax of the scene.

Finally, this scene lends itself to the "Zoo Story" exercise of observations or animal characteristics described in Chapter 9, and is an excellent alternative source for character development. The actors should reduce their animal studies suggested in the exercise to an analogous portrait of the characters revealed in this selected scene, translating individual animal traits into a comparative study of potential human behavior. The compilation of animal observations and human comparisons, including physique, peculiar vocal qualities, or posture, should capture distinct individuality in the character portraits of both the Dad and the Son; and should also provide another performance dimension of hilarious good humor or fresh insight to an interpretation of the scene.

1   **DAD:** *(Holding a doorknob sign that says "private")* **Private?**
2   **It's not really private, is it?**
3   **SON:** No.
4   **DAD:** Well, let's not have the yablons. Der fashion rests
5   particularly well. I hop da balloon fer forest waters.
6   Aged well-brood water babies. In der yablons.
7   **SON:** Huh?
8   **DAD:** Oh yeah, you're too young to understand now, but
9   one day you'll have response not too fer-well keption.
10   **SON;** Jim, do you think I could get a bicycle?
11   **DAD:** Sure you could get a bicycle. How would you pay
12   for it?
13   **SON:** Well. I don't know. I was hoping...
14   **DAD:** You see, son, a bicycle is a luxury item. You know
15   what a luxury item is?
16   **SON:** No.
17   **DAD:** A luxury item is a thing that you have that annoys
18   other people that you have it. Like our very green
19   lawn. That's a luxury item. Oh, it could be less green I
20   suppose, but that's not what it's about. I work on that
21   lawn, maybe more than I should, and I pour a little
22   bit o'money into it, but it's a luxury item for me, out
23   there to annoy the others. And let's be fair, they have
24   their luxury items that annoy me. On the corner, that
25   mailbox made out of a ship's chain. Now there's no
26   way I wouldn't like that out in front of our house but
27   I went for the lawn. What I'm getting at is that you
28   have to work for a luxury item. So if you want that
29   bicycle you're going to have to work for it. Now, I've
30   got a little lot downtown that we've had for several
31   years, and if you wanted to go down there on week-
32   ends and after school and put up a building on it, I
33   think we could get you that bicycle.
34   **SON:** Gosh.

1	DAD: Yes, I know, you're pretty excited. It's not easy
2	putting up a building, son, but these are the ancient
3	traditions, handed down from the peoples of the
4	epocian Golwanna who lived on the plains of
5	Golgotha. Based upon the precepts of Hammurabi.
6	Written in cuneiform on the gates of Babylon.
7	Deduced from the cryptograms of the Questioner of
8	the Sphinx, and gleaned from the incunables of
9	Ratdolt. Delivered unto me by the fleet-footed
10	Mercury when the retrograde Mars backed into
11	Gemini, interpreted from the lyrics of "What a Swell
12	Party." Appeared on my living room wall in blood
13	writ there by God himself and incised in the Holy
14	Trowel of the Masons. Son, we don't get to talk that
15	much, in fact, as far as I can remember, we've never
16	talked. But I was wondering several years ago, and
17	unfortunately never really got around to asking you
18	until now, I was wondering what you plan to do with
19	your life.
20	SON: Well...
21	DAD: Before you answer, let me just say that I didn't know
22	what I wanted to do with my life until I was twenty-
23	eight. Which is late when you want to be a gymnast,
24	which by the way, I gave up when I found out it was
25	considered more an art than a sport. But now, your
26	mother and I have seventeen grand in the bank, at
27	today's prices that's like being a millionaire. See, if
28	you've got a dollar and you spend twenty-nine cents
29	on a loaf of bread, you've got sixty-one cents left. But
30	if you've got seventeen grand and you spend twenty-
31	nine cents on a loaf of bread, you've still got
32	seventeen grand. There's a math lesson for you.
33	SON: All I know is, it's going to be a great life.
34	DAD: Well, son, I have no idea what you're talking about

1   **but I want to suggest that you finish school first and**
2   **go on to college and get a Ph.D. in Phrenology. But let**
3   **me just say, that no matter what in life you choose to**
4   **do, I will be here to shame you, unless, of course, you**
5   **pass the seventeen thousand mark. Then you will be**
6   **awarded my college sigma delta phuk-a-lucka pin.**
7   **Good-bye, and I hope to see you around the house.** *(He*
8   *shakes the SON's hand, exits. SON stays in the room,*
9   *takes out a purple pendant which he puts around his*
10   *neck. He then takes out a small homemade radio with*
11   *antenna, dials it; we hear glitches and gwarks, then the*
12   *sound of a solar wind.)*
13 **SON: Premier...Premier...come in Premier.**
14 **MALE VOICE: Yes?**
15 **SON: How are things on Lepton?**
16 **MALE VOICE: Three hundred and eighty-five degrees**
17   **Fahrenheit. It rained molten steel. Now that's cold.**
18 **SON: Tell me again, OK?**
19 **MALE VOICE: Again?**
20 **SON: I need it now.**
21 **MALE VOICE: How long has it been since my first visit?**
22 **SON: Ten years.**
23 **MALE VOICE: Ah, yes. You were four and you were granted**
24   **the Vision.**
25 **SON: Yes.**
26 **MALE VOICE: So much is credited to the gene pool these**
27   **days. But the gene pool is nothing compared to the**
28   **Vision. It's really what I enjoy doing most. Placing the**
29   **Vision where it's least expected. Anyway, you need to**
30   **hear it?**
31 **SON: Yes.**
32 **MALE VOICE: All right. Her skin will be rose on white. She**
33   **will come to you, her breath on your mouth. She will**
34   **speak words voicelessly which you will understand**

1 because of the movement of her lips on yours. Her
2 hand will be on the small of your back and her fingers
3 will be blades. Your blood will pool around you. You
4 will receive a transfusion of a clear liquid that has
5 been exactly measured. That liquid will be sadness.
6 And then, whatever her name may be, Carol, Susan,
7 Virginia, then, she will die and you will mourn her.
8 Her death will be complete and final in all respects
9 but this: she will be alive, and with someone else. But
10 time and again you will walk in, always at the same
11 age you are now, with your arms open, your heart as
12 big as the moon, not anticipating the total eclipse.
13 They call you a WASP, *but it's women who have the*
14 *stingers.* However, you will have a gift. A gift so
15 wonderful that it will take you through the days and
16 nights until the end of your life.
17 SON: I'm getting a gift? What is it?
18 MALE VOICE: The desire to work. *(Fade out)*
19
20
21
22
23
24
25
26
27
28
29
30
31
32
33
34

CHAPTER FIVE

SCENES FOR YOUNG ADULT MEN
(With Women/Men)

"The mask which an actor wears is apt to become his face."
— Plato

In playing scenes that feature young adult men but may also include supporting roles for women and other men, it is important that the actors observe the varying ages, physical dimensions, emotional or intellectual makeup, behavioral pattern(s) appropriate for the primary age range (23-29 years) of each featured character. There is little opportunity in these selected scenes to engage in the youthful exaggeration of posing, halting speech, or innocent pretension that frequently characterizes an inexperienced approach to playing the role in scenes for youth and young men or women. The style of performance needed here to convey the more emerging, mature, and sophisticated thoughts or emotions of the characters should be direct and immediate, with a minimum of vocal or physical effort to suggest the still limited life experiences of the stage figures.

The performance demands in playing selected scenes for young adult men may also continue to rely upon observation and creative invention in the interpretation of the selected role, but there is a more natural sense of movement and a more intense animation and energy that underscores the character's changing moods, attitudes, or responses to the given circumstances described in the scene. Although there are, no doubt, ample opportunities to invest the role-playing of scenes for young adult men with personal traits, behavior, or mannerisms, the serious actor will rely more intently upon scene analysis as part of a basic psychological profile that should reveal the meaning of character actions and attitudes in the selected scene. There is also a more conscious attempt in playing scenes for young adult men to give everyday, commonplace events a

heightened sense of personal dignity and significance to reinforce each character's self-worth and value — especially in terms
of competitive "gamesmanship" when characters call attention
to themselves to enhance their personal sense of identity and
individuality.

*In playing scenes that feature young adult men but may also include
supporting roles for women, the style of performance should be direct and
immediate, with a minimum of vocal or physical effort to suggest the still
limited life experiences of the stage figures.*

There is also a greater intensity of thought and emotions in
scenes for young adult men. They appear to *think* and *act* in a
more abrupt or aggressive manner, provoking arguments and
confrontations that often reveal interior motives or psychological motivation. More often than not, however, these scenes for
young adult men depict complex, three-dimensional characters
who are products of the emotional imbalance, inhibited social
development, or submerged neurosis that leads inevitably to
committing errors in judgment, displaying unbridled anger, or
engaging in "mock-heroic" actions to assert their physical and
mental superiority. At the same time, there is a basic goodness
and naivete in these young adult men that reveal admirable
qualities of sincerity, sympathy, and compassion to take action
against forces that appear to limit chances for personal success
or even survival.

Do not be alarmed by the emphatic or perhaps suggestive language found in scenes for young adult men. The dialog may be sprinkled with verbal slang, harsh words, or veiled crudity to more faithfully portray the speech of "angry young men" who are in rebellion against an imagined reality that more polite, formal conversational language cannot address with as much force of expression or meaning. Viewed from this perspective, the language of young adult men gains a personal significance that speaks directly and immediately to specific issues or a point of view that the character wishes to address in a more direct and subjective voice. It is important to view the language of young adult men more as a question of "attitude" than as a matter of "fact" — and to look beyond the spoken words in order to identify character motivation or character action in the given circumstances of the selected scene.

These young adult men also have a new flavor and texture of individual strength and determination that allows them to face significant obstacles without charade or pretense; and their motivations are so numerous and varied that the consequences of their actions are more likely the result of a series of miscalculations or deep-seated causes that provoke a sense of humility and a quiet dignity. In playing the role, therefore, it is important to distinguish between a character's arrogance and the nature of a character's personal, human suffering. There should be an element of strength and courage evident in each character's struggle to confront what they perceive to be insurmountable odds; and the actors should be sensitive to the despair and suffering inherent in each character's frequently bitter, pessimistic critical commentary on the futility of human relationships.

The creative invention of stage business should provide an added performance dimension when playing young adult male roles, but the actors are reminded that effective and meaningful stage business must be an authentic part of the action(s) described in the scene, and must be an integral part of the character's distinctive personality. Skillful use of hand props or occasional pantomimic action may, however, enhance character development and enrich the dynamic portrait being drawn — especially when the use of hand props or pantomimic action(s) clearly delineate a character's attitude or clearly define a character's personality traits or mannerisms. It is also important for the actors to carefully "blend" creative and authentic experiences or observations with their own distinctive personalities so that the character portraits are fresh and vibrant rather than drab imitations of playing traditional young adult men.

In approaching the selected scenes that follow, be aware of the need for the voice to be easily heard and understood, with adequate volume and rate to be determined by the demands of each character's action(s) in the episode. There should be clarity and precision in the voicing of dialog, and extremely well-formed stage diction is desirable to suggest the vocal variety needed to highlight each character's alternating attitudes or moods. The role of movement may be more active in scenes for young adult men to express the peculiar qualities of physical and mental activity that are revealed in varying situations or sequences of agitated interaction with other characters. The subtleties of *pause* and *phrasing* may also play an important role in voicing dialog in scenes for young adult men to suggest different temperaments and different emotional or mental states of mind in the given circumstances.

Scenes for young adult men have a new flavor and texture of individual strength and determination that allows them to face significant obstacles without charade or pretense, provoking a sense of humility and a quiet dignity.

Although there may be isolated moments of comic intent in the selected scenes that follow, they are subdued and easily identifiable as incidental to the primary development of the characters. It is essential to practice restraint in these comic moments and to refrain from excessive exaggeration to highlight the comic potential of the characters at the expense of the seriousness of the situation. There is generally a "biting edge" to the comic spirit in these scenes that serves to mask the exceedingly public or private despair of the character and the situation in which the humor surfaces; and it is rarely amusing in the context of the character's personal suffering.

Finally, there is an acute atmosphere of anxiety and anticipation that appears to hover over the characters in these selected scenes as they try in vain to realize personal dreams or resolve personal goals that are at odds with the other characters in the episode. Against a sometimes cold, calculating backdrop of fear and suspicion, each character is forced to confront the prejudices and self-doubts that have helped to shape their individual mistrust of one another. The insights these young adult men gain from their relationships, however, provide a meaningful glimpse of the uncommon and unexpected discovery of true friendship and comradeship that shares private confessions and respects personal confidences.

These selected scenes for young adult men are also warmly probing and striking examinations of the deeper themes of loneliness, despair, adolescent panic, and the scars of unhappy or disappointing childhoods that have severely limited the characters' ability to come of age with dignity and a sense of positive direction. Through the intimate interaction of these young adult men — sometimes humorous and sometimes painfully tragic — there is a sense of growing self-awareness that inextricably binds the characters together and prepares them for the final rites of adulthood. And it is in this powerful urge to strive to achieve all that life has to offer that these young adult men achieve their individuality and most clearly define their lives, for better or worse, in terms of their own personal struggle to survive in a world of their own making.

from *Long Day's Journey Into Night* ©
by Eugene O'Neill

In the brief space of one day — early morning until midnight — the Tyrone family comes to life on stage with almost frightening fidelity. Based upon the Nobel Prize-winning playwright's own tortured family history, the playscript vividly depicts James Tyrone (O'Neill, Sr.) as the famous but aging father/actor who is a vengeful miser; Mary (O'Neill, Sr.'s wife) as a confirmed drug addict; Jamie, Jr. (O'Neill, Sr.'s thirty or so older son) as a disillusioned, wanton drunk, and Edmund (Eugene O'Neill, the twenty- or so year-old younger son and aspiring writer) as a creative artist who suffers from tuberculosis. The doomed household of misfits and malcontents has gathered at their summer home in an eastern seacoast town and are all waiting the medical diagnosis of Edmund's "summer cold" from Dr. Hardy's recent examination. There is a shattering quiet in the family living room as emotions and tempers rise and fall in anticipation of the dreaded news that might confirm the worst fears, and the likely prospect of Edmund's confinement to a state sanatorium is never distant from the family conversation.

At the scene opens, Edmund is alone in the living room. He has just taken a drink from the whiskey bottle on the table, but quickly sits in a side chair and opens a book when he hears his older brother, Jamie, enter the room. Edmund, frail and spiritless, appears pale and gaunt; his courage and resolve vanish as he aimlessly turns the pages of the book. Jamie smiles cynically after catching sight of the bottle and glasses. He glances in the mirror and sees a self-destructive alcoholic who bears some responsibility for his younger brother's many excesses and escapades. There is an awkward, prolonged silence as the brothers cautiously begin to share confidences. There is also the tragic intrusion of the noise they hear upstairs: their mother, Mary, a once-beautiful young girl educated in a convent, is stumbling around in her dope-induced childhood dreams and memories.

The autobiographical nature of this scene punctuates the soul-shattering revelations of self-truth and self-destruction that need to be addressed objectively. There may be a tendency for the actor playing the Edmund character to interpret the author's sharp, painful sketch more as an "observer" than as an actual participant in the given circumstances, and to lose dramatic sight of the more important portrayal of the strained relationship of the brothers as they slowly gravitate toward each other after severe bouts of melancholy or alcoholism. In addition, Jamie needs to be conveyed in a more sympathetic character portrait than the one that traditionally features him as a villain or agent of corrupting influence on the younger, more vulnerable Edmund. These "haunted souls," as the playwright aptly describes them, will also exhibit more dimension if the actors focus upon the social behavior and the fanciful illusions of the brothers that are stripped away when they begin to discuss the pathetic reality of their mother, who has apparently found her own solace in a dream world of morphine escapism. Hopefully, what emerges from the egocentric games that the brothers play to establish themselves as active subjects rather than as passive objects in the Tyrone household is that their own "pipe dreams" of success and achievement have only been cheap imitations of the truth of their own failures.

1   JAMIE: Sneaking one, eh? Cut out the bluff, kid. You're a

2   rottener actor than I am.

3   EDMUND: *(Grins.)* **Yes, I grabbed one while the going was**

4   good.

5   JAMIE: *(Puts a hand affectionately on his shoulder.)* **That's**

6   better. Why kid me? We're pals, aren't we?

7   EDMUND: I wasn't sure it was you coming.

8   JAMIE: I made the old man look at his watch. I was

9   halfway up the walk when Cathleen burst into song.

10   Our wild Irish lark! She ought to be a train announcer.

11   EDMUND: That's what drove me to drink. Why don't you

12   sneak one while you've got a chance?

13   JAMIE: I was thinking of that very thing. *(He goes quickly to*

14   *the window at right.)* **The old man was talking to old**

15   **Captain Turner. Yes, he's still at it.** *(He comes back and*

16   *takes a drink.)* **And now to cover up from his eagle eye.**

17   *(He memorizes the level in the bottle after every drink.*

18   *He measures two drinks of water and pours them in the*

19   *whiskey bottle and shakes it up.)* **There. That fixes it.**

20   *(He pours water in the glass and sets it on the table by*

21   *EDMUND.)* **And here's the water you've been drinking.**

22   EDMUND: Fine! You don't think it will fool him, do you?

23   JAMIE: Maybe not, but he can't prove it. *(Putting on his*

24   *collar and tie)* **I hope he doesn't forget lunch listening**

25   **to himself talk. I'm hungry.** *(He sits across the table*

26   *from EDMUND — irritably.)* **That's what I hate about**

27   **working down in front. He puts on an act for every**

28   **damned fool that comes along.**

29   EDMUND: *(Gloomily)* **You're in luck to be hungry. The way**

30   I feel I don't care if I ever eat again.

31   JAMIE: *(Gives him a glance of concern.)* **Listen, kid. You**

32   **know me. I've never lectured you, but Doctor Hardy**

33   **was right when he told you to cut out the red eye.**

34   EDMUND: Oh, I'm going to after he hands me the bad

1   news this afternoon. A few before then won't make
2   any difference.
3   JAMIE: *(Hesitates — then slowly)* I'm glad you've got your
4   mind prepared for bad news. It won't be such a jolt.
5   *(He catches EDMUND staring at him.)* I mean, it's a
6   cinch you're really sick, and it would be wrong dope
7   to kid yourself.
8   EDMUND: *(Disturbed)* I'm not. I know how rotten I feel,
9   and the fever and chills I get at night are no joke. I
10   think Doctor Hardy's last guess was right. It must be
11   the damned malaria come back on me.
12   JAMIE: Maybe, but don't be too sure.
13   EDMUND: Why? What do you think it is?
14   JAMIE: Hell, how would I know? I'm no doc. *(Abruptly)*
15   Where's Mama?
16   EDMUND: Upstairs.
17   JAMIE: *(Looks at him sharply.)* When did she go up?
18   EDMUND: Oh, about the time I came down to the hedge, I
19   guess. She said she was going to take a nap.
20   JAMIE: You didn't tell me —
21   EDMUND: *(Defensively)* Why should I? What about it? She
22   was tired out. She didn't get much sleep last night.
23   JAMIE: I know she didn't. *(A pause. The brothers avoid
24   looking at each other.)*
25   EDMUND: That damned foghorn kept me awake, too.
26   *(Another pause)*
27   JAMIE: She's been upstairs all morning, eh? You haven't
28   seen her?
29   EDMUND: No. I've been reading here. I wanted to give her
30   a chance to sleep.
31   JAMIE: Is she coming down to lunch?
32   EDMUND: Of course.
33   JAMIE: *(Dryly)* No of course about it. She might not want
34   any lunch. Or she might start having most of her

1   **meals alone upstairs. That's happened, hasn't it?**

2   **EDMUND:** *(With frightened resentment)* **Cut it out, Jamie!**

3   **Can't you think anything but –?** *(Persuasively)* **You're**

4   **all wrong to suspect anything. Cathleen saw her not**

5   **long ago. Mama didn't tell her she wouldn't be down**

6   **to lunch.**

7   **JAMIE:**   **Then she wasn't taking a nap?**

8   **EDMUND:** **Not right then, but she was lying down,**

9   **Cathleen said.**

10   **JAMIE:**   **In the spare room?**

11   **EDMUND:** **Yes. For Pete's sake, what of it?**

12   **JAMIE:** *(Bursts out.)* **You damned fool! Why did you leave**

13   **her alone so long? Why didn't you stick around?**

14   **EDMUND:**   **Because she accused me – and you, and Papa –**

15   **of spying on her all the time and not trusting her. She**

16   **made me feel ashamed. I know how rotten it must be**

17   **for her. And she promised on her sacred word of**

18   **honor –**

19   **JAMIE:** *(With a bitter weariness)* **You ought to know that**

20   **doesn't mean anything.**

21   **EDMUND:** **It does this time!**

22   **JAMIE:** **That's what we thought the other times.** *(He leans*

23   *over the table to give his brother's arm an affectionate*

24   *grasp.)* **Listen, kid, I know you think I'm a cynical**

25   **bastard, but remember I've seen a lot more of this**

26   **game than you have. You never knew what was really**

27   **wrong until you were in prep school. Papa and I kept**

28   **it from you. But I was wise ten years or more before we**

29   **had to tell you. I know the game backwards and I've**

30   **been thinking all morning of the way she acted last**

31   **night when she thought we were asleep. I haven't been**

32   **able to think of anything else. And now you tell me she**

33   **got you to leave her alone upstairs all morning.**

34   **EDMUND:** **She didn't! You're crazy!**

1   **JAMIE:** *(Placatingly)* **All right, kid. Don't start a battle with**
2   **me. I hope as much as you do I'm crazy. I've been as**
3   **happy as hell because I'd really begun to believe that**
4   **this time** – *(He stops — looking through the front parlor*
5   *toward the hall — lowering his voice, hurriedly.)* **She's**
6   **coming downstairs. You win on that. I guess I'm a**
7   **damned suspicious louse.** *(They grow tense with a*
8   *hopeful, fearful expectancy. JAMIE mutters.)* **Damn! I**
9   **wish I'd grabbed another drink.**
10   **EDMUND: Me, too.** *(He coughs nervously and this brings*
11   *on a real fit of coughing. JAMIE glances at him with*
12   *worried pity.)*
13
14
15
16
17
18
19
20
21
22
23
24
25
26
27
28
29
30
31
32
33
34

Revue Sketches
by Harold Pinter

Harold Pinter, one of the most "literary" contemporary playwrights, has fashioned two intriguing, if not somewhat obscure, revue sketches that call attention to the sense of horror and alienation that he envisions in the searing indictments of contemporary life and times that follow. But there is humor, as well, and a hope that after meeting, talking, and tearing at one another for a time there will be a more profound understanding of the ultimate paradox of life: we are together, but also alone, in the world. It is this reflection of the "absurdist" point of view that the actors will need to understand in playing the selected revue sketches. There is also a need to bridge the unspecified gaps in time, place, and action in order to give the characters in each revue sketch a definite relationship and to clearly establish the intention(s) and motivation(s) that make the imaginary world of the stage figures so different, and yet so similar.

Perhaps a review of the basic principles of absurdism in terms of its use of the bizarre, the grotesque, and the "weird" to mask significant philosophical issues being addressed by the playwright would certainly enrich the actor's critical insight necessary to visualize this "Pinter-pair" of revue sketches that punctuate the dehumanization and automation of man. The rather impersonal nature of the two revue sketches, however, requires imaginative performance approaches that capture clearly drawn, flesh-and-blood character portraits that have distinct identities and sensitivities. Pinter himself may have provided the appropriate performance clue for an interpretation of the revue sketches when he pointed out in a recent interview with Richard Findlater in *The Twentieth Century* that "...I start off with people who come into a particular situation...and I'm convinced that what happens in my plays could happen anywhere, at anytime, in any place, although the events may seem unfamiliar at first glance."

As you approach these revue sketches, remember that the performance time spent on the stage is always the "living present," and cultivate a performance blueprint that includes *all* of the essential events or incidents that may have taken place in each of the following character's "untold" lives before the

136

selected episode began. Make sure that you seize the role-playing opportunities suggested in the revue sketches that follow and fill in the playwright's tentative, incomplete character outlines with as much imagination and inventive "self-expression" as possible to embody a character of substantial form and content. You may wish to explore the possibility of sound effects, taped music, or recordings to punctuate the responses or reactions of the characters in the revue sketches. There should also be some attention paid to a performance blueprint that includes peculiar behavior patterns, habitual "internal" conflicts and contradictions — or bodily actions, gestures, and physical mannerisms — to be more descriptive in indicating the hidden or submerged thoughts of the revue sketch characters. Finally, a detailed analysis of each revue sketch in terms of potential character-building should encourage spontaneous body images for visual characterization, and perhaps prompt inventive facial or physical expressions that help to clarify the apparent meaning of the mysterious events, incidents, and actions of these delightful but disturbing episodes that follow.

from *The Applicant* ©

The first revue sketch focuses attention on a young man of indeterminate age who simply applies for a job but suddenly finds himself in a bizarre interrogation with an aggressive administrative supervisor whose probing, relentless "psychological testing" leaves him gasping, blushing, and convulsing on the floor in a state of surprise and shock. The young man, Lamb, is apparently enthusiastic, eager, and intelligent enough to easily qualify for the vacant position, but Miss Piffs, the computerized-like bureaucrat who must review his credentials, raises such disturbing and shattering questions during the interview session that the "applicant" is left battered and defeated in a sequence of repeatedly hilarious attempts to adequately respond to the preposterous questions being asked of him.

1   PIFFS: Ah, good morning.
2   LAMB: Oh, good morning, miss.
3   PIFFS: Are you Mr. Lamb?
4   LAMB: That's right.
5   PIFFS: *(Studying a sheet of paper)* **Yes. You're applying for**
6   **this vacant post, aren't you?**
7   LAMB: I am actually, yes.
8   PIFFS: Are you a physicist?
9   LAMB: Oh yes, indeed. It's my whole life.
10 PIFFS: *(Languidly)* **Good. Now our procedure is that before**
11   **we discuss the applicant's qualifications we like to**
12   **subject him to a little test to determine his psycholog-**
13   **ical suitability. You've no objection?**
14 LAMB: Oh, good heavens, no.
15 PIFFS: **Jolly good.** *(MISS PIFFS has taken some objects out of*
16   *a drawer and goes to LAMB. She places a chair for him.)*
17   **Please sit down.** *(He sits.)* **Can I fit these to your palms?**
18 LAMB: *(Affably)* **What are they?**
19 PIFFS: Electrodes.
20 LAMB: **Oh yes, of course. Funny little things.** *(She attaches*
21   *them to his palms.)*
22 PIFFS: **Now the earphones.** *(She attaches earphones to his*
23   *head.)*
24 LAMB: I say, how amusing.
25 PIFFS: **Now I plug in.** *(She plugs into the wall.)*
26 LAMB: *(A trifle nervously)* **Plug in, do you? Oh yes, of**
27   **course. Yes, you'd have to, wouldn't you?** *(MISS PIFFS*
28   *perches on a high stool and looks down at LAMB.)* **This**
29   **helps to determine my...my suitability, does it?**
30 PIFFS: **Unquestionably. Now relax. Just relax. Don't think**
31   **about a thing.**
32 LAMB: No.
33 PIFFS: **Relax completely. Rela-a-a-x. Quite relaxed?** *(LAMB*
34   *nods. MISS PIFFS presses a button on the side of her*

1	*stool. A piercing high pitched buzz-hum is heard. LAMB*
2	*jolts rigid. His hands go to his earphones. He is propelled*
3	*from the chair. He tries to crawl under the chair. MISS*
4	*PIFFS watches, impassive. The noise stops. LAMB peeps*
5	*out from under the chair, crawls out, stands, twitches,*
6	*emits a short chuckle and collapses in the chair.)* **Would**
7	**you say you were an excitable person?**
8	**LAMB: Not – not unduly, no. Of course, I –**
9	**PIFFS: Would you say you were a moody person?**
10	**LAMB: Moody? No, I wouldn't say I was moody – well,**
11	**sometimes occasionally I –**
12	**PIFFS: Do you ever get fits of depression?**
13	**LAMB: Well, I wouldn't call them depression exactly –**
14	**PIFFS: Do you often do things you regret in the morning?**
15	**LAMB: Regret? Things I regret? Well, it depends what you**
16	**mean by often, really – I mean when you say often –**
17	**PIFFS: Are you often puzzled by women?**
18	**LAMB: Women?**
19	**PIFFS: Men.**
20	**LAMB: Men? Well, I was just going to answer the question**
21	**about women –**
22	**PIFFS: Do you often feel puzzled?**
23	**LAMB: Puzzled?**
24	**PIFFS: By women.**
25	**LAMB: Women?**
26	**PIFFS: Men.**
27	**LAMB: Oh, now just a minute, I...Look, do you want sepa-**
28	**rate answers or a joint answer?**
29	**PIFFS: After your day's work do you ever feel tired? Edgy?**
30	**Fretty? Irritable? At a loose end? Morose? Frustrated?**
31	**Morbid? Unable to eat? Unable to remain seated?**
32	**Unable to remain upright? Lustful? Indolent? On heat?**
33	**Randy? Full of desire? Full of energy? Full of dread?**
34	**Drained? of energy? of dread? of desire?** *(Pause)*

1   LAMB: *(Thinking)* **Well, it's difficult to say really...**
2   PIFFS: **Are you a good mixer?**
3   LAMB: **Well, you've touched on quite an interesting point**
4   **there –**
5   PIFFS: **Do you suffer from eczema, listlessness, or falling**
6   **coat?**
7   LAMB: **Er...**
8   PIFFS: **Are you virgo intacta?**
9   LAMB: **I beg your pardon?**
10   PIFFS: **Are are you virgo intacta?**
11   LAMB: **Oh, I say, that's rather embarrassing. I mean – in**
12   **front of a lady –**
13   PIFFS: **Are you virgo intacta?**
14   LAMB: **Yes, I am, actually. I'll make no secret of it.**
15   PIFFS: **Have you always been virgo intacta?**
16   LAMB: **Oh yes, always. Always.**
17   PIFFS: **From the word go?**
18   LAMB: **Go? Oh yes, from the word go.**
19   PIFFS: **Do women frighten you?** *(She presses a button on the*
20   *other side of her stool. The stage is plunged into redness,*
21   *which flashes on and off in time with her questions.*
22   *Building...)* **Their clothes? Their shoes? Their voices?**
23   **Their laughter? Their stares? Their way of walking?**
24   **Their way of sitting? Their way of smiling? Their way**
25   **of talking? Their mouths? Their hands? Their feet?**
26   **Their shins? Their thighs? Their knees? Their eyes?**
27   **Their...** *(Drumbeat)* **Their...** *(Drumbeat)* **Their...** *(Cymbal*
28   *bang)* **Their...** *(Trombone chord)* **Their...** *(Bass note)*
29   LAMB: *(In a high voice)* **Well, it depends on what you mean**
30   **really –** *(The light still flashes. She presses the other*
31   *button and the piercing buzz-hum is heard again. LAMB's*
32   *hands go to his earphones. He is propelled from the chair,*
33   *falls, rolls, crawls, totters and collapses. Silence. He lies*
34   *face upwards. MISS PIFFS looks at him then walks to*

141

1   *LAMB and bends over him.)*
2   **PIFFS: Thank you very much, Mr. Lamb. We'll let you know.**
3
4
5
6
7
8
9
10
11
12
13
14
15
16
17
18
19
20
21
22
23
24
25
26
27
28
29
30
31
32
33
34

from *Trouble in the Works* ©

The second revue sketch focuses attention on a young factory worker who finds himself in the precarious position of having to inform his superior that coworkers in the mill are dissatisfied with the "products" being manufactured and would like to see a new line of merchandise produced. Wills, the young factory worker, is anxious about the prospects of facing his superior, but his manner is genuine and sincere. Mr. Fibbs, the boss, simply cannot comprehend the situation or the worker's dissatisfaction, and is reluctant to abandon the highly successful commercial enterprise that has provided such quality products in the past. It is an uneasy confrontation that provides a fleeting glimpse into the murky and shallow abyss that lies between the "disturbing" products being produced by the factory workers and the perception of "distance" between management and personnel that abounds when unspoken doubts or rising tensions are not resolved.

1   FIBBS: Ah, Wills. Good. Come in. Sit down, will you?

2   WILLS: Thanks, Mr. Fibbs.

3   FIBBS: You got my message?

4   WILLS: I just got it.

5   FIBBS: Good. Good. *(Pause)* Good. Well now...Have a cigar?

6   WILLS: No, thanks, not for me, Mr. Fibbs.

7   FIBBS: Well, now, Wills, I hear there's been a little trouble

8   in the factory.

9   WILLS: Yes, I...I suppose you could call it that, Mr. Fibbs.

10   FIBBS: Well, what in heaven's name is it all about?

11   WILLS: Well, I don't exactly know how to put it, Mr. Fibbs.

12   FIBBS: Now come on, Wills, I've got to know what it is,

13   before I can do anything about it.

14   WILLS: Well, Mr. Fibbs, it's simply a matter that the men

15   have...well, they seem to have taken a turn against

16   some of the products.

17   FIBBS: Taken a turn?

18   WILLS: They just don't seem to like them much anymore

19   FIBBS: Don't like them? But we've got the reputation of

20   having the finest machine part turnover in the

21   country. They're the best paid men in the industry.

22   We've got the cheapest canteen in Yorkshire. No two

23   menus are alike. We've got a billiard hall, haven't we,

24   on the premises? We've got a swimming pool for use

25   of staff. And what about the long-playing record

26   room? And you tell me they're dissatisfied?

27   WILLS: Oh, the men are very grateful for all the ameni-

28   ties, sir. They just don't like the products.

29   FIBBS: But they're beautiful products. I've been in the

30   business a lifetime. I've never seen such beautiful

31   products.

32   WILLS: There it is, sir.

33   FIBBS: Which ones don't they like?

34   WILLS: Well, there's the brass pet cock, for instance.

1   FIBBS: The brass pet cock? What's the matter with the
2   brass pet cock?
3   WILLS: They just don't seem to like it anymore.
4   FIBBS: But what exactly don't they like about it?
5   WILLS: Perhaps it's just the look of it.
6   FIBBS: That brass pet cock? But I tell you it's perfection.
7   Nothing short of perfection.
8   WILLS: They've just gone right off it.
9   FIBBS: Well, I'm flabbergasted.
10   WILLS: It's not only the brass pet cock, Mr. Fibbs.
11   FIBBS: What else?
12   WILLS: There's the hemi unibal spherical rod end.
13   FIBBS: The hemi unibal spherical rod end? Where could
14   you find a finer rod end?
15   WILLS: There are rod ends and rod ends, Mr. Fibbs.
16   FIBBS: I know there are rod ends and rod ends. But where
17   could you find a finer hemi unibal spherical rod end?
18   WILLS: They just don't want to have anything more to do
19   with it.
20   FIBBS; This is shattering. Shattering. What else? Come on,
21   Wills. There's no point in hiding anything from me.
22   WILLS: Well, I hate to say it, but they've gone very vicious
23   about the high-speed taper shank spiral flute reamers.
24   FIBBS: The high-speed taper shank spiral flute reamers!
25   But that's absolutely ridiculous! What could they
26   possibly have against the high-speed taper shank
27   spiral flute reamers?
28   WILLS: All I can say is they're in a state of very bad agita-
29   tion about them. And then there's the gunmetal side
30   outlet relief with handwheel.
31   FIBBS: What!
32   WILLS: There's the nippled connector and the nippled
33   adapter and the vertical mechanical comparator.
34   FIBBS: No!

1   WILLS: And the one they can't speak about without trem-
2   bling is the jaw for Jacob's chuck for use on portable
3   drill.
4   FIBBS: My own Jacob's chuck? Not my very own Jacob's
5   chuck?
6   WILLS: They've just taken a turn against the whole lot of
7   them, I tell you. Male elbow adaptors, tubing nuts,
8   grub screws, internal fan washers, dog points, half
9   dog points, white metal bushes –
10   FIBBS: But not, surely not, my lovely parallel male stud
11   couplings.
12   WILLS: They hate and detest your lovely parallel male
13   stud couplings, and the straight flange pump connec-
14   tors, and back nuts, and front nuts, *and* the
15   bronzedraw off cock with handwheel and the bronze-
16   draw off cock without handwheel!
17   FIBBS: Not the bronzedraw off cock with handwheel?
18   WILLS: And without handwheel.
19   FIBBS: Without handwheel?
20   WILLS: And with handwheel.
21   FIBBS: Not with handwheel?
22   WILLS: And without handwheel.
23   FIBBS: Without handwheel?
24   WILLS: With handwheel *and* without handwheel.
25   FIBBS: With handwheel *and* without handwheel?
26   WILLS: With or without! *(Pause)*
27   FIBBS: *(Broken)* Tell me. What do they want to make in its
28   place?
29   WILLS: Brandy balls.
30
31
32
33
34

from *Eastern Standard* ©
by Richard Greenberg

This social satire and stinging exposé of a group of young, wealthy, upwardly mobile but terribly jaded New York "yuppies" who share dreams, hopes, fears, and frustrations — not to mention potential bed-partners in a pinch — is a delightfully perceptive playscript that alternates between initial disenchantment and final resignation of the value of life and what it can offer in contemporary society. The social comedy begins in a chic, trendy Manhattan restaurant where Stephen, a young architect, and his best friend Drew observe Phoebe, a Wall Street banker, and her brother Peter having lunch. Stephen is immediately attracted to Phoebe and after some awkward moments — most notably a raving, bottle throwing bag lady and an unsatisfied, long-suffering waitress who is wonderfully antic — Stephen and Phoebe strike up a conversation and the powerful attraction each discovers for the other ripens into a budding friendship.

This scene, a month later, is set at Stephen's beach house. Stephen and Phoebe are lying idyllically in each other's arms, exploring the nature of their new relationship. There is a series of fumbling exchanges in which the characters reflect on their professional careers, pontificate on the deterioration of society in general, and eventually discover that they are kindred spirits.

Each character reveals old griefs and bittersweet feelings which plague them, but there is also a refreshing honesty and authenticity in their communication that suggests they are ideally suited for each other. They each provide the other with a calming sanctuary, especially at this moment and in this hectic time zone. Although the characters' high hopes and growing self-awarenesses are evident in the scene, there are still lingering doubts about this "accidental happiness" they are sharing for, perhaps, the first time in their young adult lives. The mood of the scene is both deliciously witty and playful as the characters indulge their comic fantasies. But the characters are also anxious and self-centered as they begin to embrace the caring and understanding that only true lovers can ever comprehend.

In playing the scene it is important for the actors to focus on the characters rather than on the comic situation. The inherent problems of staging and limited opportunities for movement — after all, the characters are in a reclining position for this episode! — require a more conscious focus of attention on the characters' emotional, intellectual, and psychological states in the performance interpretation. There should be good "listening" technique evident here as well; and each character should exhibit an intense concentration on what is said by the other character, responding with an alertness and freshness that suggests this moment is unique and unlike other more familiar encounters that the characters may have experienced in their lives. Good focus and listening should help the actors intensify the shifting actions, attitudes, and moods of the characters as well; and provide a more subtle performance blueprint to compensate for the limited physical action in the scene. It might be a good idea for the actors to improvise comfortable playing positions for the characters, and to discover in the rehearsal period those convenient posture and physical space positions that will not allow potentially distracting actions like stroking hair, kissing, or embracing to interfere with the interpretation of the dialog, or interfere with the inventive stage business that may need to be explored as a basic ingredient in the characters' subsequent reactions and responses in the scene. Finally, don't forget to give the scene a spirited sense of good fun, tender moments, and a tempo that suggests the ebb and flow of the characters' emotions.

1   STEPHEN: Are you happy? *(Beat)*
2   PHOEBE: Excuse me? *(Beat)*
3   STEPHEN: What?
4   PHOEBE: I'm sorry. I was thinking of something.
5   STEPHEN: Oh. *(Beat)* I said, "A penny for your thoughts."
6   PHOEBE: It didn't sound like that.
7   STEPHEN: I said it quickly. I said: "A penny-for-your-
8   thoughts."
9   PHOEBE: Oh. *(Long pause)*
10   STEPHEN: What are you thinking about?
11   PHOEBE: IBM.
12   STEPHEN: IBM.
13   PHOEBE: Yes. I think about IBM at lot.
14   STEPHEN: Oh.
15   PHOEBE: Also NYNEX. *(Beat. She sighs.)* This is bliss.
16   STEPHEN: Thank you.
17   PHOEBE: Have I told you I love your house?
18   STEPHEN: No.
19   PHOEBE: I love your house.
20   STEPHEN: I built it myself. I designed it. I must have told
21   you that.
22   PHOEBE: It's charming.
23   STEPHEN: Thank you. *(Pause)*
24   PHOEBE: I'm still thinking about IBM though.
25   STEPHEN: That's serene.
26   PHOEBE: I'm sorry; I'm a terrible drag. I don't rusticate
27   easily, I never have.
28   STEPHEN: It takes a while.
29   PHOEBE: I've wanted to. For ages. I've wanted to move to
30   Vermont and breed maple syrup. *(Beat)* Oh, God, I'm
31   thinking of stock option indexes, I'm thinking of
32   takeover bids, the world is too much with me. What
33   are you thinking of?
34   STEPHEN: Twin gothic spires.

1   PHOEBE: Excuse me?

2   STEPHEN: It's this building we're putting up in midtown.

3   These hideous spires that make no sense. I've been

4   campaigning against them for – Oh, well, it's hope-

5   less.

6   PHOEBE: I've been meaning to ask you. How did you end

7   up at such a cheesy firm, anyway?

8   STEPHEN: Oh!...Well...

9   PHOEBE: You must have had some other offers, didn't

10   you?

11   STEPHEN: Well...I...You know...They wanted me the most.

12   PHOEBE: ...Oh.

13   STEPHEN: And I never intended to stay this long, but...I

14   was doing so much better than anybody else and

15   before I knew it –

16   PHOEBE: Well, you can't really blame yourself; you were

17   seduced.

18   STEPHEN: Yes. *(Beat)* No.

19   PHOEBE: ...What?

20   STEPHEN: No. That's a pleasant idea, but there's no such

21   thing as seduction, really. There's only the...unex-

22   pected availability of what you secretly want. I was

23   having a wonderful time! I was envied. I was in a

24   paradise of my own cleverness!

25   PHOEBE: But then your work started getting worse and

26   worse.

27   STEPHEN: No, everything else did. My work got clever and

28   clever.

29   PHOEBE: You're very talented.

30   STEPHEN: Yes, but talent becomes a nightmare when you

31   hate what you're doing with it...Oh, well. This time off

32   I'm taking, hardly anyone's ever been given that

33   before. Glassman – my boss – "Take however long

34   you need," he said. "Just come back to us." I took off

1   **because I thought it was better to be useless than to**
2   **be harmful, but some of these long days...No, it's fine.**
3   **I won't complain. I have this house, I have time,**
4   **you're here...I'll just vamp until I figure out what to**
5   **do with the rest of my life.** *(PHOEBE kisses him.)* **Was it**
6   **nice being a mogul?**
7   PHOEBE: I was hardly a mogul.
8   STEPHEN: Weren't you? I thought all people in finance
9   were moguls. But then I have no idea how the world
10   works.
11   PHOEBE: There are moguls and there are peons; I was
12   somewhere in between.
13   STEPHEN: And you loved making money hand over fist?
14   PHOEBE: I didn't make money hand over fist. I loved
15   crossing my legs in a swivel chair.
16   STEPHEN: Oh!
17   PHOEBE: And I loved turning on my computer and
18   sipping coffee from a Styrofoam cup and phoning
19   strangers and telling them what to do with their
20   money and having them *believe* me. And I loved
21   sometimes working until five in the morning and
22   having a car pick me up and just sort of crumpling
23   into it; and the city would rush by, very lavender and
24   very expensive, but I could afford it, and all the
25   people I knew seemed happy.
26   STEPHEN: But wasn't it just a lot of bad people doing evil
27   things?
28   PHOEBE: I never noticed any of that.
29   STEPHEN: Well, as I said, I have no idea how the world
30   works.
31   PHOEBE: It was a system; it thrived. I had a very good
32   time. *(Beat)* I mean I *have* a very good...
33   STEPHEN: It was very nice of the company to give you all
34   this time off.

1   PHOEBE: Yes, well, it's amazing how generous they can be
2   when you're the moll of one of the criminals who
3   brought disgrace upon them. They'd probably give
4   me the rest of my life off if I —
5   STEPHEN: Stop this, it's morbid.
6   PHOEBE: Yes. I'm sorry.
7   STEPHEN: We have to look at it this way: we're both on
8   sabbatical. We're recharging our batteries.
9   PHOEBE: Yes, that's how I'll look at it. I'm sorry. I'm being
10   impossible.
11   STEPHEN: Not at all. *(Beat)* It's the phone calls more than
12   anything that bother me, but —
13   PHOEBE: The phone calls?
14   STEPHEN: Forget it.
15   PHOEBE: What are you talking about?
16   STEPHEN: Nothing...
17   PHOEBE; Stephen...
18   STEPHEN: The ones you take and never tell me about; the
19   ones I intercept.
20   PHOEBE: They're nothing.
21   STEPHEN: This vague male voice. "Is, uh, Phoebe there?"
22   "No." "Thank you very much." Click. No identifica-
23   tion so that I don't start making connections. Of
24   course, that sends my head spinning in a thousand
25   different directions. Why the secrecy? Why the
26   clandestine —
27   PHOEBE: It's hardly clandestine.
28   STEPHEN: It's Loomis, of course, I know that, but why
29   can't you tell me?
30   PHOEBE: Yes, of course, it's Loomis. I hate him.
31   STEPHEN: How did he get this number?
32   PHOEBE: He's not without resources. *(Beat)* I gave him the
33   number.
34   STEPHEN: Ah. *(Beat)* Well.

1   PHOEBE: There's nothing to it. He started...
2   STEPHEN: What?
3   PHOEBE: He started threatening –
4   STEPHEN: What –
5   PHOEBE: – to kill himself, Stephen, all right? *(Beat)*
6   STEPHEN: Oh. *(Beat)* That's become quite a cliché among
7   the discredited, hasn't it?
8   PHOEBE: I don't believe him.
9   STEPHEN: It's just another form of extortion...Well, if you
10   don't believe him, why do you –
11   PHOEBE: It's nothing. Nothing at all. I listen. I appease
12   him. You just can't leave people in puddles. Not if
13   you're a secular humanist. The creed of secular
14   humanism is "Thou shalt listen to old lovers whine
15   incessantly." I do it. I'm among the faithful. Sue me.
16   *(Beat)*
17   STEPHEN: I'm sorry.
18   PHOEBE: No, I am.
19   STEPHEN: Talk to him all you want. I'll get on the exten-
20   sion, we'll have conference calls.
21   PHOEBE: You're insane.
22   STEPHEN: I'll lend him my knife.
23   PHOEBE: Shut up. *(She kisses him.)*
24   STEPHEN: Thank you.
25   PHOEBE: I won't let him call me anymore. I promise. It's
26   over. We'll shut everything out. There's no work, no
27   Loomis, nothing but us and this beach. Nothing has
28   ever happened in our lives and we're alone as alone
29   can be.
30
31
32
33
34

from *The Nerd* ©
by Larry Shue

This brilliantly conceived and highly entertaining comedy is deliciously sinister and side-splitting in its clever treatment of the hilarious complications that erupt when Willum Cubbert, a young adult architect living in Terre Haute, Indiana, is visited by a man he's never actually met before, but who saved his life in Vietnam during the war. The visitor, Rick Steadman, turns out to be an incredibly inept, hopelessly dense "nerd," who extends his initial welcome beyond the reasonable limits of good taste with an antic display of assorted mishaps and miscalculations that literally drive his host to despair and desperation under the zany circumstances. As Rick settles in for what appears to be a permanent visitation, his increasingly irritating attitude and behavior drives the normally calm, passive Willum to contemplate physical mayhem and violence to rid himself and his friends of "the nerd," who remains oblivious to his own chilling intruding presence.

As this scene opens, Rick appears unexpectedly at the architect's apartment as Willum and his friends, Axel and Tansy, are celebrating his thirty-fourth birthday. Willum — who had recently written Rick to say that, as long as he is alive, "[you]...will have somebody on earth who will do anything for you... "— is delighted to finally meet the fellow ex-soldier who saved his life after he was seriously wounded in Vietnam. But that delight soon fades into disbelief as it becomes painfully obvious that "the nerd" is a bumbling, stumbling oaf with no redeeming social graces, no sophistication, no intelligence, and no interpersonal skills to confront the obstacles which surely litter his lifestyle. The scene is also reminiscent of the incongruity, unpredictability, and hilarity of a rather lethal family reunion — and is as refreshingly unrestrained as the other uninhibited episodes that are found in the complete play-script itself.

In playing this "tea-time" scene, the actors will need to pay particular attention to those performance choices which generate interesting and inventive stage business and to create challenging improvisational opportunities that highlight the "inner" and the "outer" character(s) in terms of vocal or physical characterization. The characters, Axel, a jaded theatre critic, and Tansy, an aspiring television weather girl, require a finely etched oral and visual self-portrait that is uniform and unified in its ability to give these supporting roles special individuality and pinpoint accuracy in character responses and reactions to the frenzied incidents that follow as they each struggle valiantly to be amiable company in this improbable predicament. These particular characters, who find themselves in this rather improbable situation, also need to be mentally and emotionally alert and responsive as well, with no self-indulgent theatrics or distracting theatrical posing if they are to provide meaningful contrast to the predominant comic "nerd" character in the selected scene.

Here is an excellent performance opportunity for the actors playing the roles of Rick and Willum to explore the creative use of photographs, magazines, short stories, or recent television and film characterizations that might suggest a mental picture of the action, the character, or the situation described in the scene. Remember, however, that this scene's basic comic impulse revolves around the seriously inept, social outcast Rick, so the other actors in the scene should practice subtle economy in their actions and reactions to suggest the personal and private nature of their growing disdain and ridicule of "the nerd" or the humor of the situation may not be clearly understood by the audience. Finally, the actors should approach this selected scene with the same intensity, dedication, and discipline as any other performance blueprint, paying attention to analyzing each character's physical, vocal, and mental qualities as they might help to clearly define and amplify the basic motivation(s) or intention(s) of the characters in terms of mood, attitude, and point of view.

This successful discovery should reveal the nuances and spontaneous outbursts that provoke the inherent comedy of the given circumstances, and also result in a slashing, satirical edge to the character portraits being drawn.

1   TANSY: Here we are. Tea time.
2   WILLUM: Ah!
3   AXEL: Well, aren't we civilized.
4   TANSY: Why, of course. *(Offering RICK a cup)* **Rick?**
5   RICK: Thanks. Are we goeen' to eat, sometime?
6   TANSY: Won't be long now.
7   RICK: Good.
8   TANSY: Cream?
9   RICK: Nah.
10 TANSY: Lemon?
11 RICK: 'Kay. *(He takes a lemon slice.)*
12 AXEL: **We were just talking about our favorite old songs**
13   **and things.**
14 TANSY: Oh, my. *(To RICK)* **You use sugar?**
15 RICK: **Sure.** *(He takes a spoonful.)*
16 AXEL: **Memories, memories.**
17 TANSY: *(To RICK)* **Sand?**
18 RICK: *(As if unsure he has heard)* **Hunh?**
19 TANSY: **Sand?** *(Pointing to each of two bowls)* **Sugar on the**
20   **left, sand on the right.**
21 RICK: *(Pause)* **No, I'm fine. Thanks.** *(He watches the tray as*
22   *it passes to the others.)*
23 TANSY: Axel?
24 AXEL: *(Taking a cup)* 'nk you.
25 TANSY: *(To WILLUM)* And –?
26 WILLUM: *(Taking a cup)* Yes. Thanks.
27 TANSY: **Oh, yes. Those old songs – take you right back.**
28   **Just the other day, I – I'm sorry, Ax. Here.**
29 AXEL: *(Helping himself)* **Just get some cream here. And a**
30   **little sugar – a – and some sand.** *(He stirs all three into*
31   *his tea.)*
32 WILLUM: *(To TANSY)* **What were you saying?**
33 TANSY: **Oh, just that I was listening to the radio the other**
34   **day –** *(To WILLUM)* **anything?**

1   **WILLUM: Just sand, thanks.** *(He takes several spoonfuls of*
2   *sand, stirs happily.)*
3   **TANSY: – and what should come on but some old thing I**
4   **haven't heard since high school.** *(Adds lemon and sand*
5   *to her own tea.)*
6   **AXEL: Your tea is superb, incidentally.**
7   **WILLUM:** *(Sipping)* **Mmm!**
8   **TANSY: Is it?**
9   **WILLUM: Yes, indeed.**
10   **TANSY:** *(Sips.)* **Mmm. Not so bad.**
11   **WILLUM: So what was on the radio?**
12   **TANSY: Oh, some old rock-and-roll song by Rip Delahous-**
13   **saye and His All Girl Band. Remember them?**
14   **AXEL: Rip Delahoussaye. Sure.**
15   **WILLUM: Hey, they don't write songs like those anymore.**
16   **"Bumout"?**
17   **AXEL: "Bumout," yep. And "Dive Boppin' Mama"?**
18   **TANSY: "I Lost My Baby to the Great Big Train"?**
19   **WILLUM: Sure.**
20   **AXEL: Great songs.**
21   **WILLUM: Good times.**
22   **TANSY: And remember some of those old TV shows?**
23   **"Herd Busters"?**
24   **AXEL: "Herd Busters." We used to listen to that on the**
25   **radio.** *(Deep, thrilling radio voice)* **"Out of the West they**
26   **came – six tall men on a single horse!"**
27   **WILLUM: That's right. And remember "Furball and**
28   **Snorkey"?**
29   **TANSY: Sure. With his friend Bunghead the Clown.**
30   **AXEL: And Sphinctre the Dog! That's right.**
31   **WILLUM: Yeah.**
32   **AXEL: That's right.**
33   **WILLUM: Boy. Childhood in Terre Haute.**
34   **TANSY:** *(Nostalgically)* **No kidding. Do you –? I can**

1   remember – every year, right after the first snowfall,
2   my father would take his old scatter-gun down from
3   the mantel, go out into the woods, and see if he
4   couldn't bring down a plane.
5   AXEL: Yeah...
6   WILLUM: *(With a chuckle)* Man, some of the things. *(To*
7   *RICK)* You ever go to pork-dances? They'd make us all
8   go, us kids. We'd have to slow dance all night with
9   these big slabs of meat. It was supposed to be – prepa-
10   ration for later life, or something.
11   AXEL: Who knows.
12   WILLUM: I don't know.
13   AXEL: And did you ever –? Every Christmas, our family,
14   we'd take this, really, it was the intestine of a sheep –
15   and we'd stuff it full of this spicy sausage meat.
16   WILLUM: Oh, yeah?
17   AXEL: *(Warmly)* Yeah. *(Pause)* That old sheep'd get so mad.
18   WILLUM: Well, sure she would.
19   AXEL: Got to where she'd know when Christmas was
20   coming every year. We'd find her hiding.
21   WILLUM: Sure.
22   TANSY: Or we'd go out and dig in the snow, and see if we
23   couldn't find ourselves some bananas.
24   RICK: What?
25   TANSY: *(As she exits to the kitchen)* Oh, we had this crazy
26   notion we wanted to start an orchestra. *(She exits.)*
27   WILLUM: La, la.
28   AXEL: Remember old man Wormsley?
29   WILLUM: *(Warmly)* Nope.
30   AXEL: *(Happily)* Me neither. *(TANSY enters with a steaming*
31   *drum of hot tar.)*
32   TANSY: Rick? Boiling hot tar all over your face?
33   RICK: Not right now, thanks. *(TANSY exits.)*
34   WILLUM: So, Rick –

1   **WILLUM & AXEL:** *(Loud falsetto)* **Yeep! Yeep! Yeep!**
2   **WILLUM:** **– how would you compare Terre Haute life with**
3   **what you're used to?**
4   **RICK:** **'Bout the same.**
5   **WILLUM:** **Oh...** *(TANSY enters with saucers and two kinds of*
6   *foodstuff, all on a tray.)*
7   **TANSY:** **Here we go.** *(To RICK)* **Saucer?** *(He takes one.)* **And –**
8   **just help yourself.**
9   **RICK:** **What are those?**
10   **TANSY:** **Just our traditional appetizer – garbanzos and**
11   **rusks.**
12   **RICK:** **Oh.** *(He takes a rusk, then spoons a garbanzo or two*
13   *onto it. He lifts it, but the garbanzos roll off onto his*
14   *saucer. He tries again, balancing them precariously.)* **They**
15   **kinda roll around on there, don't they?** *(They drop off*
16   *again.)* **Here. Wait a minute.** *(He takes a second rusk;*
17   *then, with a rusk in each hand, he pounces on the errant*
18   *garbanzos, trapping them between improvised rusk-jaws.)*
19   **There we go.** *(He takes a bite.)* **Not bad.** *(Wisely)* **That's**
20   **really true, though. Food really tastes better when you**
21   **catch it yourself, y'know? That's what my father always**
22   **said. Departed father, I should say.**
23   **TANSY:** *(Suddenly ashamed)* **Oh, Rick. When did he die?**
24   **RICK:** *(Doesn't she have ears?)* **He didn't die. He just departed.**
25   **TANSY:** **Oh...**
26   **RICK:** **Yeah, I woke up one morneen', and he was gone. I**
27   **still remember, 'cause it was the day after I got my**
28   **tambourine.**
29   **TANSY:** **Uh-huh...**
30   **AXEL:** **Yeah...**
31   **WILLUM:** *(Crossing to AXEL for more tea. Between his teeth)*
32   **What now, Ax?**
33   **AXEL:** *(Smiling, pouring)* **Oh, something a little stronger, I**
34   **think.**

1   WILLUM: All right.
2   RICK: This is great.
3   WILLUM: Yeah.
4   RICK: Good old Terre Haute.
5   WILLUM: Right.
6   RICK: I can hardly wait till it gets winter, so we can shoot
7   some planes and stuff some sheep!
8   WILLUM: Ax –
9   AXEL: Right. Oh   old man winter. Whew! *(To RICK)* I hope
10   you brought your gear.
11   RICK: Huh?
12   AXEL: You know – parkas, space heaters. Mukluks.
13   RICK: What?
14   AXEL: Well, we'll get you some, don't worry.
15   WILLUM: *(Catching on)* Oh! Oh, sure.
16   AXEL: 'Cause it's gonna get *pretty* mean out there, starting
17   – *(Checks watch)* well, about now, really.
18   WILLUM: Oh, it's not that bad. A few months of howling,
19   bleak nothingness. But – there's no reason you
20   shouldn't – survive. *We* did.
21   TANSY: Sure. We've been lucky. *(Her expression changes.)*
22   Well, luckier than – the others.
23   RICK: What? Others?
24   TANSY: Oh, Rick.
25   AXEL: This house used to be *filled* with people.
26   TANSY: Yes...
27   AXEL: Gone now.
28   WILLUM: They couldn't take the winter.
29   RICK: Who couldn't?
30   WILLUM: *You* know. The old.
31   AXEL: The young.
32   TANSY: The sick.
33   AXEL: *(To TANSY)* Who do you miss the most?
34   TANSY: The sick, I guess.

1   AXEL: Yeah.

2   WILLUM: *(To RICK)* **Oh, Rick. You should have been here.**

3   TANSY: **This house used to ring with the laughter of the**

4   **sick.**

5   WILLUM: **No more.**

6   TANSY: **No...**

7   WILLUM: **No more.**

8   RICK: **What happened?**

9   WILLUM: **Oh – starvation.**

10   TANSY: **Marauding savages from Indianapolis.**

11   WILLUM: **Yes...and forest beasts, on the prowl – desperate**

12   **for food for their hibernating young.**

13   RICK: **Are you kiddeen? Some *beasts*?**

14   WILLUM: **Oh, yes.**

15   RICK: **What did you do when there was *beasts* comeen'**

16   **around?**

17   AXEL: **Well, if all else failed, one of the sick would go out**

18   **there and offer himself up.**

19   RICK: **Huh?**

20   AXEL: **How are you feeling?**

21   RICK: **Fine.**

22   AXEL: **Yeah?**

23   RICK: **What kind of beasts are they?**

24   WILLUM: **Oh...what. Coyotes.**

25   AXEL: **Wolverines.**

26   TANSY: **Mastodons.** *(AXEL and WILLUM look at her.)*

27   **Sometimes.**

28   RICK: **Oh, yeah. We got those.**

29   WILLUM: **You do? *Mastodons*?**

30   RICK: **Yeah, I think. Don't they have, like, real hairy**

31   **palms, or sometheen'?**

32   WILLUM: **I'm not sure.**

33   RICK; **Any pigs?**

34   WILLUM: **What? Pigs?**

1   RICK: Yeah.
2   WILLUM: No. Listen, we're talking about –
3   RICK: Good. 'Cause those are the ones I hate. Whenever I
4   see a pig, like, in a movie or sometheen'? Forget it. I'm
5   outta there. I can't take those suckers.
6   AXEL: Well, we do get *some* pigs.
7   WILLUM: Quite a few, really.
8   TANSY: Big, giant –
9   AXEL: *Mutant pigs.*
10   WILLUM: They'd as soon kill you as look at you.
11   RICK: Really?
12   TANSY: Big, hairy things. *(The kitchen timer sounds again.)*
13   Woop! Dinner time! *(She exits.)*
14   WILLUM: Oh, boy.
15   AXEL: *(To RICK)* Man, am I ready for some chow. How
16   about you?
17   RICK: Oh, yeah. I'm starveen'.
18   AXEL: Great.
19   RICK: Pigs, huh? *(WILLUM and AXEL nod. TANSY enters*
20   *with a huge tureen; puts it on the table.)* What are we
21   haveen'?
22   TANSY: Wait, Rick.
23   AXEL: Wait.
24   TANSY: First – a little surprise.
25   RICK: Huh?
26   TANSY: *(Uncovering a tureen)* Ta-da!
27   WILLUM: Oh, boy.
28   AXEL: An apple core!
29   WILLUM: Oh, we're gonna have some fun now! *(TANSY*
30   *carefully sets the core upright on the table.)*
31   AXEL: *(To RICK)* You ever do this?
32   RICK: What are we doeen'?
33   WILLUM: *(As they excitedly gather around the core)* Gonna
34   watch this baby turn *brown*.

1   **AXEL: Yeah!**

2   **RICK: Why?**

3   **TANSY: Oh – it's just our way.**

4   **RICK: Oh.** *(Pause)* **Then we're not goeen' to eat till it turns**

5   **brown?**

6   **TANSY: Right.**

7   **RICK: Because it's your *way*?**

8   **WILLUM & AXEL: Right.**

9   **RICK: Oh...**

10   **WILLUM: OK, OK. Shhh!** *(They all stare at the apple core.*

11   *Fifteen or twenty seconds pass. Occasionally someone*

12   *takes a sip of tea.)*

13   **RICK: I think maybe my side's turneen' brown a little bit.**

14   *(More seconds pass.)* **No, maybe not.** *(More seconds)*

15   **Your side turneen' brown?** *(One or two of the others*

16   *shake their heads.)* **Little bit? No?** *(Pause)* **Yeah, you**

17   **wouldn't of thought this would be that much fun, but**

18   **it really kind of is, isn't it?** *(The others keep staring,*

19   *hoping they have heard incorrectly.)* **Better than**

20   **watcheen' chalk, that's for sure. You could watch**

21   **chalk forever and it would never do anything neat**

22   **like turn brown. This is great.**

23   **WILLUM:** *(Seeing that this isn't working)* **Uh – Tansy –?**

24   **Maybe you should check –**

25   **TANSY:** *(Taking her cue)* **Ah! Sounds like the old kitchen**

26   **timer! Time for dinner!** *(She goes to the kitchen.)*

27

28

29

30

31

32

33

34

from *Saving Stonewall* ©
by John Wooten

A highly imaginative retelling of the historical events that led up to the accidental shooting of General "Stonewall" Jackson by some of his own troops in the midst of the Civil War, this scene offers an intense character study of two young adult Confederate soldiers who have been given sanctuary at the decimated plantation house of Virginia Hopewell, just outside of the Chancelorsville Battleground in Virginia. Although the historical incidents are accurate, the two young adult men are not; they are fresh, richly imaginative characters that offer devastingly different points of view on the war and on life in the "Old South" of this period. The flow of the action is enhanced by crisp dialog and by a subtle, penetrating examination of the meaning and significance of war on the heart, the mind, and the soul of these weary young participants.

Daniel, the sensitive and perceptive foot soldier recently wounded in the leg, is now confined to bed. Although he appears to be just another innocent farm boy casuality of the war-ravaged landscape, he is much more intelligent and independent thinking than his appearance might initially suggest. Jefferson, also recovering from an apparent injury, is his youthful counterpart sharing a space at the Hopewell plantation. He is the son of an influential Colonel in the Confederate Army, and has an underlying spirit of recklessness and rebellion. After a closer look at his temperament, however, it is obvious that he, too, is more complex than initial appearances might suggest. Both young men are competing for the attention of Sarah Hopewell, the attractive and fascinating young lady who — along with her servant Tessie — has been given responsibility for the care of the soldiers. After a series of haunting, terrible intrigues and dark secrets are revealed by the characters, the author also surprises us by revealing that Daniel was responsible for the mistaken attempt on the life of General "Stonewall" Jackson.

In playing the scene, the actors need to pay attention to the relative similarities of the young men in terms of their age, regional dialect, and physical type; and to be inventive in the use of gestures, mannerisms, personal habits, or vocal/physical qualities that will give each character some definite distinction and dimension. Since both young men are apparently *not* what they appear to be, the actors may need to provide a performance blueprint that explores significant psychological or emotional moments for the characters to develop in the scene; and the actors should also investigate the "cause-and-effect" relationship of the characters to highlight the consequences and implications of the actions that are identified in the scene. It might also be a good performance idea to review the basic principles of *purpose, passion,* and *perception* discussed in Chapter 3 to gain additional insight in understanding the intimate interpersonal relationship of the characters in this scene.

The selected scene also lends itself to the actors' inventive use of expressive, forceful performance "verbs" that underline the spontaneity and energy of the character's spoken dialog and physical actions. Performance verbs, however, should be carefully chosen to reinforce character subtext and the inherent meaning of character intention(s) and motivation(s) suggested in the scene. It is important, therefore, that the actors clearly isolate, define, and reveal the "hidden" facts regardig these young characters in terms of attitude, behavior, and psychology when playing the scene. Finally, do not hesitate to highlight the "inner" and "outer" nature of these characters; and encourage a natural and conversational tone of expression that gives additional depth and dimension to the thoughts, ideas, and emotions of these young men who, perhaps for the first time in their lives, are trying desperately to come to know — and to accept — each other, and themselves, for what they really are...no matter what the cost.

1 JEFFERSON: Daniel...Daniel...hey, Danny Boy!
2 DANIEL: *(Turning lantern up, half asleep)* Huh?...What's
3   wrong? What's going on?
4 JEFFERSON: How are you doing?
5 DANIEL: I'm asleep.
6 JEFFERSON: *(Smiles.)* Not anymore.
7 DANIEL: Is there something wrong?
8 JEFFERSON: Yeah, I can't sleep...you want a drink? *(Holds*
9   *out bottle.)*
10 DANIEL: No. What time is it?
11 JEFFERSON: Night. Come on.
12 DANIEL: *(Considers.)* All right. *(JEFFERSON crosses to*
13   *DANIEL's bed and sits. He takes a swig and passes the*
14   *bottle to DANIEL.)* Thanks. *(DANIEL drinks.)*
15 JEFFERSON: That's better than the other stuff.
16 DANIEL: Yeah. *(DANIEL looks at him.)*
17 JEFFERSON: *(Laughs.)* Don't worry, it ain't that good. If the
18   good Colonel wasn't planning on coming back, that
19   whiskey would tickle your tongue. My father ain't
20   gonna walk out on these women, not yet anyway...So,
21   you want to get drunk, Danny Boy?
22 DANIEL: I'm still feeling it from earlier. *(Looks around.)*
23   Where's Tessie?
24 JEFFERSON: Oh, don't let her fool you. She yes Ma'ams
25   those women all day, doesn't mean she listens to them.
26 DANIEL: Where is she?
27 JEFFERSON: Upstairs.
28 DANIEL: But there's no roof up there.
29 JEFFERSON: So? It's not raining. And if it should, I guess
30   she feels safer up there than down here with me.
31   *(Makes monster face, laughs.)* How's the leg?
32 DANIEL: OK.
33 JEFFERSON: Still hurt?
34 DANIEL: No.

1   **JEFFERSON:** Uh-huh...So, after you fell off, Mrs. Hopewell

2   **and I had a little talk.**

3   **DANIEL: What about?**

4   **JEFFERSON: What do you think?**

5   **DANIEL:** *(Perks up.)* **About what happened?**

6   **JEFFERSON: Why, yes, my young friend. You did happen**

7   **to come up in conversation.**

8   **DANIEL: And?**

9   **JEFFERSON: She made sense out of everything. Why you**

10   **were brought here. The special attention. It's all clear**

11   **as day now.** *(JEFFERSON smiles.)*

12   **DANIEL: Well?**

13   **JEFFERSON: I don't know if I should tell you.**

14   **DANIEL: What?**

15   **JEFFERSON: The truth may prove to be too distracting.**

16   **Might hamper the healing process. At least that's**

17   **what Virginia seemed to think.**

18   **DANIEL: Tell me, Jefferson.**

19   **JEFFERSON:** *(A beat. He eyes DANIEL carefully.)* **You really**

20   **don't remember anything that happened to you?...**

21   **Nothing?**

22   **DANIEL: No.**

23   **JEFFERFSON: All right. All right. Don't get yourself so**

24   **excited, soldier. Tell you what I'll do. I'll tell you what**

25   **I know little by little. But you have to promise me that**

26   **at anytime you start to remember or should you get to**

27   **feeling nervous or excited, you'll speak up.**

28   **DANIEL: Fine.**

29   **JEFFERSON: You have to promise.**

30   **DANIEL: I promise!**

31   **JEFFERSON: That's better. You also have to promise that**

32   **you won't let Virginia or Sarah know that you know. I**

33   **promised Virginia I wouldn't say anything, but you**

34   **being a good friend of mine and due to my enormous**

1   sense of duty, I felt strangely obligated to tell you.
2   Agreed?
3   DANIEL: Sarah knows?
4   JEFFERSON: She does. Agreed?
5   DANIEL: Agreed.
6   JEFFERSON: All right then...Here, you better take the
7   bottle. *(He hands it to DANIEL.)* Well, what can I say,
8   you're a hero, Daniel. A real live hero. They'll prob-
9   ably name something or somewhere after you for
10   what you did the other night. I knew you seemed a bit
11   on the patriotic side, but you really give your all for
12   your country, don't you?
13   DANIEL: A hero? What are you talking about?
14   JEFFERSON: What's the last thing you remember?
15   DANIEL: Being on watch.
16   JEFFERSON: Then it's all blank, huh? *(DANIEL nods.)* Then
17   you probably don't remember being chosen to be one
18   of General Stonewall Jackson's escorts?
19   DANIEL: No.
20   JEFFERSON: Well, you apparently were. You were chosen
21   from a group of Confederate pickets. One of the
22   riders escorting Jackson had an infected foot.
23   Couldn't ride. So they passed your company and
24   asked for a volunteer to take his place.
25   DANIEL: I volunteered?
26   JEFFERSON: Hell, yeah. Then you and some other riders
27   escorted the general behind enemy lines to get a good
28   look at the Union position. Well, I guess you all got too
29   good a look. Got too close and had to head back in a
30   hurry. You put some distance between you and the
31   Yanks and then I guess you started to relax, figuring
32   you were safe. It was a natural assumption. But
33   then...then...Hand me that bottle, will you? *(DANIEL
34   quickly hands JEFFERSON the bottle. JEFFERSON takes*

1   *a long drink.)* **This whiskey is good, isn't it?**
2 **DANIEL: Jefferson!**
3 **JEFFERSON: I guess you don't remember the next part**
4   **either?**
5 **DANIEL: No.**
6 **JEFFERSON: Well, it was late and there was Confederate**
7   **pickets watching those woods you were riding**
8   **through.** *(JEFFERSON rises, crosses away from the bed*
9   *and drinks.)*
10 **DANIEL: What?**
11 **JEFFERSON: Some nervous idiot mistakes Stonewall and**
12   **you boys for Yankees. He starts shooting, causing**
13   **everyone to fire. You must remember that?**
14 **DANIEL: No. Keep going.**
15 **JEFFERSON: They hit you and most of the others. Killing**
16   **just about everybody.**
17 **DANIEL: Jesus.**
18 **JEFFERSON: Yeah.**
19 **DANIEL: And Stonewall?**
20 **JEFFERSON: What about him?**
21 **DANIEL: Was he shot?**
22 **JEFFERSON: Yeah...afraid so.**
23 **DANIEL:** *(A beat)* **Is he dead?**
24 **JEFFERSON: Nope. See that's where you come in. Since**
25   **you were riding so close to him, they say you and your**
26   **horse provided a shield. He got shot. But only in the**
27   **arm.**
28 **DANIEL: Bad?**
29 **JEFFERSON: My father told Virginia that the surgeon had**
30   **to take it that morning.**
31 **DANIEL: His arm?**
32 **JEFFERSON: Yeah. That's why the surgeon didn't come**
33   **out the night you were brought. Shame, he could**
34   **probably save that leg.**

1   DANIEL: It don't need saving.
2   JEFFERSON: Anyway, he's alive. Went home to recover.
3   Looks like he's gonna pull through just fine.
4   Apparently, he thinks you had something to do
5   with that. He'll probably give you a commission or
6   something.
7   DANIEL: I can't believe they took his arm.
8   JEFFERSON: See, I knew I shouldn't have told you.
9   DANIEL: I'm glad you told me.
10   JEFFERSON: Listen to me, Daniel. You may have to keep
11   your mouth shut, you hear? I took a big chance telling
12   you. My father had special orders to take you out
13   here. It's a very sensitive matter, what you did. It has
14   to stay between you and me.
15   DANIEL: I don't break promises. I promised you I
16   wouldn't say I know and I won't.
17   JEFFERSON: Can you imagine that damn fool who
18   shot Stonewall? I wonder what he's thinking right
19   about now.
20   DANIEL: They ought to shoot him. *(JEFFERSON laughs.)*
21   They should.
22   JEFFERSON: Maybe you already did, Danny Boy.
23   DANIEL: What?
24   JEFFERSON: And don't be trying to steal Sarah away from
25   me just because you saved the Confederacy, you hear?
26   Oh, Christ, you gonna spend the rest of the night
27   depressed? It could be a lot worse. Imagine being the
28   damn fool who blew Stonewall's arm off.
29   DANIEL: I'd rather not.
30   JEFFERSON: You really don't remember nothing, do you?
31   DANIEL: Wish I did.
32   JEFFERSON: Don't worry about it. Here, have a drink. It
33   will make you feel better.
34   DANIEL: *(Takes bottle.)* Thanks.

1   JEFFERSON: Yes, sir. You're one bonafide hero. A real
2   credit to the Confederacy. Hallelujah.
3   DANIEL: How's the shoulder?
4   JEFFERSON: I'll be lucky if I live through the night.
5   DANIEL: What about you?
6   JEFFERSON: What about me?
7   DANIEL: How'd you get wounded?
8   JEFFERSON: I told you, I was shot.
9   DANIEL: In battle?
10   JEFFERSON: No, I was trying to get flies off my uniform.
11   DANIEL: Seriously. What happened?
12   JEFFERSON: I don't remember. Hey, quit hogging the
13   bottle.
14   DANIEL: Sorry. *(He hands him the bottle.)*
15   JEFFERSON: Boy, for a nondrinker, you learn quick.
16   DANIEL: Was it day or night?
17   JEFFERSON: Night.
18   DANIEL: Did your unit lose a lot of men?
19   JEFFERSON: I don't know.
20   DANIEL: How many men did you kill?
21   JEFFERSON: Hey, what is it with the questions? I got shot,
22   they brought me here, that's it. End of story. I'm not
23   some kind of hero like you are if that's what you're
24   getting at.
25   DANIEL: Did you lose any friends?
26   JEFFERSON: A couple.
27   DANIEL: Did you see them die?
28   JEFFERSON: Boy, you are like an old woman. Didn't I just
29   say I didn't want to remember? Didn't I just say that?
30   DANIEL: I watched a lot of men die. Most of my company.
31   They were good men. Doesn't seem fair, does it?
32   JEFFERSON: Good? I'd say well-trained, devoted, even
33   loyal. But good? You have to possess a minimal
34   amount of intelligence to be good, Danny Boy. That's

1   what separates us from the animals.
2 DANIEL: What's that supposed to mean?
3 JEFFERSON: *(Laughs.)* Exactly. My young friend, what is
4   the battlefield littered with? Well? Answer the ques-
5   tion. I answered about fifty of your damn questions.
6   You can answer one of mine. What's the battlefield
7   littered with?
8 DANIEL: Jefferson, I didn't mean to...
9 JEFFERSON: Starry-eyed little do-gooders. Boys just like
10   you. Saying how they were gonna whip up them
11   Yankees. And then they screamed like little children
12   when they were hit. Crying out for God and Mommy.
13   Bunch of fools. Don't look so tough then. Don't even
14   know what they're fighting for. Just hooked on
15   fighting. Like you, hero.
16 DANIEL: I know what I'm fighting for.
17 JEFFERSON: Do you? Oh, my captain would have loved the
18   way you talk. 'Cept you probably would have hated
19   him. He'd do anything to stay out of the fight. Smelled
20   bad too. Breath that could kill a skunk. See, he had
21   important orders from the general and broke the
22   first rule. Waited too long to attack...Well, we both
23   know you don't keep the general waiting. So, we got
24   put on burial duty. Burying all them "good" soldiers.
25   Slave duty. I got to supervise the men. First time.
26   Make sure they put enough dirt over them boys to
27   cover the stink. I was in charge while the rest of the
28   officers sat in a tent drinking cheap wine from a
29   whiskey bottle. A bottle just like this. *(He takes a*
30   *drink.)* And all them boys started to look like another.
31   We were burying one giant fool. And all the time, I
32   could hear my superiors laughing in the tent. Slave
33   duty wasn't so bad for them. I spent twelve hours
34   straight looking at them rotting boys. You can get

1   used to the sight of the dead but the stench, the
2   stench is something you never get used to. I thought
3   that damn stench was gonna kill me, I really did.
4   But then we got word we were to move out. Right
5   away. The captain was drunk – *(Laughs)* drunker than
6   I am right now. Booze gave him courage, though he
7   had trouble staying on his horse as we rode to the
8   front. We got where the fighting was and there was
9   more dead and screaming boys lying in front of us.
10   Everywhere you looked. On top of each other in some
11   spots. And they were from both sides. Though they
12   screamed the same. Couldn't tell a Yank from one of
13   us. So, we settled in. The Yanks started shooting at us
14   with odd fire, not anything to speak of. I sat there for
15   hours until I couldn't take it anymore, those fools
16   screaming, the smell...it was dark. *(Takes a long drink.)*
17   I figured what the hell...let someone else worry about
18   the poor suckers. Nobody knew any better. I was
19   gonna get shot sooner or later. Might as well be in
20   control of when and where. I sure as shit wasn't going
21   to end up in some field like the rest of them,
22   screaming for somebody to kill me. *(Takes another*
23   *long drink. Pause. He slowly looks over at DANIEL.)* **What**
24   **you looking at?**
25 DANIEL: Nothing.
26
27
28
29
30
31
32
33
34

CHAPTER SIX

SCENES FOR YOUNG ADULT WOMEN
(With Men/Women)

"The senses must be awake to what's happening and to what's being created, transforming the space, always to return to the quiet inner starting point. That quiet inner place is always there, whether you are in contact with it or not."

— Joseph Chaikin

In playing scenes that feature young adult women but may also include supporting roles for men or other women, it is important that the actors capture the certain agility, independence, and charm depicted in the basic strength of will appropriate for the primary age range (23-29 years) of each featured character. There is little opportunity in these selected scenes to engage in coy facial expressions, superficial posturing, or "chitchat" that sometimes signaled the approach to playing the role in scenes for youth and young men or women. The style of performance required here to convey the ordinary nature and "nonheroic" action of frank and honest female characters should be more deliberate and informed, with no idealization or glorification of the character's gender. There are a number of selected scenes of emotional intensity, but the emphasis is upon relationships and the relevant speeches, images, and attitudes of young adult women as independent, complex, and irrepressible characters.

The performance demands in playing scenes for young adult women are similar to those for young adult men in relying upon observation and creative invention in the interpretation of the selected role; but there are additional demands in being able to speak and move in a more distinctly personal and individual manner. There is a noticeable intensity of mood and attitude in these selected scenes for young adult women that address bold new themes and more readily reveal interior thoughts and psychological themes related to character inhibition or behavioral affliction. Surface details, minor flaws, and casual acquaintances also appear to play a major role in character development in the selected scenes for young adult women, leading a number of the characters to pursue a singleness of purpose or to actively seek "interactive" relationships with older adult women whenever possible.

In playing scenes that feature young adult women but may also include supporting roles for men or other women, the style of performance needed to convey the ordinary and "nonheroic" action of frank and honest female characters should be more deliberate and informed, with no idealization or glorification of the character's gender.

The emotional and intellectual tone of these selected scenes is rich in variety and demands versatility in each actor's performance approach. There are moments of genuine humor and gentle frivolity that suggest the bonds of compassion and mutual understanding between young adult women; and there are moments of grim and sober reality that recall painful childhood memories, adolescent scars, or frustrated wishful dreams easily recognized in similar experiences by other young adult women. The characters exhibit courage and conviction even while engaging in innocent blunders, committing errors in judgment, or displaying basic urges such as anger, fear, or anxiety. They do not, however, suffer in silence and voice their concerns in responsible and distinctly personal expressions of objectivity.

The actors should approach each selected scene in a natural, sensitive manner that indicates the friendly and intimate relationship common to all of the young adult women in these episodes; and the actors should engage in active scene study to discover the common interests that appear to emotionally and intellectually attract each of the young adult women. There should be some attention paid to the hidden despair and frustration expressed by each of the characters as they desperately try to reinforce their own sense of honesty and truthfulness. It is especially important for the actors to also be aware of the sense of independence and urgency voiced by the young adult women as they confront traditional beliefs and learned behaviors that appear to inhibit their own personal development and self-expression.

One of the interesting elements in the selected scenes for young adult women is the simple, understated spirit of adventure that reveals each character's basically gentle nature. But there are elements of fierce determination, strength, and hardened resolve that emerge to signal forceful inner conflicts as well. Look for these elements as an indication of the large personal truths that are revealed just beneath the surface of the young adult women's polite conversation and passionate exchanges of dialog. Look, also, for abrupt and serious shifts in character attitude or mood that do not permit unwarranted intrusion into highly sensitive personal or private issues, and heighten the awkwardness and insecurity each character initially feels when trying to express personal sadness or despair.

In approaching the selected scenes that follow, the actors should be inventive in capturing the comic spirit of light-hearted, genuinely funny escapades that explore the valiant struggle to confront impending adulthood and awakening or repressed sexuality. Drawing upon personal observations or youthful experiences that help to suggest descriptive walks, postures, voices, and attitudes for the young adult women characters should be beneficial in depicting their personal values and in clarifying their self-image. Although a number of the selected scenes exhibit a "bittersweet" quality in tone, what the characters inevitably discover about themselves and their relationship with others is both positive and productive in terms of achieving a greater capacity to learn and to understand more about the pain and pleasure of life and living it to the fullest!

Remember that stage figures in contemporary drama are very much "like us today," so search for the appropriate bodily actions and gestures that reinforce the character portrait; and chart believable vocal or physical changes that appear to take place in the characters during the selected scene being performed. Make sure that you give your contemporary creation distinctive, individual dimension that helps to "visualize" how the character might appear in these commonplace episodes. Relying on casual observation or planned study of everyday situations and flesh-and-blood role models may provide valuable performance information and insight, and also has the additional benefit of being current and contemporary. Such alertness to interesting and intriguing real-life role models in all walks of life may just provide the germ of inspiration that gives individuality and vitality to striking and imaginative characterization.

The challenge in playing these selected scenes for young adult women is to act instinctively, and to make daring choices in performance that build moment-to-moment anticipation and suspense that is only resolved at the climactic resolution of the episode. There is very little virtue in a timid, tepid approach to role-playing in the contemporary theatre if the actors are to achieve what Stanislavsky encouraged his own students to realize: the elusive quality of *Étonnez Moi ´* ("Astonish me!"). No small part of that imaginative astonishment is the actor's ability to fashion a gallery of character portraits that are fresh, original, and memorable in their attention to detail and in their daring.

Scenes for young adult women frequently highlight the simple, understated spirit of adventure that reveals each character's basically gentle nature; but there are also elements of fierce determination, strength, and hardened resolve that emerge to signal forceful inner conflicts as well.

As part of the initial preparation for performing the scenes that follow, the actors should focus on the "tempo" that underscores the attitude or the mood of the characters for its most immediate, meaningful impact; and should assume a performance perspective that suggests the role is being played for the "first time." There should be intense concentration only on the "present moment" described in each scene, with nothing left to random chance in capturing an incisive character portrait that is truly distinctive and individual in its nuance. What remains, of course, is for the actors to achieve the most appropriate artistic expression possible to clarify the thoughts and the actions of these most intriguing young adult women characters!

from *Isn't It Romantic* ©
by Wendy Wasserstein

The title says it all! This witty contemporary comedy is, indeed, romantic — and chock-full of bright, urbane, sentimental, and sharply humorous characters and dialog. The Pulitzer prize winning playscript itself explores a familiar feminine dilemma: the potential conflict between individual freedom and the quest for romantic fulfillment. The role models for the playwright's comic vision are two former college classmates whose professional careers and personal crises are revealed in a series of alternating, parallel scenes that capture the tender as well as the tempestuous episodes in the lives of the two carefree young adult women.

Janie Blumberg, the short, slightly plump, and definitely kooky young adult woman, is an absorbing and endearing would-be writer anticipating a relationship with a young Jewish doctor named Marty. Harriet Cornwall, the attractive, charming, and definitely competitive young adult woman, is an upscale and sophisticated corporate-seeking executive currently considering her mannered, and married, boss. Although both young adult women are valiantly struggling to escape from their parents' smothering domination and to establish their own "self-identity," neither can resist the urge to explore the fanciful dreams of romantic love and its promise of eternal fidelity.

Janie is Jewish and her life is a daily turmoil, especially complicated by doting parents who greet her on the phone by singing "Sunrise, Sunset" and march to her doorstep with a never-ending parade of parental advice and a seemingly endless supply of the oddest collection of potential husbands imaginable. Harriet is a Gentile and her life is a madcap adventure of balancing her rising executive career at Colgate-Palmolive and trying to cope with her unbalanced mother, a self-proclaimed "feminist" whose active social and political agenda does not apparently include her daughter. The two young adult women friends have both moved to New York City to carve out professional careers for themselves and to savor a bite of the "Big Apple," desperately searching for a slice of happiness, success, and romance.

In this scene, the former classmates meet in Central Park West to renew their friendship and to brush up on the latest news in their scattered lives. They are later joined by Marty, the nice Jewish doctor, who graduated from Harvard and is now introducing himself for the first time. The encounter is complete with rich and rewarding humor as the characters enjoy each other's zany conversation and unlikely company. This is also a scene that perceptively foreshadows the self-assuredness and self-confidence that each young adult woman character appears to achieve in some depth later in the playscript, especially as their mature wisdom brightens and their desperate relationship with men flickers...and fades.

The actors are encouraged to intensify the emotional and intellectual content of this scene, and to "personalize" the action being performed as part of each character's imagined life. The *illustrative* approach to character building — giving a life and meaning to the circumstances, images, and objects associated with each character — should be an essential ingredient of the performance blueprint as well. The inventive use of stage business may also help to advance the storyline of this scene, especially if the stage business can suggest an appropriate tempo or rhythm for the action and reaction of each character. For example, cigarettes, handbags, glasses, briefcases, shopping bags, or other small props that establish a sense of familiarity and intimacy between the characters might be extremely effective in this particular scene.

1   HARRIET: Hi ho, hi ho, it's off to work we go...I think I just
2   got a job. *(They hug.)* Hi, Janie.
3   JAMIE: Hi, Harriet.
4   HARRIET: Thank God you're here.
5   JANIE: Of course I'm here. I got your message last night.
6   HARRIET: The man I interviewed with was very im-
7   pressed I took a year off in Italy to look at pictures. I
8   liked him. He was cold, aloof, distant. Very sexy. Can I
9   have a hit of your Tab?
10   JANIE: Sure.
11   HARRIET: I can't stay for breakfast. I told him I could
12   come right back to Colgate for a second interview.
13   Janie, I think our move back home to New York is
14   going to be very successful.
15   JANIE: It is?
16   HARRIET: Of course there's absolutely no reason why you
17   should believe me.
18   JANIE: You have an M.B.A. from Harvard. Of course I
19   believe you.
20   HARRIET: You sound like your mother.
21   JANIE: No. Tasha would believe you 'cause you're thin.
22   Look at us. You look a Vermeer and I look like an
23   extra in *Potemkin.*
24   HARRIET: Janie, I think someone's watching us.
25   JANIE: *(Fluffing her hair)* Do I look all right? You know
26   what I resent?
27   HARRIET: What?
28   JANIE: Just about everything except you. I resent having to
29   pay the phone bill, be nice for super, find meaningful
30   work, fall in love, get hurt – all of it I resent deeply.
31   HARRIET: What's the alternative?
32   JANIE: Dependency. I could marry the pervert who's
33   staring at us. No. That's not the solution. I guess I
34   could always move back to Brookline. Get another

1   masters in something useful like "Woman's Pottery."

2   Do a little freelance writing. Oh, God, it's exhausting.

3   HARRIET: He's coming. *(MARTY STERLING enters Down*

4   *Left. JANIE's mother's dream come true. A nice Jewish*

5   *doctor from Harvard. A prince and a bit of a card.)*

6   MARTY: You're Harriet Cornwall. I sat behind you in

7   Twentieth-Century Problems. I always thought you

8   were a beautiful girl. *(He extends his hand.)* Marty

9   Sterling.

10   HARRIET: *(Shaking it)* Hi. And this is Janie Blumberg.

11   MARTY: Sure. I remember you. I saw you and Harriet

12   together in Cambridge all the time. You always looked

13   more attainable. Frightened to death, but attainable.

14   I'm not attracted to cold people anymore. Who needs

15   that kind of trouble?

16   HARRIET: I don't know.

17   MARTY: So what do you do?

18   JANIE: Oh, I scream here on Central Park South. I'm

19   taking a break now.

20   HARRIET: Janie and I just moved back to New York

21   together. Well, at the same time. I lived in Italy for a

22   year, and Janie was lingering in Brookline, Mass.

23   MARTY: Good old Brookline. Ever go to Jack and Marian's

24   restaurant? Unbelievable kasha varnishka.

25   HARRIET: Excuse me.

26   MARTY: Kasha. Little noodle bow ties with barley. Uh, my

27   father's in the restaurant business. Are you familiar

28   with Yee Olde Sterling Tavernes?

29   HARRIET: Sure. That's a national chain.

30   MARTY: My father's chain.

31   HARRIET: *(Impressed)* Well!

32   JANIE: Well.

33   MARTY: Well. I'm on call. I'm a doctor. Kidneys.

34   HARRIET and JANIE: *(Very impressed)* Well.

1   JANIE: Well, maybe you two should sit for a minute, remi-
2   nisce about Twentieth-Century Problems.
3   MARTY: I wish I could. Good-bye.
4   HARRIET: Good-bye. *(MARTY starts to exit, stops, turns.)*
5   MARTY: Janie Blumberg. Is your brother Ben Blumberg?
6   HARRIET: Yup. That's her brother Ben.
7   MARTY: I went to Camp Kibbutz with Ben Blumberg
8   when I was nine.
9   JANIE: Yup, that's my brother Ben.
10 MARTY: Would you tell your brother Murray Schlimovitz
11   says hello.
12 JANIE: Who's Murray Schlimovitz?
13 MARTY: Me. Before my father owned the Sterling
14   Tavernes, he owned the Schlimovitz Kosher Dairy
15   restaurants in Brooklyn. But around fifteen years
16   ago all the Schlimovitz restaurants burned down. So
17   for the sake of the family and the business, we
18   changed our names before I entered...uh, uh
19   Harvard. Nice to see you. 'Bye. *(MARTY exits.)*
20 HARRIET: What were you doing? "Maybe you two should
21   sit and reminisce about Twentieth-Century Problems"?
22 JANIE: Marty Sterling could make a girl a nice husband.
23 HARRIET: Now you really sound like your mother.
24 JANIE: Hattie, do you know who that man's father is?
25 HARRIET: Uh-huh. He's an arsonist.
26 JANIE: No. He's a genius. Mr. Sterling, the little man who
27   comes on television in a colonial suit and a pilgrim
28   hat to let you know he's giving away free popovers at
29   Yee Olde Salade and Relish Bar; that guy is Milty
30   Schlimovitz, Doctor Marty Sterling's father.
31 HARRIET: It's all right. I can make do without Doctor
32   Murray Marty and his father's popovers. I have to get
33   to that interview. My friend Joe Stine, the head-
34   hunter, says they only have you back if they're going

1   to hire you.
2 JAMIE: Well, if you don't marry Marty Sterling, I'll marry
3   him. Wait till I tell my parents I ran into him. Tasha
4   Blumberg will have the caterers on the other
5   extension.
6 HARRIET: I'm afraid marrying him isn't a solution. Will
7   you walk me back to Colgate?
8 JANIE: Sure. If I can get myself up.
9 HARRIET: Do I look like a successful professional single
10   woman?
11 JANIE: Well.
12 HARRIET: What, well?
13 JANIE: Hattie, you know the wisdom of Tasha Blumberg?
14 HARRIET: Which one?
15 JANIE: Always look nice even when you throw out the
16   garbage, you never know who you might meet. Put on
17   your jacket, sweetheart. Always walk with your head
18   up and your chest out. Think "I am."
19 HARRIET: I am. *(Putting on jacket, lifting her head and chest)*
20 JANIE: Now I can be seen with you. *(JANIE slumps. They exit*
21   *arm in arm.)*
22
23
24
25
26
27
28
29
30
31
32
33
34

from *The Baltimore Waltz* ©
by Paula Vogel

There is a great deal more to this 1992 Obie Award-winning comedy/drama for "Best New American Play" than initially meets the eye. The playwright dedicates the playscript to her beloved brother, Carl, who we are told "...invited me to join him in a joint excursion to Europe [1986]. Due to pressures of time and money, I declined, never dreaming that he was HIV positive. *The Baltimore Waltz* is a journey with Carl to a Europe that exists only in the imagination." From this rather searing, thought-provoking personal tragedy, however, emerges a giddy, fun-hearted, and fanciful flight of fantasy that is at once comic/tragic, dearly clever, and hopelessly romantic in its heart-breakingly lovely tribute to the imaginary "dream vacation" the author and her brother were never able to share. It is a madcap fantasy of misadventure, mayhem, and malice that tickles and tantalizes with hope, love, and compassion.

The playwright's comic vision translates personal tragedy into a sardonic wit and wisdom that is sure to perform well in the scene that follows. In this imaginative version of the tragic event, Anna (playwright), an unmarried schoolteacher, has been diagnosed with ATD — "Acquired Toilet Disease" — a fatal affliction that is peculiarly associated with elementary school-teachers! She and her brother, Carl, immediately take flight and book passage to Europe, where Anna vows to consume her remaining days pursuing the insatiable delights of food, sight-seeing, and sensual pleasures. Carl, on the other hand, struggles to find a cure for his sister and innocently becomes entrapped in a wild, wacky Third Mannish espionage scheme complete with mistaken identities, conspiracy, and comic confrontations that lead nowhere. Carl's quest to find a cure for his sister's illness also leads nowhere, and the European excursion — idyllic and idiotic — suddenly ends with Carl's surprising death. It is then that we realize the entire playscript was Anna's valiant attempt to ennoble her brother's spirit when she could not save his life, and that the slides of their "trip" to Europe were only wishful dreams that were never realized outside of Baltimore.

The scenes that follow are concerned with Anna's initial diagnosis, when she is informed — rather clinically by the dour, distant doctor — that she is suffering from "Acquired Toilet Disease," and Carl's sympathetic intervention to make sense of the doctor's diagnosis as well as to keep his sister's spirits from collapsing. There is excellent satire here on the medical profession and Carl's "happy idea" to flee to Europe in quest of a cure for his sister's malady. The tone of the scene is heightened anxiety, but the characters' actions are at once screwball and ruthlessly forward-thinking. The actors will need to maintain an active, energetic tempo for the scene, but also allow for potentially pathetic and "life-threatening" moments of fragile denial and hysterical disbelief to emerge as well. There is also a spirit of manic rage in these scenes that must be handled delicately so that the irony and the "dark humor" are not lost in the initial wailing and bemoaning of Anna's predicament. The scenes, after all, are a crazy, desperate-quilt patchwork of delightful character reactions and responses to a potentially tragic situation — but they are filled with a wildly antic blend of comic larceny and sober lessons in living life to its fullest that prevent the scenes from becoming morose or mauldin.

1   **from Scene One**
2
3   ANNA: Explain it to me. Very slowly. So I can understand.
4   Excuse me, could you tell me again?
5   DOCTOR: There are exudative and proliferative inflam-
6   matory alterations of the endocardium, consisting of
7   necrotic debris, fibrinoid material and disintegrating
8   fibroblastic cells.
9   CARL: Oh, sweet Jesus.
10   DOCTOR: It may be acute or subacute, caused by various
11   bacteria: streptocci, staphlococci, enterocci, gram
12   negative bacilli, etc. It may be due to other micror-
13   ganisms, of course, but there is a high mortality rate
14   with or without treatment. And there is usually rapid
15   destruction and metastases.
16   CARL: Anna –
17   ANNA: I'm right here, darling. Right here.
18   CARL: Could you explain it very slowly?
19   DOCTOR: Also known as Loffler's syndrome, i.e.,
20   eosinophilia, resulting in fibroblastic thickening,
21   persistent tachycardia, hepatomegaly, splenomegaly,
22   serious effusions into the pleural cavity with edema.
23   It may be Brugia malayi or Wuchereria bancofti –
24   also known as Weingarten's syndrome. Often seen
25   with effusions, either exudate or transudate.
26   ANNA: Carl –
27   CARL: I'm here, darling. Right here.
28   ANNA: It's the language that terrifies me.
29
30   **from Scene Two**
31
32   CARL: Medical Straight Talk: Part One.
33   ANNA: So you're telling me that you really don't know?
34   DOCTOR: I'm afraid that medical science has only a small

1	foothold in this area. But of course, it would be of
2	great benefit to our knowledge if you would consent
3	to observation here at Johns Hopkins –
4	CARL: Why? Running out of laboratory rats?
5	ANNA: Oh, no. I'm sorry. I can't do that. Can you tell me at
6	least how it was...contracted?
7	DOCTOR: Well – we're not sure, yet. It's only a theory at
8	this stage, but one that seems in great favor at the
9	World Health Organization. We think it comes from
10	the old cultus ornatus –
11	CARL: Toilet seats?
12	ANNA: Toilet seats! My God. Mother was right. She always
13	said –
14	CARL: And never, ever, in any circumstances, in bus
15	stations –
16	ANNA: Toilet seats? Cut down in the prime of youth by a
17	toilet seat?
18	DOCTOR: Anna – I may call you Anna? You teach school, I
19	believe?
20	ANNA: Yes, first grade. What does that have –?
21	DOCTOR: Ah, yes. We're beginning to see a lot of this in
22	elementary schools. Anna – I may call you Anna?
23	With assurances of complete confidentiality – we
24	need to ask you very specific questions about the
25	body, body fluids and body functions. As mature
26	adults, as scientists and educators –. To speak
27	frankly – when you needed to relieve yourself, where
28	did you make wa-wa?
29	ANNA: There's a faculty room. But why – how –?
30	DOCTOR: You never, ever used the johnny in your class-
31	room?
32	ANNA: Well, maybe once or twice. There's no lock and
33	Robbie Matthews always tries to barge in. Sometimes
34	I just can't get the time to – surely you're not

1   suggesting that –
2   DOCTOR: You did use the johnny in your classroom? *(The*
3   *DOCTOR makes notes from this.)*
4   CARL: Is that a crime? When you've got to go, you've got to –
5   ANNA: I can't believe that my students would transmit
6   something like this –
7   DOCTOR: You have no idea. Five-year-olds can be deadly.
8   It seems to be an affliction, so far, of single school-
9   teachers. Schoolteachers with children of their own
10   develop an immunity to ATD...Acquired Toilet Disease.
11   ANNA: I see. Why hasn't anybody heard of this disease?
12   DOCTOR: Well, first of all, the Center for Disease Control
13   doesn't wish to inspire an all-out panic in communi-
14   ties. Secondly, we think education on this topic is the
15   responsibility of the NEA, not the government. And
16   if word of this pestilence gets out inappropriately,
17   the PTA is going to be all over the school system
18   demanding mandatory testing of every toilet seat
19   in every lavatory. It's kindling for a political
20   disaster.
21   ANNA: *(Taking the DOCTOR aside)* I want to ask you
22   something confidentially. Something that my
23   brother doesn't need to hear. What's the danger of
24   transmission?
25   DOCTOR: There's really no danger to anyone in the imme-
26   diate family. You must use precautions.
27   ANNA: Because what I want to know is...can you transmit
28   this thing by...by doing – what exactly do you mean by
29   precautions?
30   DOCTOR: Well, I guess you should do what your mother
31   always told you. You know, wash your hands before
32   and after going to the bathroom. And never lick
33   paper money or coins in any currency.
34   ANNA: So there's no danger to anyone by...what I mean,

1   Doctor, is that I can't infect anyone by –

2   DOCTOR: Just use precautions.

3

4   **from Scene Three**

5

6   CARL: *(Agitated)* I'll tell you what. If Sandra Day O'Connor

7   sat on just one infected potty, the media would be

8   clamoring to do articles on ATD. If just one grand-

9   child of George Bush caught this thing during toilet

10   training, that would be the last we'd hear about the

11   space program. Why isn't someone doing something?

12   I'm sorry. I know you're one of the converted. You're

13   doing...well, everything you can. I'd like to ask you

14   something in confidence, something my sister

15   doesn't need to hear. Is there any hope at all?

16 DOCTOR: Well, I suppose there's...always hope.

17 CARL: Any experimental drugs? Treatments?

18 DOCTOR: Well, they're trying all sorts of things abroad.

19   Our hands are tied here by NIH and the FDA, you

20   understand. There is a long-shot avenue to explore,

21   nothing, you understand, that I personally endorse,

22   but there is an eighty-year-old urologist overseas

23   who's been working in this field for some time –

24 CARL: We'll try anything.

25 DOCTOR: His name is Dr. Todesrocheln. He's somewhat

26   unorthodox, outside the medical community in

27   Vienna. It's gonna cost you. Mind you, this is not an

28   endorsement.

29 ANNA: You hear the doctor through a long-distance

30   corridor. Your ears are functioning, but the mind is

31   numb. You try to listen as you swim toward his

32   sentences in the fluorescent light in his office. But

33   you don't believe it at first. This is how I'd like to die;

34   with dignity. No body secretions – like Merle Oberon

1   in *Wuthering Heights*. With a somewhat becoming
2   flush and a transcendental gaze. Luminous eyes
3   piercing the veil of mortal existence. The windows
4   are open to the fresh breeze blowing off the moors.
5   Oh. And violins in the background would be nice, too.
6   *MUSIC:* Violins playing Strauss swell in the background.
7
8
9
10
11
12
13
14
15
16
17
18
19
20
21
22
23
24
25
26
27
28
29
30
31
32
33
34

from *Laundry and Bourbon* ©
by James McLure

The comic action of this scene revolves around the lives of small town wives whose occupational hazards include marriages that have gone sour, watching television to relieve their boredom, engaging in juicy tidbits of local gossip and, of course, folding laundry and sipping bourbon — with just a splash of coke! It is a hot, dusty summer afternoon in Maynard, Texas, as Elizabeth and her friend Hattie parade to the front porch to celebrate their gratifying ritual of "laundry and bourbon." The adult women are polite, honest, and extremely sensitive to each other's frustrations; and there is a wrenching sadness in their relationship that is poignant and yet subtly understated in their solemn echoes of past dreams and present, unpleasant apprehension.

Elizabeth, the more resilient of the two adult women, is intuitively quiet and soft-spoken, but radiates an inner strength of conviction and compassion that indicates her dignity and deep-seated reservoir of resolve. She is especially alarmed by the turmoil and disruption that has become part of her life with the return of her husband, Roy, from the Vietnam war. Hattie, on the other hand, is sometimes brusque and sometimes a busybody but always a good listener and a good friend, a highly amusing and sharply observant adult woman who ultimately impresses as a sincere, caring companion with special strengths that nurture others in their time of pain and sorrow.

In playing the scene, the actors need to extend a potentially amusing situation — folding laundry and sipping bourbon —

beyond the range of biting humor and comic gossip toward the pathos and poignancy that is revealed as the characters gently probe into each other's lives and the crises they must face individually. At times, the conversation may be polite and patronizing; but at other times it may be laced with self-recrimination, edged with regret, or soul-searing in its directness. But the special friendship that these adult women enjoy also reverberates with glints of gentleness, tenderness, and genuine understanding that indicates there is more here than surface appearances might suggest at first glance. The actors will need to read this scene with discerning insight, and unravel the sequence of action(s) and event(s) in order to give creative license to an imaginative interpretation of each character.

If possible, the performance blueprint should include a subtle, suggestive accent that might be appropriate to the rural, Southern locale; but the accent should be well-polished and authentic if it is to capture the vivid speech and imagery voiced by these characters. Attention should also be paid to the momentum suggested in the dialog and in the action of the scene, especially the inevitable build to a climax when Hattie places Elizabeth's current life situation in clear, direct focus for her. It might be appropriate for the actors to explore the role that "mental symbols" might play in clearly defining each character as well. As you recall from the previous discussion in Chapter 2, mental symbols indicate the character's desire, what actions the character is willing to commit to achieve the desire, and the fateful price that must be paid by the character for the desire. Careful isolation of each character's primary motivation should also help to clarify the actor's mental symbol and stimulate the action and reaction that follows in the performance of the scene.

1   ELIZABETH: God, I hate laundry.

2   HATTIE: Try doing it for three kids.

3   ELIZABETH: Week in. Week out. It's the same old clothes.

4   HATTIE: You can only look at so many pairs of Fruit of the

5   Loom before you want to puke.

6   ELIZABETH: I'd like to burn everything in this basket and

7   start all over. Everything except this shirt.

8   HATTIE: Why that shirt's all frayed.

9   ELIZABETH: It is now, but I remember the first time Roy

10   wore this shirt.

11   HATTIE: When was that?

12   ELIZABETH: On our first date. He drove up in that pink

13   Thunderbird in this shirt with all the pearl buttons.

14   He looked just like Paul Newman in *Hud*. *(HATTIE*

15   *holds up a pair of boxer shorts.)*

16   HATTIE: God, these shorts are big.

17   ELIZABETH: What?

18   HATTIE: These jockey shorts...they're so big. They're not

19   that wide. They're for a narrow body, but they're so

20   long...

21   ELIZABETH: I suppose.

22   HATTIE: ...Why're they so long?

23   ELIZABETH: Roy likes them big. Says he needs a lot of

24   room. *(Pause)*

25   HATTIE: Whew, it's hot out here. *(Pause)* Lordy, how's a

26   body supposed to keep cool?

27   ELIZABETH: Nothing to do but fix a bourbon and coke

28   and just sit and sweat.

29   HATTIE: I can't do that.

30   ELIZABETH: You can't sweat?

31   HATTIE: No. Fix a drink in the afternoon in front of

32   the kids.

33   ELIZABETH: Why not?

34   HATTIE: Children learn by example.

1   ELIZABETH: So?
2   HATTIE: Well, all I need is to come to a house full of kids
3   sitting around drinking margaritas. You don't know
4   what it's like raising a family.
5   ELIZABETH: No, I don't.
6   HATTIE: And lemme tell you, summertime is the worst.
7   ELIZABETH: What do you do?
8   HATTIE: I send them outside.
9   ELIZABETH: In this heat.
10   HATTIE: I give 'em a salt pill and say, play outside.
11   ELIZABETH: Don't they collapse from heat prostration?
12   HATTIE: Anything to slow them down.
13   ELIZABETH: I wish you'd let me take them sometimes.
14   HATTIE: Elizabeth, you're not used to kids. The strain
15   would kill you. Elizabeth, what are you staring out at
16   the road for?
17   ELIZABETH: No reason. There's nothing to see.
18   HATTIE: That's the truth. Nothing green to look at. God,
19   it's depressing living on the edge of the desert.
20   ELIZABETH: But just think, millions of years ago all this
21   land was under water.
22   HATTIE: Well...at least it would have been cool.
23   ELIZABETH: I like this land, but sometimes it gets too hot
24   and burnt for people. It's still too wild and hard for
25   anything to grow. *(Pause)* Oh, look, Hattie!
26   HATTIE: What is it?
27   ELIZABETH: Look at that cloud.
28   HATTIE: It's just a cloud.
29   ELIZABETH: Yeah, but look how it's throwing a shadow
30   across the land. God, doesn't that shadow look
31   peaceful gliding over the land. Doesn't it look cool? It
32   reminds me of a cool hand stroking a hot surface.
33   *(Pause)* Lately I've felt so hot and hollow inside I've
34   wanted something to come along and touch me

1 like that.

2 **HATTIE: Elizabeth, what's the matter with you?**

3 **ELIZABETH: Nothing, Hattie, nothing.**

4 **HATTIE:** *(Pause)* **You're doing it again, staring out at that**
5 **hill. There ain't nothing out there but the highway**
6 **and the road up to the house. Now, what're you**
7 **expecting to see?**

8 **ELIZABETH: I was hoping to see a 1959 pink Thunderbird**
9 **convertible come over that hill.**

10 **HATTIE: You've got tears in your eyes! Don't you tell me**
11 **nothing's the matter! What is it?** *(Pause)*

12 **ELIZABETH: Roy's been gone two days.** *(Pause)*

13 **HATTIE: Why, that son of a bitch! No wonder you've been**
14 **so weird. Here, you sit yourself down here. I'm gonna**
15 **fix you a drink and you're gonna tell me all about it.**

16 **ELIZABETH: I don't want another drink.**

17 **HATTIE; Hush up. Hattie's taking care of you now. The**
18 **doctor is in.** *(ELIZABETH sits. HATTIE exits to kitchen,*
19 *talking.)* **I knew there was something wrong the**
20 **minute I laid eyes on you. First you didn't answer the**
21 **doorbell, and as soon as I saw you I could tell some-**
22 **thing was the matter. That son of a bitch.** *(HATTIE*
23 *returns, having mixed drinks in record time.)* **Well, what**
24 **brought it on this time?**

25 **ELIZABETH: I don't know. Things haven't been the same**
26 **since he came back.**

27 **HATTIE: From Vietnam?**

28 **ELIZABETH: Yeah.**

29 **HATTIE: I know. I seen the change. But believe me, you've**
30 **been perfect about it.**

31 **ELIZABETH: I haven't been anything. I haven't done**
32 **anything. He was the one that went off for two years.**
33 **He was the one got shot up. He's the one that**
34 **has nightmares.**

1   HATTIE: Nightmares.

2   ELIZABETH: Yeah, almost every night. *(Pause)* Anyway,

3   now he's back and he can't seem to get nothing

4   started. He made me quit the job at the pharmacy. He

5   worked some out at his Dad's place. He's done some

6   roughnecking out in the oil fields. But then he always

7   gets in fights and gets himself fired.

8   HATTIE: Well...what's he got to say for himself?

9   ELIZABETH: He says he's looking for something.

10   HATTIE: Hmmm. What?

11   ELIZABETH: He doesn't know what. He says everything

12   has changed here in Maynard.

13   HATTIE: Nothing's changed in Maynard since the Civil

14   War.

15   ELIZABETH: I want him back the way he used to be.

16   HATTIE: Elizabeth, he's always been wild and unman-

17   ageable.

18   ELIZABETH: *(Flaring)* I don't want to manage him. I don't

19   want to break his spirit. That's why I married him, his

20   spirit. Roy Caulder wasn't going to take no crap from

21   anyone or anything. He and Wayne Wilder were

22   gonna shake up the world.

23   HATTIE: Need I remind you that Wayne Wilder is

24   currently serving five to ten for car theft?

25

26

27

28

29

30

31

32

33

34

from *The Role of Della* ©
by John Wooten

This scene is an especially significant inclusion for a scene-book in performance because it reveals in inexplicable detail the "insanity" involved in the contemporary audition process — especially the "cattle call" of an open audition! It is a riveting, riotous look at the theatrical ritual and performer rites associated with active competition for a role in the amateur or professional ranks, especially considering that each aspiring actor may only have two or three minutes to impress a casting director with that memorable monolog or that "winning personality" that stands head and shoulders above the other competitors. The scene is a critical commentary on the intrigue and deception that sometimes reveal themselves quite unexpectedly in the worst of all possible audition situations. And there is an important lesson to be learned here from the hardened war stories and battle scars that emerge from this audition excursion with a truly seasoned theatre warrior who seizes the opportunity to clearly define the meaning of "*stealing* the scene."

In this scene, two aspiring actors are competing at an open audition in New York City. Emma, the more experienced performer, is immediately in control of the situation as she assumes the demeanor of a production staff employee and interviews a rival actor for the role she covets for herself. There is an abrupt contradiction in her alternating moods of cool wisdom and degrading rudeness that becomes increasingly, and menacingly, more apparent as the scene unfolds. Elizabeth, the eager and inexperienced performer attending her first open audition, is completely open and trusting. She exhibits potential and promise in the improvisations and line readings that Emma ruthlessly savages with critical commentary, and exhibits an intuitive sensitivity and creativity that is transparent in spite of Emma's badgering. There is also the authentic woman staff worker coordinating the audition process who enters the scene after Elizabeth has exited; and she should add a sense of normalcy and kind efficiency to the scene.

The actors should suggest the complexities of expression revealed in each character's motivation and intention surrounding the audition process when playing the scene; and should convey the surprising truth about this particular audition intrigue that lies just beneath the surface of the given circumstances. It is especially important for the actor portraying Emma to be subtle in her posing scheme to punctuate the "ironic twist" that is revealed at the conclusion of the scene. The actors should also make a clear distinction between their "theatrical" persona as it is generally observed in a more traditional *stage* performance and the "personality" persona that needs to be revealed here in the *backstage* performance. That is why it is important to cultivate a performance style that has a simplicity as well as a sincerity that masks the true nature of the typical audition battlefield. In addition, the actors are encouraged to pursue the comic impulse inherent in the scene, and to be inventive in incorporating those extraneous theatrical complementaries — props, costumes, taped music, furniture, theatrical makeup, or other distracting accessories — that are *not* generally recommended for the competitive audition but may add a refreshingly colorful tone that provides good balance to the more mature and menacing elements suggested in the scene.

1	*(Lights up on an audition studio. EMMA stands in front*
2	*of a table. She carefully examines a few head shots which*
3	*are spread about the table. She notices one of interest*
4	*and slowly sits down in a chair in front of the table. ELIZ-*
5	*ABETH slowly sticks her head into the room.)*
6	**ELIZABETH: Excuse me.** *(Startled, EMMA quickly puts the*
7	*head shot on the table. She begins to rise.)* **No, don't get**
8	**up. I'm a little early. There was no monitor out front.**
9	**I saw the door open. I didn't know if I should come**
10	**straight in...or if I should wait... I'll come back in a**
11	**few minutes.** *(Starts out.)*
12	**EMMA: Do you have your audition card?**
13	**ELIZABETH: Oh, yeah.** *(With a smile)* **I wouldn't lose this. I**
14	**had to get here at six a.m. to wait in line and I still**
15	**barely got a slot. Some girl offered me fifty dollars for**
16	**this card. Just for a chance to audition. It's like a zoo**
17	**out there.**
18	**EMMA: Hand it to me, please.**
19	**ELIZABETH: Sure.** *(She crosses to her. Offers hand.)* **I must**
20	**say it's a great pleasure to meet you, Ms. Stewart. I've**
21	**heard great things about your theatre.**
22	**EMMA:** *(Shakes hand.)* **Thank you. The card.**
23	**ELIZABETH: Oh, right.** *(She hands EMMA the audition*
24	*card.)* **Sorry. Just a little nervous.**
25	**EMMA: That's all right. I understand.**
26	**ELIZABETH: John Wyatt says hello.**
27	**EMMA: Really.**
28	**ELIZABETH: He's doing great. He just booked...**
29	**EMMA: Do you have a resumé?**
30	**ELIZABETH: Of course.** *(She hands EMMA her resumé.)*
31	**EMMA:** *(Takes a moment, looks at the head shot.)* **No, I need**
32	**your resumé.** *(ELIZABETH laughs.)* **Is something funny?**
33	**ELIZABETH: I don't understand.**
34	**EMMA:** *(Deliberately slow)* **I need your resumé.**

1   ELIZABETH: That is my resumé.
2   EMMA: No.
3   ELIZABETH: Yes, that's me.
4   EMMA: Really? You've gained a few pounds since this
5   picture was taken, haven't you?
6   ELIZABETH: I beg your pardon?
7   EMMA: What role are you interested in?
8   ELIZABETH: Della.
9   EMMA: Della? Really? The ingénue?
10   ELIZABETH: *(A beat)* Yes.
11   EMMA: *(Chuckles to herself.)* OK. Why not. What piece are
12   you doing?
13   ELIZABETH: Uh...Today, I...
14   EMMA: Can you move back a little, please?
15   ELIZABETH: Sure. Sorry. *(She moves back, away from*
16   *table.)* Good morning. My name is Elizabeth Ryan.
17   Today, I will be doing a selection from...
18   EMMA: Just do the monolog.
19   ELIZABETH: I'm sorry?
20   EMMA: You only have two minutes, you know.
21   ELIZABETH: Yes.
22   EMMA: *(A beat)* Well? The clock's ticking.
23   ELIZABETH: *(She turns and takes a breath. She turns back*
24   *around and begins.)* "Oh, we would get into terrible
25   arguments, my mother and I."
26   EMMA: Do I have something on my face?
27   ELIZABETH: Pardon?
28   EMMA: Why are you looking at me?
29   ELIZABETH: Is it OK if I direct my piece to you?
30   EMMA: What do you think?
31   ELIZABETH: *(Begins again, awkwardly directing piece to*
32   *chair.)* "One, when I was twelve or thirteen, I told her
33   that God was a moronic fairy tale – I think I'd spent
34   an entire night..."

1 EMMA: I'm sorry... Do you have anything else?
2 ELIZABETH: Excuse me?
3 EMMA: Do you have another monolog? *(ELIZABETH looks*
4   *confused.)* Anything? I've already heard that twice
5   today and if I hear it slaughtered one more time, I
6   think I'll have no choice but to shoot myself.
7 ELIZABETH: *(Taken aback)* I'm sorry. If you'd like to give
8   me a direction with it, I'd be happy to...
9 EMMA: This is not an acting class, Elizabeth. Besides,
10   what you need is an interpretation class. *Agnes of*
11   *God* is not a melodrama.
12 ELIZABETH: No, of course not. I wasn't trying to...
13 EMMA: Don't make excuses. Just do something else.
14 ELIZABETH: I don't have anything else prepared. I
15   thought that piece was appropriate.
16 EMMA: Actors do not think, Beth. Those who think, think.
17   Those who act, act. Those who think they can act,
18   spend more time thinking than acting.
19 ELIZABETH: Of course. Can I please try again?
20 EMMA: No. Tell me a story...Something funny.
21 ELIZABETH: Funny?
22 EMMA: Yes. Make me laugh.
23 ELIZABETH: Just like that?
24 EMMA: You want this job, don't you? You want to play
25   Della?
26 ELIZABETH: Of course. OK...Let's see...When I was a little
27   girl, my friend Carol and I found this old doll's house
28   in her attic. We sneaked it carefully downstairs and
29   cleaned it off. Carol had a pet mouse, Binkey. So we
30   dressed Binkey up in this white Barbie dress and...
31 EMMA: *(Ignoring her)* So, I see here that you've listed
32   Sandy in *Grease* as one of your credits.
33 ELIZABETH: Oh, yes. It was a great experience. Working
34   with Paul Jones. Do you know him?

1   EMMA: Didn't anyone ever tell you not to lie on your
2   resumé?
3   ELIZABETH: I didn't.
4   EMMA: Oh, come now.
5   ELIZABETH: I didn't. I swear I didn't.
6   EMMA: There's no character listing here by *The Glass*
7   *Menagerie.* Was it done in the absurdist style or did
8   you play the gentleman caller?
9   ELIZABETH: I played Laura.
10   EMMA; That must have been some time ago.
11   ELIZABETH: Last summer.
12   EMMA: I'm sorry, I didn't mean to interrupt your little
13   story.
14   ELIZABETH: That's OK...Uh, where was I...So, after we
15   dressed Binkey up in the Barbie costume, we placed
16   him inside the doll house and he crawled right into
17   the miniature bathroom as if he wanted to take a
18   bath...
19   EMMA: Add a Southern accent.
20   ELIZABETH: *(Adding a Southern accent)* **Then he got stuck**
21   **in the miniature hall closet and we had to shake the**
22   **doll house up and down and then Binkey popped out**
23   **but he was all hyper and we couldn't catch him so he**
24   **ran downstairs and Carol's mom was having this big**
25   **ritzy dinner party and Binkey ran right into...**
26   EMMA: Let's see a little Spanish.
27   ELIZABETH: *(ELIZABETH switches to a Spanish accent.)*
28   **...the middle of Carol's mother's boss's legs. She**
29   **screamed, leaped up onto the couch and pulled up**
30   **her dress. Well, she wasn't wearing...**
31   EMMA: Faster.
32   ELIZABETH: **Then Carol's mother's boss's husband tried**
33   **to grab her but instead he knocked her off into the**
34   **double salsa cream dip and...**

1   **EMMA: Faster!**

2   **ELIZABETH: ...and Binkey got scared and ran into the**

3   **front yard and the whole party went outside to look**

4   **for him except Carol's mother's boss's husband and**

5   **Carol's mother's boss who was crying, not because of**

6   **the double salsa dip or even the flashing incident but**

7   **more because she couldn't fit into Carol's mother's**

8   **clothes, so she had to wear Carol's mother's**

9   **husband's raincoat and then just as she put it on,**

10   **Binkey ran into the house followed by the neighbors...**

11   **EMMA:** *(Dryly)* **Wait a second. You're bowling me over**

12   **here. Please, let me take a breath. I can't stand it. You**

13   **are a laugh riot, Liz. I'll never be the same. Ever.**

14   **ELIZABETH:** *(A long beat. On the verge of tears)* **Why are you**

15   **being so rude to me?**

16   **EMMA:** *(Innocently)* **Rude. Am I being rude? I'm sorry,**

17   **Elizabeth. Please continue your lovely story.**

18   **ELIZABETH: I don't want to. I'm leaving.**

19   **EMMA: Leaving. You sure? You still have a few seconds left.**

20   **ELIZABETH: If you didn't think I was right for the role**

21   **you should have just said so.**

22   **EMMA: Right? You're perfect. I just wanted to make sure**

23   **you could handle all the terrible things Della must**

24   **endure.**

25   **ELIZABETH: Really?**

26   **EMMA: Oh, yeah.**

27   **ELIZABETH: And?**

28   **EMMA: There is no doubt in my mind that you think you**

29   **would be perfect for this role. I don't think I've ever**

30   **seen an actress quite like you before.**

31   **ELIZABETH: Thank you!**

32   **EMMA: But out of fairness I have to finish out the day. I'll**

33   **call you tomorrow. Mind you, it will be late. Between**

34   **eleven p.m. and ten a.m. Make sure you're awake and**

1   by the phone. If you don't pick up after the first ring,
2   I'll offer Della to someone else.
3 ELIZABETH: Don't worry. I won't sleep a wink.
4 EMMA: Good.
5 ELIZABETH: Anything I should know about the char-
6   acter? Keep in mind?
7 EMMA: Leave the wig at home. It doesn't fit.
8 ELIZABETH: Wig?
9 EMMA: And work on combining the Spanish accent with
10   the Southern. You can talk faster too.
11 ELIZABETH: Even faster?
12 EMMA: Pace is everything.
13 ELIZABETH: OK. I'll work on it tonight.
14 EMMA: All right. Run along now. I'll be in touch.
15 ELIZABETH: Thank you. Thank you very much!
16 EMMA: No, thank you. *(ELIZABETH exits. EMMA watches*
17   *her off. She picks up ELIZABETH's head shot, crosses to*
18   *the wastebasket and throws the head shot away, giggling*
19   *to herself. A WOMAN enters with coffee and takes out a*
20   *bag.)*
21 WOMAN: Hi, can I help you?
22 EMMA: *(Startled)* Yes. *(A wide-eyed smile suddenly appears.)*
23   Hi. I'm a little early. I saw the door open. Should I
24   wait outside?...I'll wait outside.
25 WOMAN: No, that's OK. Do you have your audition card?
26 EMMA: Yes. *(Hands her ELIZABETH's card.)* Here you go...I
27   must say it's a pleasure meeting you. I've heard great
28   things about your theatre.
29 WOMAN: Well, thank you. We try.
30 EMMA: *(Trying to be sincere)* John Wyatt says hello.
31 WOMAN: John! How is he?
32 EMMA: Great.
33 WOMAN: Do you have your resumé with you?
34 EMMA: Sure do. *(Crosses to bag and pulls out her resumé.)*

1   WOMAN: It's like a zoo out there.
2   EMMA: I know. I had to get here at six a.m. just to get an
3   audition card. *(Hands the WOMAN her resumé.)*
4   WOMAN: Great. And what role would you like to be
5   considered for?
6   EMMA: *(A beat)* **Della.** *(Blackout)*
7
8
9
10
11
12
13
14
15
16
17
18
19
20
21
22
23
24
25
26
27
28
29
30
31
32
33
34

CHAPTER SEVEN

SCENES FOR ADULT MEN AND WOMEN

"Love the art in yourself, not yourself in the art."
— Stanislavsky

"There are no small roles — only small actors."
— Motto of the Moscow Art Theatre

In playing scenes that feature adult men and women it is important that the actors approach the role with special care, not allowing the emotional or intellectual context or content of the episode to serve as the primary ingredients of the performance, and not allowing the illuminating little details appropriate for the age range (35 years or more) of each character to surface as distracting performance principles of the characterization. Although scenes for adult men and women demand more sustained performance expertise and training, they also promote the greatest demands on the actor's "inner resources" and inventive imagination to capture the spirit of "truth" in the role. The actors who are tempted to resort to tricks like playing only the *age* of the character with cliché habits like emphasizing only the "body" and the "voice" of the character have not properly prepared the role and will not realize the potential of the role.

Reliance upon sustained performance experience and training alone, however, may be of value in the initial exploration of the role but should not dictate the actor's own creative approach to an interpretation of the character in the given circumstances of the selected scene. *Individuality* is still the hallmark of playing scenes for adult men and women, and successful actors will utilize the reservoir of their own considerable experience — both personal and performance — coupled with creative imagination to forge an inspired, insightful character portrait that leaves a peculiar, unique imprint on the role.

There is no substitute for experience and ingenuity in playing scenes for adult men and women!

The performance demands for more experienced actors in playing scenes for adult men and women grow more naturally from playscript analysis and interpretation than from line readings of the dialog or in "theatre games" and "improvisation" to capture the spirit of the character. There is more introspective scene study to discover moment-to-moment character action(s) and interaction; and there is more concentrated focus on isolating the central action and the conflict of the scene. Experienced actors may choose, however, to improvise selected moments in the scene or to create "new" scenes independent of the playscript for the characters to define and develop; or they may compile "interior monologs" based upon a character's dialog or action(s) to better understand the motivation and the subtext of a character in the given circumstances of the episode. Experienced actors may also place the characters in "real-life" settings different from those detailed in the playscript and improvise character relationships or paraphrase lines of dialog to better understand the context of the scene or to stimulate imaginative character vocal/physical interactions that may generate inventive character stage business.

Actors playing the roles in scenes for adult men and women generally rely more consciously upon their "memory book" of life experiences or complementary behaviors and mannerisms only to add subtle nuances to the composite character portrait being drawn. In the carefully planned period of analysis, the actors initially determine what the character is thinking or feeling in the selected scene and then define the character's attitude, action, and motivation in relationship to other characters in the episode. In addition, the actors explore performance opportunities for meaningful movement and experiment with descriptive bodily actions or gestures that might more clearly communicate character ideas, emotions, and thoughts. In the process of planned analysis, some experienced actors may actually begin to "assume" the basic ingredients of character attitude or mood; and, in the rehearsal period devoted to vocal and physical discovery, may actually give form and shape to a "visual" character!

As actors become better acquainted with their own performance strengths and weaknesses — and with perceptive skills in playscript analysis and interpretation — they become more sensitive and aware of the need to creatively transfer what has been learned or observed from their everyday lives into realistic, believable character sketches for the stage. In playing more complex and complicated characters like adult men and women, for example, experienced and exacting actors cultivate a catalog of emotional and sensory images that might be recalled when needed to more accurately depict a character; or they maintain a current "performance blueprint" that is alert to people, places, and events in their observation of everyday life that might provide the local color, the gesture, the attitude, the voice, the walk, the look, the behavior, or the mannerism appropriate to realize a dynamic, three dimensional character portrait.

In playing scenes that feature adult men and women, more experienced actors explore performance opportunities for meaningful movement and experiment with descriptive bodily actions or gestures that might more clearly communicate character ideas, emotions, and thoughts.

As valuable as all of these preliminary resources may be in playing adult men and women roles, experienced actors continue to rely upon the basic building blocks of *hearing* and *seeing* to clearly distinguish their stage figures. They listen to what others say and notice how they express themselves verbally and nonverbally; and they are attentive to different tones of speech, patterns of inflection, rates of speaking, and distinct pitch levels to discover interesting vocal patterns that might later be of potential performance value in voicing imaginative stage characterizations.They also look at others for interesting physical characteristics or body types in varying heights, weights, and ages to discover what might later be of potential performance value in enriching a character with movement, bodily actions, or physicalization. All of these vocal and physical elements based upon "hearing" and "seeing" are closely interrelated to character building, and help to capture an authentic spirit and temperament in communicating characterization in performance.

In approaching the selected scenes that follow, the actors should cultivate a relaxed throat and neck to achieve greater flexibility and range in pitch or tone; and movement patterns, posture, and physical reactions should accurately reflect the characters' inner thoughts, mental or emotional states, and points of view. Variety in rate and volume is essential to suggest character mood, tempo, emphasis, or disposition, and should be appropriate to both the context of the dialog and the content of the selected scene. The body should suggest the character's prevailing mood or attitude; and any physical reactions should be fluid and yet clearly indicative of what the character is thinking or anticipating in the given circumstances of the episode. The mutual harmony of voice and body "working together" in performance creates a dramatic sense of externalizing the character's action or motivation and gives added emphasis and meaning to a character portrait that is authentic and honest.

If there is a lesson to be learned in playing scenes for adult men and women it is to "visualize" the character images suggested in the episode and to underscore the basic similarity between a character's *thought* and a character's *action*, translating abstract ideas or concepts into specific performance strategies that actively engage the voice and the body in mental and physical characterization. This "poetic conception" is what the gifted theatre artist Robert Edmond Jones had in mind when he wrote in *The Dramatic Imagination* that "...our work on this stage is to suggest the immanence of a visionary world all about us." When all of these theatrical performance principles are skillfully blended into this poetic conception, the actors playing scenes for adult men and women will have achieved the most compelling and truthfully artistic expression possible!

As you approach the following scenes give some attention to the "poetic conception" suggested by Robert Edmond Jones to reveal the "heart" and the "soul" of the adult men and women characters reflected in the selected scenes. Your personal identification and understanding of the actions and thoughts expressed in the scenes should enhance the artistic and creative interpretation of the characters, and should also provide a personal, specialized performance approach that encourages an honest and authentic character portrait in playing the scenes. Finally, remember that adult men and women characters are inextricably entwined in each of these scenes and it is only through their specific action and interaction that they distinguish themselves as complex, three-dimensional stage figures.

Scenes for adult men and women encourage the actor to "visualize" the character images suggested in the episode and to underscore the basic similarity between a character's thought and a character's action, translating abstract ideas or concepts into specific performance strategies that actively engage the voice and the body in mental and physical characterization.

from *The Bald Soprano* ©
by Eugene Ionesco

Eugene Ionesco has been called an "anti-playwright" primarily because of his apparent dislike for traditional theatre and its emphasis upon popular culture and commercialism. In this scene he uses hollow slogans, pitiful phrases, clichéd sentiments, dreary social statements, and trite questions to frame an absurdist view of the human condition. The two characters in the scene, Mr. and Mrs. Martin, are a middle-aged, middle-class married couple who are trying rather late in life — to discover their "true" identity. In what is a very human and comic situation at times — perhaps the "midlife crises" — the characters wrestle with cosmic questions of marginal importance and trivial details that appear to be of major significance in their daily lives. There are unsolvable mysteries about the human condition that remain unanswered; and there is woeful wondering, pitiful pleading, and ridiculous riddles that are all left unheeded.

What *is* evident, however, in these calmly dispassionate, somewhat compulsive, characters is a stinging assessment of the ridiculousness of everyday polite conversation, and a sharp, satiric indictment of patronizing communication. While the absurdism of the given circumstances and the far-fetched author point of view often are perplexing, the dialog is punctuated with brightly humorous lines, lighthearted refrains, and sharply drawn banter that underscores the need for compassion and understanding of the human predicament. There is also a "black comedy" undertone just beneath the surface of the utterly outrageous behavior of the characters that threatens to burst forth at the slightest provocation.

In playing the scene, there are a number of potential performance problems that will need to be addressed if the actors are to achieve powerful, thought-provoking character portraits. First, the playwright has indicated in the stage directions that the actors must frequently appear to be "bored." Second, the characters are confined to chairs placed at Center Stage and there is no movement indicated in the scene until the final two lines of dialog. Third, there is very little distinction suggested in each character's attitude, mood, or point of view — indeed, in the absurdist tradition, these characters might be seen as two sides of the same personality. The actors will need to immediately gain the interest of the audience or the scene may become dull, tedious, and static. Some performance thought should be given to improvising the given circumstances initially, and then to play the scene as the playwright indicates. In any event, the actors will need to bring a degree of vitality to the tempo of the scene, rely upon "vocal coloring" to highlight significant lines of dialog, and be inventive in bodily actions or reactions to highlight character responses while confined to a chair!

The novelty of the scene, however, should provide sufficient audience interest if the characters are truly inventive; and imaginative use of pauses, facial expressions, "double-takes," hand props, repetitive gestures, peculiar mannerisms, or active stage business should enrich — and certainly enliven! — each character portrait. It will also be important for the actors to carefully "blend" their own distinctive personality traits into the character portraits to "flesh-out" the surface details and incidental events described in the episode, and to be responsive to what is happening *in* the moment of each character's theatrical life — even if that moment, at first glance, may appear to be uneventful, uninspired, or unreal.

1 MR. MARTIN: Excuse me, madam, but it seems to me,
2   unless I'm mistaken, that I've met you somewhere
3   before.
4 MRS. MARTIN: I, too, sir. It seems to me that I've met you
5   somewhere before.
6 MR. MARTIN: Was it, by any chance, at Manchester that I
7   caught a glimpse of you, madam?
8 MRS. MARTIN: That is very possible. I am originally from
9   the city of Manchester. But I do not have a good
10   memory, sir. I cannot say whether it was there that I
11   caught a glimpse of you or not!
12 MR. MARTIN: Good God, that's curious! I, too, am origi-
13   nally from the city of Manchester, madam!
14 MRS. MARTIN: That is curious!
15 MR. MARTIN: Isn't that curious? Only I, madam, I left the
16   city of Manchester about five weeks ago.
17 MRS. MARTIN: That is curious! What a bizarre coinci-
18   dence! I, too, sir, I left the city of Manchester about
19   five weeks ago.
20 MR. MARTIN: Madam, I took the 8:30 morning train
21   which arrives in London at 4:45.
22 MRS. MARTIN: That is curious! How very bizarre! And
23   what a coincidence! I took the same train, sir, I too.
24 MR. MARTIN: Good Lord, how curious! Perhaps then,
25   madam, it was on the train that I saw you?
26 MRS. MARTIN: It is indeed possible; that is, not unlikely.
27   It is plausible and, after all, why not! – But I don't
28   recall it, sir!
29 MR. MARTIN: I traveled second class, madam. There is no
30   second class in England, but I always travel second
31   class.
32 MRS. MARTIN: That is curious! How very bizarre! And
33   what a coincidence! I, too, sir, I traveled second class.
34 MR. MARTIN: How curious that is! Perhaps we did meet in

217

1   second class, my dear lady!

2 MRS. MARTIN: That is certainly possible, and it is not at

3   all unlikely. But I do not remember very well, my

4   dear sir!

5 MR. MARTIN: My seat was in coach number eight,

6   compartment six, my dear lady.

7 MRS. MARTIN: How curious that is! My seat was also in

8   coach number eight, compartment six, my dear sir!

9 MR. MARTIN: How curious that is and what a bizarre

10   coincidence! Perhaps we met in compartment six, my

11   dear lady?

12 MRS. MARTIN: It is indeed possible, after all! But I do not

13   recall it, my dear sir!

14 MR. MARTIN: To tell the truth, my dear lady, I do not

15   remember it either, but it is possible that we caught a

16   glimpse of each other there, and as I think of it, it

17   seems to me even very likely.

18 MRS. MARTIN: Oh! truly, of course, truly, sir!

19 MR. MARTIN: How curious it is! I had seat number three,

20   next to the window, my dear lady.

21 MRS. MARTIN: Oh, good Lord, how curious and bizarre. I

22   had seat number six next to the window, across from

23   you, my dear sir.

24 MR. MARTIN: Good God, how curious that is and what a

25   coincidence! We were then seated facing each other,

26   my dear lady! It is there that we must have seen each

27   other!

28 MRS. MARTIN: How curious it is! It is possible, but I do

29   not recall it, sir!

30 MR. MARTIN: To tell the truth, my dear lady, I do not

31   remember it either. However, it is very possible that

32   we saw each other on that occasion.

33 MRS. MARTIN: It is true, but I am not sure of it, sir.

34 MR. MARTIN: Dear madam, were you not the lady who

1   asked me to place her suitcase in the luggage rack
2   and who thanked me and gave me permission to
3   smoke?
4   MRS. MARTIN: But of course, that must have been I, sir.
5   How curious it is, how curious it is, and what a coin-
6   cidence!
7   MR. MARTIN: How curious it is, how bizarre, what a coin-
8   cidence! And well, well, it was perhaps at that
9   moment that we came to know each other, madam?
10   MRS. MARTIN: How curious it is and what a coincidence!
11   It is indeed possible, my dear sir! However, I do not
12   believe that I recall it.
13   MR. MARTIN: Nor do I, madam. *(A moment of silence. The*
14   *clock strikes twice; then once.)* Since coming to London,
15   I have resided in Bromfield Street, my dear lady.
16   MRS. MARTIN: How curious that is, how bizarre! I, too,
17   since coming to London, I have resided in Bromfield
18   Street, my dear sir.
19   MR. MARTIN: How curious that is, well then, well then,
20   perhaps we have seen each other in Bromfield Street,
21   my dear lady.
22   MRS. MARTIN: How curious that is, how bizarre! It is
23   indeed possible, after all! But I do not recall it, my
24   dear sir.
25   MR. MARTIN: I reside at number nineteen, my dear lady.
26   MRS. MARTIN: How curious that is. I also reside at
27   number nineteen, my dear sir.
28   MR. MARTIN: Well then, well then, well then, well then,
29   perhaps we have seen each other in that house, my
30   dear lady?
31   MRS. MARTIN: It is indeed possible but I do not recall it,
32   dear sir.
33   MR. MARTIN: My flat is on the fifth floor, number eight,
34   my dear lady.

1   MRS. MARTIN: How curious it is, good Lord, how bizarre!
2   And what a coincidence! I too reside on the fifth floor
3   in flat number eight, dear sir!
4   MR. MARTIN: *(Musing)* How curious it is, how curious it is,
5   how curious it is, and what a coincidence! You know,
6   in my bedroom there is a bed, and it is covered with a
7   green eiderdown. This room, with the bed and the
8   green eiderdown is at the end of the corridor between
9   w.c. *[i.e., bathroom]* and the bookcase, dear lady!
10   MRS. MARTIN: What a coincidence, good Lord, what a
11   coincidence! My bedroom, too, has a bed with a green
12   eiderdown and is at the end of the corridor, between
13   the w.c., dear sir, and the bookcase!
14   MR. MARTIN: How bizarre, curious, strange! Then,
15   madam, we live in the same room and we sleep in
16   the same bed, dear lady. It is perhaps, there that we
17   have met!
18   MRS. MARTIN: How curious it is and what a coincidence!
19   It is indeed possible that we have met there, and
20   perhaps even last night. But I do not recall it, dear sir!
21   MR. MARTIN: I have a little girl, my little daughter, she
22   lives with me, dear lady. She is two years old, she's
23   blond, she has a white eye and a red eye, she is very
24   pretty, her name is Alice, dear lady.
25   MRS. MARTIN: What a bizarre coincidence! I, too, have a
26   little girl. She is two years old, has a white eye and a
27   red eye, she is very pretty, and her name is Alice, too,
28   dear sir!
29   MR. MARTIN: *(In the same drawling, monotonous voice)*
30   How curious it is and what a coincidence! How
31   bizarre! Perhaps they are the same, dear lady!
32   MRS. MARTIN: How curious it is! It is indeed possible,
33   dear sir. *(A rather long moment of silence. The clock*
34   *strikes twenty-nine times. Mr. Martin, after having*

1   reflected at length, gets up slowly and, unhurriedly,
2   moves toward Mrs. Martin, who, surprised by his solemn
3   air, has also gotten up very quietly.)
4   **MR. MARTIN:** *(In the same flat, monotonous voice, slightly*
5   *singsong)* **Then, dear lady, I believe that there can be**
6   **no doubt about it, we have seen each other before and**
7   **you are my own wife...Elizabeth, I have found you**
8   **again!** *(MRS. MARTIN approaches MR. MARTIN without*
9   *haste. They embrace without expression. The clock*
10 *strikes once, very loud. This striking of the clock must be*
11 *so loud that it makes the audience jump. The MARTINS*
12 *do not hear it.)*
13 **MRS. MARTIN: Donald, it's you darling!** *(They sit together*
14 *in the same armchair, their arms around each other, and*
15 *fall asleep. The clock strikes several more times...)*
16
17
18
19
20
21
22
23
24
25
26
27
28
29
30
31
32
33
34

from *Late/Late...Computer Date* ©
by Ludmilla Bollow

An affecting and touchingly conceived family drama of two eccentric spinster sisters who live alone in genteel clutter, *Late/Late...Computer Date* offers warm, offbeat adult women characters whose haunted present-day lives evoke sad memories of past events that have estranged them from the outside world, while at the same time fortified their own dependence on one another. The depth of their feeling and understanding has grown more intimate — and perhaps intimidating — than the casual reader may wish to admit; but there is a pathos and a poignancy here that speaks volumes about the valiant struggle to hold onto and to treasure a way of life, a set of values, and a code of commitment that is, sadly, absent from contemporary society and — for that matter — from contemporary drama as well. There is also a profound sense of genuine affection and self-sacrifice expressed by the sisters that becomes more pronounced as the events of the following scene unfold and circumstances beyond control of either human nature or individual destiny lead one sister to a shattering act of cruelty in order to express the ultimate gift of genuine caring and compassion for the other sister.

In this scene, Veronica — who occasionally needs rescue from her imaginary world — is nervously anticipating her "first date," a computer match with a compatible gentleman. Isobel, her older sister, has spent the last of Mama's insurance money to insure that her sister's first date will be memorable — a final tribute to Isobel's life mission in promising Mama "to take care of Veronica." At first, Veronica adamantly refuses to go on her computer date; but after the more domineering Isobel cajoles and literally pushes her out of the door, Veronica exits wearing Mama's wedding gown, now dyed peach. Isobel is now left alone to await Veronica's return and to hear all the news of this first venture out alone — fully expecting that life will return to its uneventful routine thereafter. Veronica, however, inadvertently — and unmistakably as Isobel observes — dances into another world of "real-life fantasy" and alarms Isobel when she returns from her computer date. A subtle but suspenseful battle for control follows, resolved only when Isobel is able to finally regain mastery of her sister through a courageous act of conscious cruelty.

In playing the scene the actors are cautioned to treat the spinster sisters with respect and to concentrate on the intensifying shift of actions, attitudes, and moods that surface in the character relationships. There may be an initial tendency to focus upon the eccentric behavior or rather bizarre given circumstances of the scene, but these performance principles should be vigorously resisted in favor of a more restrained and penetrating exploration of the character's lingering memories and revealing truths to capture the essentially warm-hearted and truly compassionate relationship between these aging, colorfully awakening adult women. It may be important to establish a meaningful dramatic presence for Admiral Bird, the also aging parrot whose eerie stage figure looms ominously over the scene, and who serves as the final witness to the powerful and provocative shared tragedy but is unable to voice any incisive commentary on the overall irony of the scene's climactic resolution. There is, finally, a need for the actors to review the basic performance principles of "looking out" and "looking in" discussed in Chapter 2 as a potential performance approach to achieve the concentrated physical and vocal focus required in this scene, and to gain a perceptive understanding of each character's express intention or motivation in the given circumstances.

1   *(ISOBEL rests her head on table. Music box has stopped.*
2   *She's fallen asleep. Lights dim for a few moments.*
3   *VERONICA enters quietly, carrying her shoes. Bumps*
4   *into chair.)*
5   **ISOBEL:** *(Startled)* **Veronica! When did you come home?**
6   **VERONICA: Just now** – *(There seems to be a new vagueness*
7   *about her.)*
8   **ISOBEL: I waited. But I guess I was overtired.**
9   **VERONICA: That's all right.**
10   **ISOBEL: Did you come right home?**
11   **VERONICA: Yes.**
12   **ISOBEL: Didn't he take you anywhere?**
13   **VERONICA: Well, you see** –
14   **ISOBEL:** *(Fully awake)* **Sit down. Tell me all about it.**
15   **VERONICA: Couldn't we wait till tomorrow? I'm really**
16   **quite tired.**
17   **ISOBEL: I'm anxious to hear** –
18   **VERONICA:** *(Sits. Hesitates.)* **There's not much to tell–**
19   **ISOBEL: What did he look like? Did you like him?**
20   **VERONICA: Well, you see** – **I got there in time.**
21   **ISOBEL: I should hope so.**
22   **VERONICA: And I was so frightened. I didn't want to go in.**
23   *(Stops.)*
24   **ISOBEL: Go on. Go on** –
25   **VERONICA: Computer Palace, it was like a huge barn. Not**
26   **like a dance hall at all** – **there were printed signs all**
27   **over** –
28   **ISOBEL: That's not important right now.**
29   **VERONICA: When you came in, they took your computer**
30   **card and put it in a big machine that lit up and made**
31   **all kinds of noises, and you were given a special**
32   **number** –
33   **ISOBEL: Will you please get on to Arthur** –
34   **VERONICA: – and you waited in a special blocked-off**

1   section till your partner arrived. And all night long,
2   numbers were called over the loudspeaker. Almost
3   like bingo, with people jumping up when their
4   number was called –
5 ISOBEL: Will you please tell me what happened when
6   Arthur came?!
7 VERONICA: *(Looking down)* He never came.
8 ISOBEL: What?! He never showed up?!
9 VERONICA: His number was never called.
10 ISOBEL: Are you sure you listened carefully. Weren't
11   daydreaming as usual?
12 VERONICA: I listened very closely. And they would repeat
13   the number if no one came forward.
14 ISOBEL: I think that's terrible. I think you should get a
15   refund. All that expense. Taxi. Wig. Wasted!
16 VERONICA: It wasn't wasted. *(Takes off fur.)*
17 ISOBEL: I suppose you enjoyed sitting on the sidelines as
18   usual.
19 VERONICA: No, the waiting was awful.
20 ISOBEL: Let's go to bed. I'm so angry, I don't even feel like
21   hot tea. And no wine for you tonight. You've had
22   enough.
23 VERONICA: I don't want any.
24 ISOBEL: One night. Just one night, I wanted you to have a
25   good time. Why, if I knew that Arthur's number, I'd
26   call him this very minute. Well, we'll call Computer
27   Suitor first thing in the morning. Didn't you
28   complain to anyone?
29 VERONICA: No, you see –
30 ISOBEL: Well, I certainly would have let someone know.
31   They had his number. They could have called him.
32   How humiliating. To have to sit there all night, while
33   the others danced. I didn't want you to be a wall-
34   flower. That's why I paid for this dance. One special

1   night we planned for all these years –

2   **VERONICA:** But I didn't sit all night –

3   **ISOBEL:** What?

4   **VERONICA:** I danced.

5   **ISOBEL:** With who? Did they find you a substitute? Well,

6   we aren't paying for substitutes.

7   **VERONICA:** No, well, you see, I was sitting there, all

8   nervous, and this gentleman, nearby – he was sitting

9   and waiting too.

10   **ISOBEL:** You didn't talk to him, did you? Without an intro-

11   duction – without knowing anything about him!

12   **VERONICA:** Not right away. But after awhile, he said, "Is

13   that Paris Nights perfume you're wearing?"

14   **ISOBEL:** You are so naive about things.

15   **VERONICA:** I said "yes," and moved further away, so the

16   perfume wouldn't bother him.

17   **ISOBEL:** You mean, so he wouldn't bother you.

18   **VERONICA:** Then he said, "That was my wife's favorite

19   perfume – and you remind me of her."

20   **ISOBEL:** "You remind me of her –" What an old line. I

21   hope you didn't fall for it...But then you've never been

22   out alone. Oh, I should have known...

23   **VERONICA:** He proceeded to ask me if my date had shown

24   up. I said "no." He said his hadn't either, and that

25   whether we matched or not, we should dance, not

26   waste the whole evening.

27   **ISOBEL:** You didn't, did you?!

28   **VERONICA:** *(Rises, looking out.)* I don't know, Isobel. All of

29   a sudden I was relaxed. I didn't know anything about

30   him, and he didn't know anything about me. And I got

31   up, and followed him. And there was this lovely waltz

32   music, and they turned the lights low so you didn't

33   even see the signs on the walls, only the crystal ball,

34   shimmering like a huge bright star.

1   ISOBEL: So you danced – with a perfect stranger.

2   VERONICA: Yes. I could do it, Isobel. It was like floating.

3   ISOBEL: I think we better retire. You can tell me the rest

4   in the morning. You must be quite exhausted after all

5   that dancing.

6   VERONICA: I don't feel tired. In fact, I feel like I'm still

7   floating.

8   ISOBEL: I knew you shouldn't have taken that wine before

9   you went – *(Flustered)* Well, tomorrow – you'll feel

10   different when things are back to normal. *(Puts things*

11   *together on table.)*

12   VERONICA: *(Quietly)* He asked to come and see me.

13   ISOBEL: *(Stops what she's doing.)* What?!

14   VERONICA: *(Not facing her)* He wanted to take me home.

15   But I said "no."

16   ISOBEL: I should hope so.

17   VERONICA: I was so afraid that once we left everything

18   would turn ugly, like in Cinderella.

19   ISOBEL: I don't know what's got into you tonight,

20   Veronica. I don't know at all. Let's go to bed, and

21   tomorrow –

22   VERONICA: He asked for my phone number, so he could

23   call me.

24   ISOBEL: *(New alarm)* You didn't give it to him, did you? You

25   couldn't have been so stupid as to give your phone

26   number to a perfect stranger. Living alone on this

27   empty road like we do.

28   VERONICA: I didn't know what to do.

29   ISOBEL: You really can't be trusted out alone, can you?

30   VERONICA: We had only practiced what to say to Arthur.

31   This was so different. So, when he asked me for my

32   phone number –

33   ISOBEL: You never give your phone number to a perfect

34   stranger! I've been thinking of having the phone

1   disconnected anyway. No one calls here anymore. Just
2   advertising. Needless expense. End of the month the
3   phone goes! That's it! No more telephones in this
4   house!
5   VERONICA: I didn't give him my number.
6   ISOBEL: At least you showed some sense.
7   VERONICA: But he gave me his.
8   ISOBEL: What?!
9   VERONICA: *(Gets card from her purse.)* See. He wrote it on
10   the back of my computer card. He said I should think
11   it over. He didn't want to rush me. And, after I
12   thought it over, to call him. Because he really wanted
13   to see me again.
14   ISOBEL: *(Snatches card from her.)* This is all very ridicu-
15   lous, you know. Picking up with a perfect stranger.
16   VERONICA: *(Taking card back)* He wasn't a stranger. He was
17   a computer date.
18   ISOBEL: But not yours! You knew nothing about him.
19   VERONICA: I liked it better now knowing whether he was
20   a butcher or baker.
21   ISOBEL: Why didn't *his* date show up? Probably some-
22   thing wrong with him.
23   VERONICA: He told me all about himself.
24   ISOBEL: And you believed it?
25   VERONICA: Why not? We believed what Arthur said on
26   his card.
27   ISOBEL: Those were true facts.
28   VERONICA: Were those true facts you put down on my
29   card? You can put anything on those cards. But when
30   you sit next to a person, look them right in the eye,
31   you know if they're telling the truth or not.
32   ISOBEL: Your mind is really clouded tonight. All this
33   excitement has just been too much for you.
34   *(Deliberately)* I wouldn't be surprised if you made all

1   this up. Just another one of your stories –
2   VERONICA: It's not a story. It really happened.
3   ISOBEL: You've always made up stories. Invented charac-
4   ters –
5   VERONICA: He wasn't made up. He was real.
6   ISOBEL: Veronica, I don't want to spoil all these nice new
7   fantasies of yours, but, if you knew men like I do – all
8   the things they will say, well, just to get you alone –
9   for certain purposes.
10   VERONICA: He was a perfect gentleman!
11   ISOBEL: There! But once he had you alone – Do you
12   remember that movie I took you to, about this strange
13   man, and this lonely lady – and what he did to her...
14   VERONICA: I don't care, Isobel! I liked him. I really did.
15   And I'm going to bed now and sleep on it, and think
16   about it. You can't stop me from thinking about it.
17   You never know what goes on in my head.
18   ISOBEL: And sometimes you don't either.
19   VERONICA: – And if I still feel the same in the morning,
20   I'm going to call him.
21   ISOBEL: You're not going to call him!
22   VERONICA: *(A new strongness)* I'll decide about that in the
23   morning.
24   ISOBEL: You'll wake up tomorrow, and it'll be like a far-
25   away dream. Why, you won't remember if it happened
26   or not.
27   VERONICA: I'll remember. The rest of my life... *(Picks up*
28   *fur. Nonchalantly)* I think I'll go to bed now. I'm really
29   quite tired.
30   ISOBEL: Yes, go to bed. You'll feel better – different, in the
31   morning. Just leave your things here.
32   VERONICA: *(Starts to leave, then goes to ISOBEL.)* Thank
33   you, Isobel, for making me go. You always make me
34   go places I don't want to, and then I end up having

1   such a good time.
2   ISOBEL: Yes, you do, don't you. *(Takes her hands and pats*
3   *it.)* You see, I've always known what's best for you,
4   haven't I?
5   VERONICA: Aren't you coming along?
6   ISOBEL: No, you just go ahead. Use the bathroom first. I
7   have a few things to take care of here.
8   VERONICA: *(Just a bit of the old fright back)* Good night,
9   Isobel.
10   ISOBEL: Good   night,   Veronica.   Pleasant   dreams.
11   *(VERONICA leaves. ISOBEL straightens things up. Sees*
12   *computer card with phone number on it. Hesitates, then*
13   *walks over to parrot and tears it up into tiny pieces,*
14   *letting them flutter to the floor like snow in front of the*
15   *perch. Scolding)* Admiral Bird, did you get hungry and
16   eat up Veronica's computer card with that man's
17   phone number on it? That was naughty. That wasn't a
18   Polly cracker. That was one of Veronica's souvenirs.
19   *(Walks away.)* And now she won't have any souvenirs
20   left anymore. Nothing to save from tonight for her
21   memory board... *(Sits wearily. Staring vacantly ahead.*
22   *An inward cry)* No souvenirs left at all...Nothing worth
23   saving...Nothing...Nothing...
24
25
26
27
28
29
30
31
32
33
34

from *Brilliants* ©
by Jack Heifner

Here is a rather "brilliant" satirical sketch that should have a special appeal for the theatre aficionado who enjoys an occasionally gentle, self-mocking, and highly unapologetic look at "show business!" There is a biting edge to the sketch, but it captures the eternal spirit of the creative genius behind the scenes of mega-hit theatre productions and there is buoyant joy and winsome sophistication in both the dialog and the given circumstances that is sure to inspire an inventive — if not arresting — performance. The seemingly lighthearted sketch is set in the lobby of the elegant Algonquin Hotel on West 44th Street in New York City, but the scene could be representative of any locale or occasion where "true artists" might gather to voice their piercing and penetrating judgments on the aching condition of the theatre.

Lee Francis, a fabulously successful playwright, and Jamie Petty, an equally famous stage director, are being questioned by a very pushy and persistent female Interviewer on the professional impact of their longest-running show in the history of American theatre. It is a solemn occasion — one that requires multiple Bloody Marys! — to provide the tantalizing answers to a number of the intriguing questions posed by the conscientious Interviewer; and it is an occasion for each of the artists to indulge their worldly wise reflections on such penetrating topics as "what's happening?", "what are you doing now?", and "what have you accomplished in the last decade?" The interview itself is a moving examination of those rare, creative talents that inspire the avant-garde — and also provoke serious, if not silly, social commentary.

The playwright has indicated that the male characters are *not* "theatrical types," so this is an excellent opportunity for the actors to explore traditional approaches to performance that include "observation," "objectivity," and "role-playing" that are described in the "Zoo Story" exercise in Chapter 9. Perhaps a good beginning in the initial development of the character portraits in this sketch is a compilation of animal observations and human comparisons that capture distinct individuality in voice, body, and movement, and that is easily applicable to the imaginative character definitions of the playwright, the stage director, and the interviewer in the satirical sketch that follows. It may also be a good performance approach for the actors to explore alternative, nontraditional approaches to characterization here — especially in terms of inventive performance "metaphors" related to machines, slogans, events, or literary and real-life personalities.

In playing the role, however, the actors should not lose sight of the basic wit and satire in the sketch; and careful attention should be paid to the playwright's description of imagery, setting, and staging to better understand the potential comic effect that the character's behavior, attitude, and mannerisms may have on an interpretation of the sketch. It is also valuable in this sketch for the actors to be *in* the atmosphere detailed by the playwright — and to be imaginative in revealing specific bodily actions, personal traits, intrinsic behavior patterns, and gestures that give animation and vitality to the character portraits. Finally, don't be hesitant to give each character an impression of elegance and sophistication to underscore the unmistakable voices of these artists — and how fortunate we are to be in their company!

1   INTERVIEWER: Lee Francis and Jamie Petty are the bril-
2   liant playwright and director of the longest-running
3   show in the history of the American theatre. I met
4   them recently for drinks and talk at the famed
5   Algonquin Hotel.
6   LEE: A Bloody Mary.
7   JAMIE: I'll have a Bloody Mary.
8   INTERVIEWER: So what's happening, fellas? What are
9   you two working on?
10   JAMIE: He's working on his den.
11   LEE: I've been moving the furniture about trying to find
12   the position that will make me start writing again.
13   INTERVIEWER: That's not exactly what I meant, but...tell
14   me, I've heard that you guys were very old friends.
15   JAMIE: That's right.
16   LEE: That's right.
17   INTERVIEWER: And where did you first meet?
18   LEE: On our college campus. We were both in the art
19   department and we ended up pledging the same
20   fraternity.
21   JAMIE: Then I dropped out of the fraternity.
22   LEE: And I dropped out of the fraternity.
23   JAMIE: And I dropped out of the art department.
24   LEE: Then I dropped out of the art department.
25   JAMIE: And we both ended up in the theatre department.
26   LEE: At the time we were doing things simultaneously.
27   INTERVIEWER: And that's where you did your first play
28   together?
29   JAMIE: Yes, indeed. Lee wrote this eccentric musical
30   called *Sqush the Mush* and all the characters
31   were mushrooms. If you were naughty you got
32   punished. You were thrown into a beef stroganoff. It
33   was horrifying.
34   LEE: Talk about horrifying. Every night, before the show,

1   Jamie locked the entire cast in the men's room. For
2   preparation he made them wail and scream and
3   carry on for an hour...in character, of course.
4   JAMIE: I, at the time being heavily into Gestalt, also locked
5   the theatre. The audience literally got up and stood
6   against the doors waiting for the intermission. We
7   thought that was the neatest thing in the world.
8   LEE: We upset so many people.
9   JAMIE: It's a pity we can't alienate audiences now.
10   INTERVIEWER: And what are you doing now? In the last
11   ten years, since your show has been running, you
12   haven't done another one. Why is that?
13   JAMIE'S: Well, I had to take a little time off. I started
14   painting again...first time since college. I rented an
15   estate in Connecticut, and I began by painting the
16   autumn colors. The leaves. Exteriors. Then it got
17   colder and I had to come inside...so I started a series
18   of paintings of the chairs which were in the house.
19   Then the wallpapers. And finally, one day I was
20   painting and I looked at the canvas and focused for
21   the first time in about eight years...and I realized I
22   was painting the pattern of the carpet! And I said to
23   myself, if I continue staying here and continue
24   painting, I will soon be painting the bristles of the
25   brush. Soon I will be painting the paint. I've got to get
26   out of here! I've got to get back to the theatre.
27   INTERVIEWER: I see? So, Lee...what have you accom-
28   plished in the last decade? Have you been painting,
29   too?
30   LEE: Actually, I wrote one other play. A fifteen-minute
31   piece. It begins with someone holding a salad bowl
32   and singing, "Now I cut the lettuce and put the lettuce
33   in." They do that...then sing, "Now I cut the tomato
34   and put the tomato in." And "Now I put on the

1   dressing." And the final twelve minutes consist of

2   furious tossing. Never produced.

3   JAMIE: All our great ideas are never done.

4   LEE: We're both heavily into nonlinear work and someday

5   we hope to make it big in the noncommercial theatre.

6   JAMIE: Right now we're both just destroyed that what

7   we've done is so commercial that we can't do real art.

8   INTERVIEWER: Oh, come on. I'm sure you're not

9   destroyed by the fame and money that comes from

10   having a long-running smash.

11   LEE: But we can't be silly anymore.

12   JAMIE: We have definitely stopped being silly.

13   LEE: I mean, you can't be really silly when you're trying to

14   create a serious new show

15   INTERVIEWER: Ah ha! So that's what you've been up to?

16   JAMIE: Oh, you've caught us! Yes, we're forced to admit

17   we've been trying to work on a monumental new

18   idea.

19   LEE: It's going to be like this time *I* give the audience beef

20   stroganoff and then ask *them* to write the recipe.

21   INTERVIEWER: *(To JAMIE)* And what exactly does that

22   mean?

23   JAMIE: Oh, I don't know what it means...but it's brilliant.

24   LEE: Exactly, I don't know what it means but it's brilliant.

25   JAMIE: And I think we've got ourselves another hit.

26   LEE: Unfortunately. Another Bloody Mary?

27   JAMIE: I'll have another Bloody Mary.

28   INTERVIEWER: And that's how my interview went with

29   the playwright and director of Broadway's longest-

30   running show. I don't have a clue what they mean,

31   but I'll have a double Bloody Mary.

32

33

34

from *Speed-the-Plow* ©
by David Mamet

The setting for this scene by the Pulitzer Prize-winning play-wright David Mamet is the Hollywood apartment of mogul and production head Bobby Gould, an adult man of about forty years who is the current "messiah" and "tycoon" of the film-making industry. He is joined by Karen (a role originally played on Broadway by the pop singer and rock star Madonna), an attractive young woman in her twenties who is Gould's ambitious, tempo-rary office assistant. Provocative and ornery with an overdose injection of bitter irony and satire on the moral corruption of the "business" of the motion picture industry, the playscript is another seething Mamet "black comedy" that this time focuses attention on characters caught up in the overwhelming pursuit of authority and power at the expense of personal virtues and values. The playscript is also a revealing metaphor for spiritually bankrupt American principles as they are reflected in contempo-rary society and Gould appears to be the most articulate spokesperson of the playwright's merciless point of view.

Although the playscript is a wry glance at the gripping authority and ruthless power of the new breed of film moguls, this scene has moments of tenderness and compassion that may surprise. Karen, who has been asked to give a "courtesy read" to a prospective book/script project entitled "The Bridge; or, Radiation and the Half-Life of Society," dutifully completes the assignment and meets at Gould's apartment late at night. The book/script about the death and destruction of society caused by uncontrolled radiation leaks, is sure to be a box-office "downer," but it provides the impetus for the characters to explore their own lost lives and discover a refreshing, but fleeting, sense of purpose and passion. As the two characters sit alone reading aloud from the book/script and sharing tender, poignant reflec-tions of feeling and truth, there is a fragile bonding that adds an unmistakably enchanted and romantic flavor to the evening's encounter. Gould's transparent vulnerability and inherent basic goodness are revealed in this brief scene, but the "reincarnation" is short-lived and the conclusion of the playscript finds him shaken and unsure of his experience with Karen, but he is also resigned to return to his gruff, hard-nosed fate: "We're here to make a movie."

In playing the selected scene the actors should clearly define the tidbits of character action and reaction suggested and concentrate on a single performance objective. For the actor playing the role of Gould it is important to cultivate a "selective" rather than the representative character portrait that is detailed in the more complete playscript, especially since this episode reveals a more sensitive and sympathetic image of the character than is revealed in earlier or later action(s) of the playscript. The actor playing the role of Karen should be attentive to the delicate balance of genuine, idealistic sincerity and remarkably believable honesty that is embodied in the young woman's apparent candor and stirring perceptions of this magical, perhaps mystical, moment. Since the characters are inextricably entwined in this scene, it is also important for the actors to clearly define each action, intention, and motivation suggested to achieve the interpersonal "connection" described by the playwright.

The actors may wish to review the basic performance principles of Stanislavsky's "units of action," in Chapter 3, to isolate the catalog of multiple goals and objectives each character pursues in this scene as well; and concentrate on the "super objective," or each character's overarching emotional and intellectual desire in the given circumstances, in order to more clearly amplify the primary motivating forces that drive the characters to realize their stated goals and objectives. This is a good performance opportunity for the actors to explore the role of "body image" as well in indicating the emotional or mental state of the characters and in visualizing the action of the scene. In addition, a well-conceived and well-defined character body image may enrich the interpretation in "externalizing" the character relationships being described by the playwright. Finally, "movement phrases" like "flowering bud," "self-disclosure," or "speed-the-plow" may also help the actors make the expressive intention or submerged subtext more clearly visible in giving shape and form to the characters.

1   GOULD: Thank you.
2   KAREN: No, I thank *you*. Do you know what he's talking
3   about? Fear. A life lived in fear, and he says, It Says In
4   The Book, it doesn't have to *be* so; that those things
5   we have *seen...you* know, and you think "I, am I the
6   only one on the whole planet who knows how *bad* it
7   is...that it's *coming*... that it's sure to come."
8   What...don't you see? What can I do...? And you *can't*
9   join a convent, or "cut off your hair," or, or, or, you
10   see, this is our pain, I think, we *can't* embrace Jesus.
11   *He*, you see, and he says, "I know. And you don't have
12   to be afraid." And I realized: I haven't *breathed*. How
13   long? In *years*. From, I don't know. From terror,
14   perhaps ever. And you say, how can you say it? Is our
15   life so bad? No. No. But that it's ending. That our life
16   is ending. Yes. It's true. And he says that, that these
17   are the Dark Ages. *(Pause)* They aren't to come, the
18   Dark Ages – they are now. We're living them. *(Reads.)*
19   "In the waning days...in the last days"..."Yes," he says,
20   it's *true*, and you needn't deny it...and I felt such *fear*,
21   because, of course, he's right. Then he says: "do not
22   be afraid." The story...when you, when you read it, the
23   story itself. Down below the bridge, I'll tell you:
24   written with such love... *(Pause) Such* love... *(Pause)*
25   God. A thing to be thankful for. Such love.
26   GOULD: You've done a fantastic job.
27   KAREN: I have?
28   GOULD: Yes.
29   KAREN: I have? Doing what?
30   GOULD: On the book. *(Pause)*
31   KAREN: I...?
32   GOULD: In your report on the book. It means something,
33   it means a lot, I want to tell you, if you want to "do"
34   something out here. A *freshness*, you said a *näiveté*,

1   but call it a "freshness," and a capacity to get
2   involved...I think that it's fantastic. And, you know,
3   you dream about making a connection; but I feel I've
4   *done* it.
5   KAREN: You've made a connection...
6   GOULD: Yes. And you reached out to *me*.
7   KAREN: I did...
8   GOULD: You shared this thing with me.
9   KAREN: ...the book...
10 GOULD: You did it. Someone does something...*totally*...
11 KAREN: ...yes...
12 GOULD: And you say "yes"..."That's what I've been
13   missing."
14 KAREN: ...you're saying...
15 GOULD: That's what I've been missing. I'm saying, you
16   come *alive*, and you see everyone's been holding their
17   *breath* in this town, twenty years, forever, *I* don't
18   know...and then...
19 KAREN: Yes...
20 GOULD: So rare, someone shows, shows some *enthu-*
21   *siasm*...it becomes, it becomes *simple*. You know what
22   I mean...
23 KAREN: Yes. I do.
24 GOULD: N'I want to thank you. *(Pause)*
25 KAREN: Um...it's nothing.
26 GOULD: *(Simultaneously with "nothing")* It's something.
27   No. Let, let, let, let me *help* you. That's what I want
28   to do.
29 KAREN: *(Pause)* I'm confused.
30 GOULD: I'm saying I *thank* you; I want to do something for
31   you.
32 KAREN: No, no...
33 GOULD: And, whatever, I'm saying, if I can, that you would
34   like to do, in, in the *Studio*, if you would like to do it,

239

1   if I can help you with it, then I would like to help you.
2   KAREN: Yes. *Thank* you. *(Pause)* I absolutely do. You *know*
3   what I want to do?
4   GOULD: I...?
5   KAREN: I want to work on the film.
6   GOULD: All right. If we can. The *Prison* film...
7   KAREN: No. On this. *This* film. The Radiation film and I
8   don't care. I don't care in what capacity, well, why
9   *should* I, 'cause I don't have any skills...*that's*
10   presumptuous, of *course*, in any way I could. But I'd
11   just like, it would be so important to me, to *be* there.
12   To help. *(Pause)* If you could just help me with that.
13   And, seriously, I'll get coffee, I don't care, but if you
14   could do that for me, I would be... *(Pause)*
15 GOULD: Hmmm.
16 KAREN: I've put you on the spot.
17 GOULD: No. Yes, a little.
18 KAREN: I'm serious. I'd do *anything*...
19 GOULD: *(Pause)* Look... *(Pause)* This was a "courtesy read."
20 KAREN: I know that, but...
21 GOULD: As I told you, the chances were, were astronomi-
22   cally slim that it would...
23 KAREN: Of course, but you said, you, you wanted to
24   *investigate*...
25 GOULD: ...yes...
26 KAREN: "because once in awhile"...
27 GOULD: ...yes.
28 KAREN: And once in awhile one finds a pearl...
29 GOULD: Yes...
30 KAREN: And *this* book...I'm *telling* you, when you *read* it...
31 GOULD: Karen, it's about the End of the World.
32 KAREN: That's what I'm *saying*. That's why it...
33 GOULD: It's about the End of the World.
34 KAREN: Uh huh, uh huh. *(Pause)* This book... *(Pause)* This

1   book... *(Pause)* **But you said someone's job was to read**
2   **the manuscripts.** *(Pause)*
3   GOULD: Someone reads the manuscripts. Yes.
4   KAREN: ...that come in...
5   GOULD: ...yes. *(Pause)* We have readers.
6   KAREN: Now: why do the readers read them?
7   GOULD: *(Simultaneously with "read")* I get it. I get it. Yes. As
8   I said. Yes. Once in awhile, in a great while, yes, that...
9   KAREN: Why not this? I'm telling you...
10 GOULD: Look: I'm going to pay you the compliment of
11   being frank. *(Pause)* I'm going to talk to you. *(Pause)*
12   Power, people who are given a slight power, tend to
13   think, they think that they're the only one that has
14   these ideas, pure ideas, whatever, no matter. And,
15   listen to me. Listen. I'm going to tell you. This book.
16   Your book. On the End of the World which has meant
17   so much to you, as I see that it has: Won't Make a Good
18   Movie. OK? I could tell you many things to influence
19   you. But why? I have to respect your enthusiasm. And
20   I *do* respect it. But this book, you want us to make,
21   won't Get the Asses in the Seats. Sounds crass?
22   Whatever the thing just may be. My job: my job, my
23   new job...is not even to "make," it is to "suggest," to
24   "push," to champion...good work, I hope...choosing
25   *from* Those Things Which the Public Will Come In to
26   See. If they don't come to see it, what's the point? You
27   understand? *(Pause)* This is what I do. You said a
28   certain kind of courage to embrace a fact? *(Pause)*
29   This is the fact here.
30 KAREN: Why do you... *(Pause)* Your job is to make movies
31   people will come see.
32 GOULD: That's right.
33 KAREN: Why do you think they won't come see this one?
34   *(Pause)* Are you ever wrong? Do you see what I'm

1   asking? Just because you think it is "too good"...I...I...I
2   think they would come see it. *(Pause) I* would. It's
3   about...it's about what we feel. *(Pause)*
4 GOULD: It is?
5 KAREN: Yes.
6
7
8
9
10
11
12
13
14
15
16
17
18
19
20
21
22
23
24
25
26
27
28
29
30
31
32
33
34

from *The Whole Shebang* ©
by Rich Orloff

A wonderfully whimsical excursion into the world of intellectual "future shock," this award-winning National One-Act Play Contest comedy is a tongue-in-cheek satire about the mad creation of an ideal universe, and the even madder creators who are responsible for the astonishing, far-fetched vision of contemporary humanity. The playscript features cleverly imaginative and inventive "comic strip" characters to voice hilariously devastating social commentary on the "real world," and offers absorbing insights into modern education as well. Brilliantly original in its point of view, this comedy makes outrageous fun of present-day topics and events in a good-humored examination of the absurd conditions of our own day.

In this scene, set in a college classroom, the enthusiastic young adult Student is anxiously awaiting an oral examination on a special project: an independent study in which he "...created the heavens and the earth" in a new universe. The panel of learned scholars assembled for the examination includes the wise and patient Dean; the skeptical and critical Professor A; and the passionate and supportive Professor B. After a brief summary of the project, the Student surprises the professors by announcing the anticipated arrival of two typical human beings, John and Mary Doe, who will serve as living examples of the beauty and wonder to be found in the new universe. Unfortunately, it is Harvey Doe, John's brother, and his wife Edna who appear to complicate the situation. It appears that John and Mary are on vacation and that Harvey and Edna have taken time from their house-sitting duties to offer their own stirring perceptions and engrossing glimpses into the Student's universe project. The intimacies and intricacies that follow are a deft and frantic frolic into the humdrum lives of two average, unexceptional adult human beings struggling desperately to make sense of the cosmic nonsense goings-on!

In playing the scene, the actors are reminded that there is a minimum of overt action that helps to define the characters; but a wealth of narrative and dialog that should reveal the comic "inner truth" of each character's secret dreams and private fantasies. Play the role(s) with an emphasis upon the special relationship established by the characters in the rather absurd setting; and concentrate on a performance blueprint that clearly communicates the basic ingredients of each character's changing mood or attitude in the given circumstances. Be sure, also, that each character portrait gives comic depth and dimension to the implausible action being described so that distinct personalities as well as idiosyncrasies are highlighted. Don't forget to pay special attention to the "comic book" nature of each character as they struggle to express unique views on human relations or contemporary social values in conflicting exchanges with the other characters in the selected scene.

Finally, be aware of the fierce sense of independence and plaintive urgency in the characters as they struggle to understand the situation; and look for potential performance opportunities to interact or share meaningful interpersonal reactions and responses whenever possible. Finding an expressive visual performance *metaphor* may help to clearly underline each character's spoken dialog or subsequent physical action and enrich an authentic character portrait in playing the scene. So search for the bodily actions, gestures, and vocal qualities that best indicate character emotions and thoughts; and integrate appropriate physical mannerisms that might help the audience to visualize each character in performance.

1   PROFESSOR A: Harvey and Edna, what would you say has
2   been the best moment of your lives?
3   EDNA: Oh, that's easy. It was the day Harvey proposed to
4   me. It was the first nice day of spring, and we were
5   having a picnic in the park. I had made chicken salad
6   sandwiches and potato salad and carrot-raisin salad
7   and macaroni salad...
8   PROFESSOR B: Did Harvey make anything?
9   HARVEY: I think I picked up a six-pack.
10   EDNA: No, you were going to, but since I had to go back to
11   the store to pick up more mayonnaise, you decided to
12   let me get it.
13   DEAN: Why couldn't Harvey purchase the mayonnaise
14   when *he* went to buy the six-pack? *(HARVEY and EDNA*
15   *look at each other. Apparently, this idea never occurred*
16   *to them.)*
17   EDNA: Anyway, so we were having this picnic, and when
18   we finished eating, I wiped Harvey's mouth with my
19   napkin, and he wiped my mouth with his –
20   HARVEY: It's this thing we do.
21   EDNA: And, and I remember, I remember Harvey looking
22   right in my eyes and saying..."Let's make it legal." And
23   I thought, this man knows what I want.
24   PROFESSOR A: And was that day the best moment of your
25   life, too, Harvey?
26   HARVEY: Uh, yeah, yeah, of course, yeah.
27   EDNA: You don't have to lie to them. You told me what you
28   thought was the best.
29   HARVEY: Well, the day I proposed was one of the best.
30   PROFESSOR B: What was the best?
31   HARVEY: Well, OK, um, it was last summer, and well, I was
32   having this really lousy day, I mean, one-hundred
33   percent sucko lousy.
34   DEAN: "Sucko"?

1   **PROFESSOR B:** A colloquial adjective from the verb "suck."

2   **HARVEY:** The important thing is, the day stunk. It was

3   maybe a hundred degrees out, and maybe a hundred

4   percent humidity, and it was even worse in the house

5   because all of our air conditioners had just been

6   repossessed. And the the mail came, and it was all

7   bills, big bills, and I got so upset I didn't know what to

8   do, and so I turned on the TV. It didn't break, thank

9   uh – *(Glimpses at the STUDENT)* – whatever, and then

10   I just left the house and went into the backyard.

11   **PROFESSOR A:** And that was the best moment of your

12   life?

13   **HARVEY:** I'm getting to it. So on my way to – you know, I

14   hate being interrupted – on my way to the backyard, I

15   stopped in the kitchen and got myself a beer. Now I

16   don't know if any of you guys are beer drinkers...I guess

17   not. Usually, when you drink beer, it's either too cold,

18   or not cold enough, or it's got too much foam, or it's just

19   a lousy brand. And you still drink it, because that's

20   what life's about, accepting the beer you're given, but

21   it's nothing that, nothing you'd ever get *enthused*

22   about. But this beer, it was delicious. Just right. I can

23   still remember sitting in my backyard thinking, "I'm

24   broke, I'm unemployed, and I have lousy reception. But

25   this moment, this moment is perfect."

26   **STUDENT:** I really must interrupt –

27   **DEAN:** I told you –

28   **STUDENT:** But I don't think it's fair to judge the whole

29   human race based on such a limited sample.

30   **HARVEY:** Hey, take a little responsibility for your own

31   actions, why don't you?

32   **EDNA:** We're going to Hell, I know it.

33   **HARVEY:** He said we could say what we want.

34   **EDNA:** *(Whispering to HARVEY)* Yes, but we don't know if

1   he's going to be loving and forgiving or righteous and
2   vindictive.
3   STUDENT: Why do you insist upon giving me human qual-
4   ities? It's quite a projection.
5   HARVEY: Hey, you created us.
6   STUDENT: But I gave you free will!
7   HARVEY: That's it. Pass the buck.
8   STUDENT: I am not passing the buck.
9   HARVEY: You and your "free will." What good is it, huh? I
10   exert my free will all over the place, and all it does is
11   get me thrown out of bars.
12   STUDENT: You don't understand the concept. I gave you
13   choices –
14   HARVEY: Yeah, like being able to vote for a president and
15   then making all the candidates jerks?
16   STUDENT: There's more to it than that.
17   HARVEY: Hey, if I really had free will, do you think this is
18   the life I would have free-willed?
19   STUDENT: Maybe it is!
20   HARVEY: Yeah, well, let me tell you, if you designed me so
21   that I'd make the free will choice of *this* life, then
22   you're *really* sick.
23   EDNA: Harvey!
24   STUDENT: You could have made better choices.
25   HARVEY: I can't afford better choices! My credit cards are
26   already up to the limit!
27   DEAN: Excuse me –
28   EDNA: Harvey –
29   HARVEY: It's like everything that's great about life, he's
30   supposed to get credit for, and everything that's lousy
31   is supposed to be our fault. Well, it's not fair!
32   EDNA: Harvey, please.
33   HARVEY: It's just not fair!
34   DEAN: Excuse me...I'm sorry, but our time is almost over.

1   **PROFESSOR B:** If I may, one final question.

2   **DEAN:** Go ahead, Professor.

3   **PROFESSOR B:** *(To the HUMANS)* **Do you think the world is**

4   **getting – better or worse?**

5   **HARVEY:** Oh, worse.

6   **EDNA:** Much worse. Everyone knows that.

7   **PROFESSOR A:** Then why do you keep living?

8   **HARVEY:** Whaddaya mean?

9   **PROFESSOR A:** Your lives vary in quality from boring to

10   dismal. Your future holds no promise. Why do you

11   keep living? *(HARVEY and EDNA think for a moment,*

12   *look at each other.)*

13   **EDNA:** I just dropped ten pounds. I'm not going to die

14   now.

15   **HARVEY:** Yeah.

16   **PROFESSOR A:** And this is why you keep on living?

17   **EDNA:** Well, well, we also have to stick around for our

18   kids.

19   **HARVEY:** Yeah!

20   **EDNA:** After all, if it weren't for us, who'd be their role

21   models? *(The PROFESSORS exchange looks with each*

22   *other.)*

23   **HARVEY:** *(To EDNA)* I think you just blew it.

24   **EDNA:** They're good kids.

25   **HARVEY:** I know, I know, they're great kids. But you can't

26   tell that by looking at 'em.

27   **EDNA:** They're going to be fine, eventually. They're just

28   going through a difficult phase.

29   **HARVEY:** Yeah, it's called life.

30   **PROFESSOR A:** I still don't understand. With your atti-

31   tudes, why do you two keep living?

32   **HARVEY:** Hey, if you're suggesting I drop dead, *forget* it.

33   It'd make too many people happy.

34   **EDNA:** There are things in life to look forward to, you

1   know. Special things, things that make life worth
2   living.
3   PROFESSOR A: Name three.
4   EDNA: Well...every Thursday the paper has double-
5   discount coupons...and on weekends, I get to sleep in
6   late...oh, and about every six months, I'll give out a
7   phone number and somebody'll say "thank you" like
8   they really mean it.
9   PROFESSOR A: Don't you think those are rather trivial
10   things?
11   EDNA: So? I lead a rather trivial life. I know it.
12   HARVEY: I don't think you guys realize how hard it is
13   being a human being.
14   PROFESSOR B: Is it difficult?
15   HARVEY: You bet it is.
16   EDNA: You never feel like you have enough brains.
17   HARVEY: And you're always getting these impulses –
18   these urges – that make no sense whatsoever.
19   EDNA: Your kids look to you for answers, and you can't
20   think of anything. So you end up giving them the
21   same stupid answers your parents gave you.
22   HARVEY: When I think there are people dumber than I
23   am, I get scared. *(To the STUDENT)* So why'd you do it?
24   STUDENT: Do what?
25   HARVEY: Why'd you make us so messed up?
26   STUDENT: You're missing the point! I didn't create the
27   human being so that each one would work perfectly.
28   I created the human being so that humanity as a
29   whole would work perfectly.
30   HARVEY: But humanity as a whole doesn't work perfectly!
31   EDNA: It doesn't work perfectly at all. And we have it
32   better than most people.
33   DEAN: Do you?
34   EDNA: Oh, yes. Most people, if they get through childhood

1   **without dying of hunger or disease, all they got left is**
2   **a life of misery, pain, and injustice.**
3   **STUDENT: But I gave human beings all the resources they**
4   **need. Why, I've given you the ingredients for**
5   **paradise.**
6   **EDNA: Ohhh...you're a real tease, you know that?**
7   **STUDENT: What do you mean?**
8   **EDNA: You made the world so wonderful, and our lives so**
9   **difficult. I mean, maybe we're not the best examples**
10   **of human beings, but, well, we're trying as hard as we**
11   **can, and, and we want to be decent people and we**
12   **want our kids to turn out right and we want to have**
13   **happy lives, and, we're trying so hard, but...** *(Breaks*
14   *into tears.)* **You know what it's like to know you're**
15   **doing your best and that your life still stinks?**
16   **HARVEY:** *(To the STUDENT)* **Good work, buddy.** *(Com-*
17   *forting EDNA)* **Hey, come on. Don't cry. You do OK.**
18   **EDNA: I do not.**
19   **HARVEY: You do, too. You're a good mother, you're a good**
20   **wife, and you're one of the best damn directory assis-**
21   **tance operators in Dayton.**
22   **EDNA: You really think so?**
23   **HARVEY: Hey, as far as I'm concerned, anyone who needs**
24   **a phone number and who calls you is a lucky man.**
25   **EDNA: Thanks.**
26   **HARVEY: And if our kids turn out OK –**
27   **EDNA: If?**
28   **HARVEY: And** *when* **our kids turn out OK, it'll be all**
29   **because of you.**
30   **EDNA: Well, you had a lot to do with –**
31   **HARVEY: I hope they don't end up like me at all. That's** *my*
32   **hope for the future.**
33   **DEAN: I think we're ready to decide your grade.**
34   **STUDENT: But all humans aren't like this. If only you had**

1   met John and Mary.

2   HARVEY: Of course. Show off a couple of bozos you've

3   made life easy for.

4   STUDENT: I gave them the exact same universe I gave you.

5   HARVEY: You sound just like my dad sometimes, you

6   know that?

7   STUDENT: *(To the PROFESSORS)* John and Mary have done

8   so much with their lives.

9   HARVEY: John's the biggest kiss-ass in Dayton.

10   STUDENT: He is not!

11   HARVEY: Oh, yes, he is. Even when he goes to church, it's

12   not to pray. He just wants to suck up to you.

13   PROFESSOR A: I see.

14   HARVEY: And Mary's worse.

15   PROFESSOR B: Is she, Edna?

16   EDNA: Do I have to be honest?

17   DEAN: We'd appreciate it.

18   EDNA: Well then, Mary – who, for the record, no longer

19   has the nose you gave her – I mean, she may spend all

20   day curing people, but have you ever tried to just sit

21   down and have a nice conversation with her? "I

22   healed so many people today, Edna. Of course, not as

23   many as you gave phone numbers to."

24   HARVEY: They're great human beings, all right. I'm sure

25   they would have given you all the answers you

26   wanted.

27   EDNA: And for the rest of our lives, they would have bored

28   us at dinner parties saying, "We helped the Almighty

29   get an A."

30   STUDENT: Can I just say one thing on my behalf?

31   DEAN: Go ahead. This is your chance.

32   HARVEY: Yeah, go ahead.

33   EDNA: Yeah.

34   PROFESSOR B: Please.

1   PROFESSOR A: We're listening.

2   STUDENT: I...um... *(Sighs, then)* **They looked so good on**
3   **paper.**

4   DEAN: **Thank you. We'll caucus now to decide your final**
5   **grade.** *(The TEACHERS gather together and start to*
6   *whisper. We occasionally hear some arguing tones.)*

7   EDNA: **They decide right on the spot?**

8   STUDENT: **Yes.**

9   HARVEY: **What degree are you going for, anyway?**

10   STUDENT: **My M.U.**

11   HARVEY: **M.U.?**

12   STUDENT: **Master of the Universe.** *(We hear some heated*
13   *mumbling.)*

14   PROFESSOR B: **You have to consider the exquisite beauty**
15   **of their design.**

16   PROFESSOR A: **But they're not practical.**

17   HARVEY: *(To the STUDENT)* **Can I ask you a question about**
18   **the universe that has troubled me since I was**
19   **a kid?**

20   STUDENT: **Sure.**

21   HARVEY: **How come there's maple walnut ice cream and**
22   **butter pecan ice cream, instead of maple pecan and**
23   **butter walnut?**

24   STUDENT: **I don't think I can answer that one.**

25   HARVEY: **Nobody can.**

26   DEAN: **Despite all their flaws, they have survived for thou-**
27   **sands and thousands of years.**

28   PROFESSOR B: **And they have such nice feet.**

29   PROFESSOR A: **Their feet are indeed nice. It's from the**
30   **ankles up that they make me nervous.**

31   PROFESSOR B: **Still, their genetic engineering is most**
32   **advanced.**

33   DEAN: **And they're also biodegradable.**

34   HARVEY: *(To EDNA)* **This is going to make some story to**

1   **tell our friends.**
2   **STUDENT: Oh, I'm afraid once you're teleported back to**
3   **Earth, you won't remember a thing.**
4   **HARVEY:** *(To EDNA)* **Oh, well. There goes the movie sale.**
5   **EDNA: And I had already decided what I was going to wear**
6   **on the talk shows.**
7   **HARVEY: Let's face it. We're going to have to spend the rest**
8   **of our lives as average people.**
9   **EDNA:** *(Softly)* **Damn.**
10   **DEAN: Yes, yes, yes. There is much wrong with the project.**
11   **I still don't think it's fair to call the student an**
12   **underachiever.**
13   **PROFESSOR A: I don't know why he created them; they**
14   **serve no useful purpose.**
15   **PROFESSOR B: Maybe they're not perfect, but there is**
16   **something so beautiful and special about them.**
17   **EDNA:** *(To the STUDENT)* **Is it, is it OK if I take off my**
18   **slippers?**
19   **STUDENT: Go right ahead.**
20   **EDNA: Thanks.** *(EDNA takes off her slippers and rubs her*
21   *feet. Without the STUDENT noticing, this gets PROFESSOR*
22   *B's attention.)*
23   **HARVEY: Your bunions acting up again?**
24   **EDNA:** *(Defensively)* **Yes.**
25   **HARVEY: You gotta stop buying those teeny shoes. You**
26   **don't got teeny feet.**
27   **EDNA: I buy shoes the right size.**
28   **HARVEY: No, you don't. You keep insisting your feet are**
29   **smaller than they are. That's why your feet are always**
30   **in such lousy shape.** *(PROFESSOR B walks over to*
31   *EDNA and examines her foot.)*
32   **PROFESSOR B: I'm changing my grade.** *(PROFESSOR B*
33   *returns to the other TEACHERS.)*
34   **EDNA: What did I do?**

1   **STUDENT: Nothing.** *(The TEACHERS end their conference.)*
2   **DEAN: We've decided your grade.** *(The TEACHERS resume*
3   *their previous positions.The STUDENT and the HUMANS*
4   *face them.)*
5   **DEAN: There is much that is commendable about your**
6   **project, both in Earth's evolutionary ability and its**
7   **astonishing variety of beauty. The human being is**
8   **wondrous and fascinating. Nevertheless –**
9   **HARVEY:** *(To EDNA)* **Uh, oh.**
10   **EDNA: Shhh.**
11   **DEAN: The three of us agree that the human being's**
12   **design is tragically flawed. Look at them. They're so**
13   **scared and confused by their own drives. What good**
14   **are all their noble qualities when by adulthood, most**
15   **of them have developed a grudge against life itself?**
16   **I'm afraid we're going to have to give you a C plus.**
17   **STUDENT: C plus?!**
18   **EDNA and HARVEY:** *(Simultaneously)* **C plus?!**
19   **DEAN: I'm sorry.**
20   **HARVEY: Wait a second. We do not live in a C-plus**
21   **universe.**
22   **EDNA: It's at least a B.**
23   **STUDENT: I created fruits and vegetables and birds that**
24   **fly and fish that swim and artists and athletes and**
25   **thinkers and leaders, and all I get is a C plus? I gave**
26   **this project everything I had. Everything!**
27   **PROFESSOR A: Some of us felt the grade was generous.**
28   **HARVEY:** *(To the PROFESSORS)* **All I can say is – it's easy to**
29   **sit back and judge. Real easy. How do you guys know**
30   **you're not just somebody else's science project? Huh?**
31   **Huh? I bet right now some higher being is giving your**
32   **entire dimension a D.**
33   **PROFESSOR B: I don't understand. After all of your**
34   **complaints –**

1   HARVEY: So I was in a bad mood! You got us at a bad time.

2   EDNA: It was just before bedtime.

3   HARVEY: And on Saturday night, if you get my drift.

4   EDNA: Those six minutes mean a lot to us.

5   HARVEY: *(To EDNA, surprised)* They do?

6   EDNA: You know they do.

7   HARVEY: Well, I sorta hoped, but, uh, I never assumed...

8   EDNA: Well, of course.

9   HARVEY: I keep worrying one day they'll come up with a

10   silicon chip –

11   EDNA: No...never.

12   PROFESSOR A: *(Getting ready to go)* I don't see why they go

13   on living. I really don't.

14   EDNA: *(Fed up)* I'll tell you why!

15   DEAN: Why?

16   EDNA: *(Straining hard to think of a reply)* Well...because...

17   *(Suddenly inspired)* because things could get better,

18   that's why!

19   HARVEY: That's right. Things could always get better.

20   PROFESSOR B: And what makes you think that?

21   HARVEY: *(To EDNA)* Tell 'em.

22   EDNA: I haven't the slightest idea. I guess we were just

23   designed that way. When push comes to shove, I guess

24   we were designed to have...faith. *(Everyone looks at the*

25   *STUDENT. He smiles and nods.)*

26   HARVEY: *(To the PROFESSORS)* See? He's not as big a jerk

27   as you think he is.

28   DEAN: I'm sorry. The grade is final.

29   PROFESSOR A: *(To the STUDENT)* You want my advice?

30   Next time, don't design them in your own image. It's

31   very narcissistic. *(PROFESSOR A exits.)*

32   PROFESSOR B: *(To the HUMANS)* Take care of your feet,

33   and always treat cows with respect. *(PROFESSOR B*

34   *exits.)*

1   **DEAN:** *(To the STUDENT)* **Now don't be too hard on your-**
2   **self. You did your best.**
3   **STUDENT: That makes it even more depressing.**
4   **DEAN: It's only a universe. It'll pass.** *(The DEAN exits. The*
5   *STUDENT starts to clean up.)*
6   **EDNA: Uh...I'm sorry if we blew your grade.**
7   **STUDENT: It's my fault. I should've never goofed off on**
8   **the seventh day.**
9   **EDNA: Well, if it means anything, we** *are* **glad you created**
10   **us.**
11   **STUDENT: Are you?...Are you, Harvey?**
12   **HARVEY: Well, all in all, when I think about it, I mean,**
13   **life's not that bad, once you get over the disappoint-**
14   **ment that it stinks.**
15   **STUDENT: I'll remember that.**
16   **HARVEY: So you want to grab a brew?**
17   **STUDENT: I better have you teleported back to Earth.**
18   **HARVEY: Oh, yeah, well, sure.**
19   **EDNA: By the way, if there is such a thing as reincarna-**
20   **tion –**
21   **STUDENT: I really can't discuss such things –**
22   **EDNA: You don't have to tell me, but if it does exist, could**
23   **you bring me back as a bunny rabbit? Everybody likes**
24   **bunny rabbits.**
25   **HARVEY: And could you bring me back as an eagle?**
26   **EDNA: An eagle?**
27   **HARVEY: Yeah. Just once I'd like to fly real high on my**
28   **own power, real high, so I could look down and get a**
29   **clear view of the whole shebang.**
30   **STUDENT: That's a very nice desire, Harvey.**
31   **HARVEY: Yeah, well, I got my moments.**
32   **STUDENT: Shall we go?**
33   **HARVEY: OK.**
34   **STUDENT: After you.** *(HARVEY and EDNA exit. The*

1   *STUDENT is about to go, but then he turns around and*
2   *picks up the globe. Shrugs to himself.)* **I think it's good.**
3   *(The STUDENT sighs, puts the globe under his arm and*
4   *exits. The lights fade.)*
5
6
7
8
9
10
11
12
13
14
15
16
17
18
19
20
21
22
23
24
25
26
27
28
29
30
31
32
33
34

CHAPTER EIGHT

AUDITION MONOLOGS FOR MEN AND WOMEN

"Calm down! Only your whole career depends on this scene!"

— Alfred Hitchcock

The anticipated success of the actor's audition monolog involves much more than just a basic appreciation of traditional theatrical techniques or an understanding of the basic principles of playscript interpretation. Indeed, the successful audition monolog is carefully researched, staged, and "voiced" with a performance knowledge and experience that is polished and positive. Before discussing a specific performance blueprint that the actor needs to pursue in preparing for the audition or the "call-back," let's review the primary ingredients involved in conventional calls or casting tryouts for a production.

Long before the actual auditions are posted for a call, the director may have already begun to "see" and to "hear" the characters in the playscript and think of the audition as a simple, efficient device to discover "who" among the assembled performers most clearly resembles the director's initial concept (vocal/physical) of the stage figures being cast. The audition process in this respect is very similar to a job interview, except that in the audition the actor is *performing* answers to the questions asked by the director! It is important, therefore, to devise an orderly personal and professional system of preparation and rehearsal that will address any potential audition scenario, especially those devoted to such additional audition elements like the "interview" that may follow the monolog, the "improvisation" that may be requested, or the "movement sequence" demonstration that is typically a part of the audition occasion.

The actor should consider the audition as a "conversation" in which a number of talents — voice, body, movement, intellect, sensitivity, and interpretation — are on display *simultaneously* in a rather limited audition time frame of three to five minutes!

It is essential in the audition monolog to immediately project a stage pres-ence that is memorable for its radiant aura of authenticity and to promote that indescribable "life spirit" of the character being portrayed in an honest, natural, spontaneous, and familiar performance.

That is why it is essential to immediately project a stage presence that is memorable for its radiant aura of authenticity and to promote that indescribable "life spirit" of the character being portrayed in an honest, natural, spontaneous, and familiar performance. Because there are as many methods of conducting auditions as there are imaginative and demanding directors, the following performance blueprint is provided as a working model for the actor who wishes to score a favorable — and lasting — impression using the audition monolog.

At first, it is well to read the monolog like a *story*, with an active ear for interpretation hints or clues to the locale, time period, and given circumstances of the selected episode or incident. The first reading should indicate the character's intellectual and emotional thought, and should reveal the degree of personal association or familiarity that is needed by the actor to perform the character description with naturalness and accuracy. A second reading of the monolog should be more critical and objective than the first, and should concentrate on discovering the inherent "meaning" and any implied "subtext" being conveyed in the words or the actions of the character. The second reading invariably reveals the character's point of view in the monolog and may help the actor to detail the visual and aural approach needed to clearly define characterization as well.

As valuable as all of these preliminary investigations may be, however, the actor's most vital performance resource remains "self-image" enriched by personal imagination and creativity. The style of audition performance needs to be carefully rehearsed to mirror a relaxed and yet distinctly professional manner; and there should be no evidence of an overly precise use of the voice, exaggerated movement, or theatrical posing. Remember that the *actor's* primary objective of the audition is to demonstrate a "performance personality" that is capable of achieving that "indescribable" character the director has already begun to imagine as part of the stage figures in the production. It would help, of course, if the actor's audition also featured a memorable character performance that was infectious, spontaneous, and true-to-life!

The actor's expectations for preparation and performance should also include attention to the following basic principles of "audition etiquette" to observe in promoting a healthy and competitive attitude in presenting monologs publicly as part of the audition process. For instance, general or "open" audition monologs are memorized and a time limit may be posted. If possible, try to become acquainted with the actual audition space before the scheduled audition time; and don't litter the audition or the space with extraneous costumes, props, taped music, furniture, theatrical makeup, or other distracting accessories. Remain faithful to the dialog of the playscript and avoid ad-libbing a character's lines; or, if there are unavoidable mistakes in voicing the dialog, try to continue the lines and incorporate the mistakes into the characterization if possible. Give thought also to the "physical" life of the character as well as to the speech of the character; and "warm up" the emotional, intellectual, physical, and vocal demands of the monolog *before* the audition rather than during the audition!

The style of audition performance needs to be carefully rehearsed to mirror a relaxed and yet distinctly professional manner; and there should be no evidence of an overly precise use of the voice, exaggerated movement, or theatrical posing.

Additional dimensions of performance expectations to make regarding monologs relate to how the character looks, speaks, and moves during the audition. It will be important, therefore, for the actor to have ease and freedom of movement, to project vocal variety as well as vocal control, and to demonstrate an emotional honesty and concentration that suggests the potential for a realistic, stage-worthy performance. The actor's preparation for the audition should include sensory responses that may help to enrich the tempo of the monolog. It would also be wise to review the general characteristics associated with "playing the role," discussed in Chapter 2, and "playing the scene," discussed in Chapter 3, before allowing an uninformed performance technique to reveal itself in the public audition.

The monologs that follow are representative of the competitive material the actor might select for audition performance. As part of the preparation for performance, however, it will be necessary to read the *complete* playscript in order to determine the special context in which the monolog reveals the character's intention, motivation, or point of view in this isolated moment of time, place, and action. Remember that each monolog is an intimate, fleeting glance of an individual character whose brief time on stage must be "focused" directly toward the audience to achieve its most immediate, meaningful impact. Assume an audition performance attitude that concentrates on the "present" moment and embraces the character as if playing the role for the "first time" to achieve the most memorable theatrical response.

The selected monologs have also been compiled to provide a convenient beginning, middle, and end for each episode; and a preliminary character analysis, evaluation, and interpretation has been provided to stimulate distinction and individuality in the performance. The actor should not leave everything to imagination, however, but should remain alert to events in everyday life or casual observation to more completely define each character, or to more completely delineate each character intention in the monolog. After all, as the professional actor/director Tom Markus reminds us in the *Professional Actor:* "Your audition is the second most important performance you will give. The opening night performance, or the one that gets reviewed, is the most important. If you give a poor performance at the audition, you'll never have an opportunity to give another!"

from *The Actor's Nightmare* ©
by Christopher Durang

A rather timid young adult accountant named George
Spelvin is suddenly pushed center stage to replace an ailing
actor, victim of a car accident, in this uproarious theatre spoof of
"the show must go on!" — apparently at *any* cost! The playbill for
the evening may be Noel Coward's *Private Lives,* Samuel
Beckett's *Checkmate,* or William Shakespeare's *Hamlet,* but in
the chaos and confusion that ensues, who can really tell? George,
costumed as Hamlet in this monolog, fumbles through one
missed cue after another, stumbles all over the stage setting, and
mumbles his lines of dialog so miserably that the rest of the cast
jumps ship before this leaking theatre craft sinks from the
weight of heavy-handed theatrics and bombastic acting. The
monolog, however, is a grand moment for the actor to summon
forth inventive stage business or vocal/bodily actions to reinforce the absurdity of the moment and the insanity of the
performer.

In playing the monolog the actor may wish to review the
"presentational" style of performance discussed in Chapter 2
and make *no* attempt to present the hilarious stage action as if it
were "lifelike," or may devise a performance blueprint that is

"nonrealistic" and rely more frankly on the theatrical and audience-centered manners, movements, or behaviors that might be appropriate to the Shakespearean character being portrayed in this episode. There are also imaginative performance opportunities for the actor to indulge in artificial posing or posturing, to take extended pauses following mishaps, and to engage in boisterous buffoonery to indicate the amateurish nature of the character/performer. The actor should be cautious, however, not to allow the performance to become a comic caricature. There still must be a sense of control and discipline in the interpretation and in the theatrical execution that is more than a one-dimensional display of vocal and physical anxiety and apprehension of the character being thrust into this ludicrous situation. Moderation and restraint can be meaningful performance principles as well; and the disciplined actor will emphasize the urgency or the futility of the significant moments in the monolog rather than the madness and the mayhem.

1   GEORGE: Oh, don't go. *(Pause; smiles uncomfortably at the*
2   *audience.)* **Maybe someone else will come out in a**
3   **minute.** *(Pause)* **Of course, sometimes people have**
4   **soliloquies in Shakespeare. Let's just wait a moment**
5   **more and maybe someone will come.** *(The lights*
6   *suddenly change to a dim blue background and one*
7   *bright, white spot Center Stage. GEORGE is not standing*
8   *in the spot.)* **Oh, dear.** *(He moves somewhat awkwardly*
9   *into the spot, decides to do his best to live up to the*
10   *requirements of the moment.)* **To be or not to be, that is**
11   **the question.** *(Doesn't know anymore.)* **Oh, maid!** *(No*
12   *response; remembers that actors call for "line.")* **Line.**
13   **Line! Ohhh. Oh, what a rogue and peasant slave am I.**
14   **Whether 'tis nobler in the mind's eye to kill oneself,**
15   **or not killing oneself, to sleep a great deal. We are**
16   **such stuff as dreams are made on; and our lives are**
17   **rounded by a little sleep.** *(The lights change. The spot*
18   *goes out, and another one comes up Stage Right.*
19   *GEORGE moves into it.)* **Uh, thrift, thrift, Horatio.**
20   **Neither a borrower nor a lender be. But to thine own**
21   **self be true. There is a special providence in the fall**
22   **of a sparrow. Extraordinary how potent cheap music**
23   **can be. Out, out, damn spot! I come to wive it**
24   **wealthily in Padua; if wealthily, then happily in**
25   **Padua.** *(Sings.)* **Brush up your Shakespeare; start**
26   **quoting him now; Da da...** *(Lights change again. That*
27   *spot goes off; another one comes on Center Stage, though*
28   *closer to audience. GEORGE moves into that.)* **I wonder**
29   **whose yacht that is. How was China? Very large,**
30   **China. How was Japan? Very small, Japan. I pledge**
31   **allegiance to the flag of the United States of America**
32   **and to the republic for which it stands, one nation,**
33   **under God, indivisible with liberty and justice for all.**
34   **Line! Line! Oh, my God!** *(Gets idea.)* **O my God, I am**

1	heartily sorry for having offended thee, and I detest
2	all my sins because I dread the loss of heaven and the
3	pains of hell! But most of all because they offend
4	thee, my God, who are all good and deserving of all
5	my love. And I resolve to confess my sins, to do
6	penance, and to amend my life, Amen. *(Friendly)*
7	That's the act of contrition that Catholic school chil-
8	dren say in confession in order to be forgiven for
9	their sins. Catholic adults say it too, I imagine. I don't
10	know any Catholic adults. Line! *(Explaining)* When
11	you call for a line, the stage manager normally gives
12	you your next line, to refresh your memory. Line! The
13	quality of mercy is not strained. It droppeth as the
14	gentle rain upon the place below, when we have shuf-
15	fled off this mortal coil. Alas, poor Yorick. I knew him
16	well. Get thee to a nunnery. Line. Nunnery. As a child,
17	I was taught by nuns, and then in high school I was
18	taught by Benedictine priests. I really rather liked
19	the nuns, they were sort of warm, though they were
20	fairly crazy too. Line. I liked the priests also. The
21	school was on the grounds of the monastery, and my
22	junior and senior years I spent a few weekends
23	joining in the daily routine of the monastery –
24	prayers, then breakfast, then prayers, then lunch,
25	then prayers, then dinner, then prayers, then sleep. I
26	found the predictability quite attractive. And the food
27	was good. I was going to join the monastery after high
28	school, but they said I was too young and should wait.
29	And then I just stopped believing in all those things,
30	so I never did join the monastery. I became an
31	accountant. I've studied logarithms, and cosine and
32	tangent... *(Irritated)* Line! *(Apologetic)* I'm sorry. This is
33	supposed to be *Hamlet* or *Private Lives* or something,
34	and I keep rattling on like a maniac. I really do

1   apologize. **I just don't recall attending a single**
2   **rehearsal. I can't imagine what I was doing. And also**
3   **you came expecting to see Edwin Booth and you get**
4   **me. I really am very embarrassed. Sorry.** *Line!* **It's a**
5   **far, far better place I go to than I have ever been**
6   **before.** *(Sings the alphabet song.)* **A, b, c, d, e, f, g, h, i, j,**
7   **k, l, m, n, o, p, q, r, s, t...** *(As he starts to sing, enter ELLEN*
8   *TERRY, dragging two large garbage cans. She puts them*
9   *side by side, gets in one.)* **Oh, God. Are you Ophelia? Get**
10   **thee to a nunnery.** *(She points to the other garbage can,*
11   *indicating he should get in it.)* **Get in? OK.** *(He does.)*
12   **This must be one of those modern** *Hamlets*. *(Lights*
13   *change abruptly to "Beckett lighting.")*
14
15
16
17
18
19
20
21
22
23
24
25
26
27
28
29
30
31
32
33
34

from *A Woman Called Truth* ©
by Sandra Fenichel Asher

The well-documented, historical figure of the African-American adult woman Sojourner Truth is an inspiring chronicle of faith, courage, and indomitable will that is warmed by the simplicity of compassion and understanding at its shining, gentle best. Sold away from her family as a slave, she later regained her freedom and embarked upon a remarkable campaign to pull together the shattered strands of her life. In the triumphant journey, she also became a truly persuasive advocate for abolition and women's rights; and was a monumental force in helping to resist the disturbing lessons which a study of the past history of slavery so clearly reveals.

This narrative monolog — recalled as an older adult — paints an incisive portrait of "Sojourner," the woman, who has become increasingly restive and disturbed by the poverty of charity and compassion she has witnessed in her detractors, and "Truth," the prophet, who ordains with superior intellect and gifted revelation that social salvation is at hand. In playing the monolog, the actor must take into account the historical perspective of the character and pay attention to the significant tradition that is part of this character's heritage. There should *not*, however, be a conscious performance blueprint that seeks to "re-create" the historical figure in terms of vocal/physical qualities, manners, or behaviors that might have been discovered in an archeological study of historical events.

Sojourner Truth was, after all, a flesh-and-blood human being — sometimes cynical in her wit and sometimes deeply affecting in her wisdom — who should emerge in performance with the warmth, humor, and conviction that characterized her authentic life. It it important, therefore, to approach the monolog with directness and simplicity; and to envision a performance blueprint that expresses universal human qualities which might suggest a stage character "like us today." A convenient starting point for the actor is to determine the character's emotional *and* psychological state in this monolog and to explore the inner limits of the character's obvious human suffering with a fierce determination that reveals courage and dignity in the gruesome face of oppression.

1   **SOJOURNER:** *(Resuming narrative)* **I began walking east**
2   **again, as I'd walked before toward freedom. Though I**
3   **could neither read nor write, I could talk and I could**
4   **sing. I would wander the country, talking and**
5   **singing, until the people heard, and understood, and**
6   **made wrong things right. In parlors and in lecture**
7   **halls, on street corners and in revival tents, I told my**
8   **story – as I'm telling it to you – to any and all with a**
9   **moment to listen. I spoke out against slavery and**
10   **poverty and ignorance. I cried out for justice.**
11   **"Sojourner," I became, a wanderer among the**
12   **people. "Lord," I cried, "Thy name is truth," and I**
13   **took for my own the name of my last and greatest and**
14   **only master. My name, my free name, my own name:**
15   **Sojourner Truth.** *(She speaks from lectern as if*
16   *addressing a public gathering. Others ad-lib responses as*
17   *at opening.)* **Children, I have come here tonight like**
18   **the rest of you, to hear what I have got to say.** *(She*
19   *laughs at her own joke.)* **Children, I talk to God, and**
20   **God talks to me. I go out and talk to God in the fields**
21   **and the woods. This morning I was walking out, and**
22   **I got over the fence. I saw the wheat holding up its**
23   **head, looking very big. I went up and took hold of it.**
24   **You believe it? There was no wheat there! I said, "God,**
25   **what is the matter with this wheat?" And He says to**
26   **me, "Sojourner, there's a little weevil in it." Now, I**
27   **hear talk about the Constitution and the rights of**
28   **man. I come up and I take hold of this Constitution. It**
29   **looks mighty big and I feel for my rights, but there**
30   **aren't any there. Then I say, "God, what *ails* this**
31   **Constitution?" And He says to me, "Sojourner, there's**
32   **a little weevil in it." Well, now, don't these little**
33   **weevils just eat up this country's crop?** *(Others*
34   *applaud. She steps to side of lectern.)*

1   In my travels, I met Frederick Douglass, fighting
2 **for the black people, and Susan B. Anthony, fighting**
3 **for the woman's right to vote. Harriet Beecher Stowe,**
4 **Ulysses S. Grant.** *(She takes a small book from her*
5 *pocket and shows it.)* **Got all their autographs right**
6 **here. I call this my Book of Life.** *(She opens book and*
7 *runs her fingers over a signature, reciting rather than*
8 *reading.)* **Says "October 29, 1864," doesn't it? "A.**
9 **Lincoln."** *(She smiles affectionately at the page.)* **Shook**
10 **his hand at the White House. Yes, I did. I said, "Mr.**
11 **Lincoln, I never heard of you before you ran for pres-**
12 **ident." He said, "Sojourner, I have heard of *you*."** *(She*
13 *pauses, saddened.)* **Saw him one last time...to say good-**
14 **bye. Rest well, Father Abraham. So much done; so**
15 **much left to do.** *(She returns to the cube RD of the*
16 *podium, where she sits as at the opening of the play.*
17 *Others take their places for final scene as if gathering for*
18 *a public meeting.)*
19   **It was with Frances Gage at a women's rights**
20 **convention in Ohio that I gave one special talk of**
21 **mine. Some folks liked it; plenty didn't. But every-**
22 **body listened, and they all remembered.**
23
24
25
26
27
28
29
30
31
32
33
34

from *The Transfiguration of Benno Blimpie* ©

by Albert Innaurato

A shocking and shattering recital of the pathetic life of a young man who is considered a "freak" by others, the monolog that follows is a powerful and thoroughly haunting confession of a social misfit in isolation from the world at large. Benno Blimpie, a youth weighing five-hundred pounds, desperately unhappy, unloved, and unfulfilled, is literally eating himself to death while barricaded in his room. Rejected by his family and a society which ridicules him, Benno sits Center Stage and watches with fascination and bitterness as scenes from his early life are played out all around him. Scene after gruesome scene details his hopeless failure as a human being; and heaps derision and scorn upon him and his twisted, tormented life.

In playing the monolog the actor should give *no* thought to the character's excessive — perhaps theatrically exaggerated — physical portrait. The primary performance principle here is an interpretation of the character's mood, attitude, and point of view in the given circumstances. It is important to understand the effect that behavior, heredity, and society may have had on conditioning the character's action(s) in the monolog; and to realize that beneath the character's apparently gross and distorted exterior is a sensitive, caring human being with very real and urgent thoughts and emotions that cry out for attention and compassion.

The actor needs to look beyond the superficial trappings of the character's isolation, frustration, and humiliation to approach the role with *sensitivity* and *selectivity*. It may be a good idea to chart the vocal and physical changes that appear to take place in the character during the monolog, and to visualize the character as objectively as a scientist might record an experiment. The actor may also wish to review the exercise "And the 'Beat' Goes On," in Chapter 9, to discover the potential "action maps" that might help to chart the character's alternating intentions in the monolog as well; and to address significant character turns in action, thought, or mood with corresponding bodily responses, vocal/physical changes, gestures, or inventive stage business that provide additional relief in the monolog's tempo and staging. All of these potential performance principles, hopefully, may provide valuable insights and reveal the subtext of the character's point of view in this enterprising monolog.

1   **BENNO:** *(He starts slowly, with little expression.)* **Benno**
2   **loved to draw. And he loved drawings. As soon as he**
3   **was old enough he stole car fare from his mother's**
4   **purse and went to the big museum. He snuck in. He**
5   **ran to the Renaissance paintings. And he stared at**
6   **them. He stared at their designs, most particularly at**
7   **their designs. And at their colors. But the designs to**
8   **begin with were the most significant to him. The**
9   **circle, for instance, fascinated him; and the right**
10   **angle as used in a painting like "The Last Supper"**
11   **thrilled him. He would trace the angles and the**
12   **circles in these paintings with his fingers when the**
13   **guards weren't looking. Then, on paper napkins and**
14   **the dirty lined paper from the Catholic school, he**
15   **would make designs like those. He draws arcs and**
16   **circles, and angles and lines trying to vary them with**
17   **the deception and subtlety of the masters. He wasn't**
18   **interested in drawing people. He knew what they**
19   **looked like. Think of the structure of the foot. The**
20   **lines bend, then they curve. The arch juts up, then**
21   **juts down; two angles, like a roof. Underneath there**
22   **is the inverse. The sole is like a barreled vault. Then,**
23   **at the front, five straight lines – but with rounded**
24   **tips. Benno drew idealized feet, or distorted them in**
25   **his own way. He was not interested in the imperfec**
26   **tions of real feet. Benno's make-believe feet were**
27   **curved or gracefully inclined. Real feet are crooked**
28   **and crushed. One day, out of guilt, Bennos' pop-pop**
29   **bought him a paint set with a Social Security check**
30   **that bounced or something and caused some discom-**
31   **fort. Benno painted – he colored in his designs. He**
32   **painted hour upon hour. He lulled himself asleep**
33   **planning paintings as though they were battle**
34   **campaigns. He dreamed colored designs and designs**

1   of colors and waking, tried to copy these. Once, once
2   when he had finished painting six straight lines care-
3   fully, he stared at his painting and heard...heard
4   music played up the back of his spine. It made no
5   difference. When he had finished a painting, Benno
6   was still fat, ugly, and alone. Nothing makes a differ-
7   ence, nothing alters anything. It took Benno a very
8   long time to learn this. And Benno wasn't sure he had
9   learned it, really, until he started eating himself to
10   death. Then Benno knew he had learned. For all that
11   matters is the taste of our own flesh. It tastes
12   horrible, particularly if we are fat and sweat a lot. But
13   there are no disappointments there; and those feel-
14   ings of horror and disgust at chewing ourselves are
15   the only feelings we can be sure of. Benno will put his
16   eyes out soon. Then there will be no seductive angles
17   or circles. Benno will be left to stumble about his
18   filthy room, the windows nailed shut, biting at
19   himself. Thank you.
20
21
22
23
24
25
26
27
28
29
30
31
32
33
34

from *The Baltimore Waltz* ©
by Paula Vogel

Encore! This monolog is from Scene One of the delicious comedy/drama *The Baltimore Waltz* that is included in the Chapter 6 scenes for young adult women. Here, however, the featured character is Carl, the young adult man whose fatal HIV illness inspired his sister to write the playscript as a lasting tribute to the imaginary "dream vacation" the author and her brother were never able to share. Carl is the head librarian of literature and languages at the San Francisco Public Library; an intelligent, sensitive, professional who speaks six languages. He is also a devoted educator and teacher who sets high standards for the children in his class. His recent illness, however, has taken an obvious toll on his energy and now he musters up a last round of courage and conviction to share with his young students and their visiting parents the awful truth revealed in the monolog: he has been suspended from his position!

In what has to be the most hilarious, outrageous grade school farewell ever voiced in a public library with parents in stunned silence, Carl percolates with flavorful tidbits of revelation and revenge as he shares the recent news of his suspension with the youthful, innocent, and unsuspecting children. He speaks out on issues grade school youngsters could not possibly comprehend; but his satiric tirade is filled with colorful language and intoxicating innuendo that is sure to be an adult crowd-pleaser. The children are attentive, even spellbound by the presentation and Carl abruptly exits with a flourish — unapologetic and unavailable for further comments, thank you!

In playing the monolog it is important for the actor to

remain in the "here and now" of the library/classroom setting, and to treat the dialog in a more conversational, personal tone of voice to suggest intimacy and quiet urgency. The dialog does not actively suggest forceful gestures or bodily actions to call attention to the piercing wit of the lines; and the actor should avoid distracting facial expressions or cliché posing or posturing. Finally, the actor should practice economy in the use of subtle actions or reactions to suggest the "private and personal" nature of this single, solitary character's confession to the children; and the actor should allow the character to pay the price of this tragedy with an exit that has dignity as well as comic delight in having spoken the last word on the subject.

1   CARL: Good morning, boys and girls. It's Monday
2   morning, and it's time for "Reading Hour With Uncle
3   Carl" once again, here at the North Branch of the San
4   Francisco Public Library. This is going to be a special
5   reading hour. It's my very last reading hour with you.
6   Friday will be my very last day with the San Francisco
7   Public Library as children's librarian. Why? Do any of
8   you know what a pink slip is? *(Holds up a rectangle of*
9   *pink.)* It means I'm going on a paid leave of absence
10   for two weeks. Shelley Bizio, the branch supervisor,
11   has given me my very own pink slip. I got a pink slip
12   because I wear this. *(Points to a pink triangle on his*
13   *lapel.)* A pink triangle. Now, I want you all to take the
14   pink construction paper in front of you, and take
15   your scissors, and cut out pink triangles. There's tape
16   at every table, so you can wear them too! Make some
17   for Mom and Dad, and your brothers and sisters. Very
18   good. Very good, Fabio. Oh, that's a beautiful pink
19   triangle, Tse Heng. Now before we read our last story
20   together, I thought we might have a sing-along. Your
21   parents can join in, if they'd like to. Oh, don't be shy.
22   Let's do "Here We Go Round the Mulberry Bush."
23   Remember that one? *(Begins to sing. He also demon-*
24   *strates.)* "Here we go round the mulberry bush, the
25   mulberry bush, the mulberry bush; Here we go round
26   the mulberry bush, so early in the morning." "This is
27   the way we pick our nose, pick our nose, pick our
28   nose; This is the way we pick our nose, so early in the
29   morning." Third verse! *(Makes a rude gesture with his*
30   *middle finger.)* "This is the way we go on strike, go on
31   strike, go on strike; This is the way we go on strike, so
32   early in the – "What, Mrs. Bizio? I may leave immedi-
33   ately? I do not have to wait until Friday to collect
34   unemployment? Why, thank you, Mrs. Bizio. Well,

boys and girls, Mrs. Bizio will take over now. Bear with her, she's personality impaired. I want you to be very good and remember me. I'm leaving for an immediate vacation with my sister on the east coast, and I'll think of you as I travel. Remember to wear those triangles. *(To his supervisor)* I'm going. I'm going. You don't have to be rude. They enjoyed it. We'll take it up with the union. *(Shouting)* In a language you might understand, up-pay ours-yay!

from *Special Offer* ©
by Harold Pinter

Here's an offer you won't be able to refuse! Harold Pinter presents an interesting monolog that uses striking and unexpected role reversal to punctuate his social, highly satirical, point of view on the commercialism of the sexes from a woman's point of view. The obvious tongue-in-cheek British humor may be a trifle droll at first, but with continued rereading the actor will discover that the given circumstances are filled with subtle and wry opportunities to explore sophisticated performance approaches to genteel comedy in a "risk-free" rehearsal period. There is also interesting character subtext here to unravel in what appears to be a delicately textured but highly unsolvable "personal issue" that involves a young adult woman. The lady in question, a secretary for the British Broadcasting Corporation (BBC), has received a most unusual "special offer" while visiting a rest room at the fashionable Swan and Edgars.

In playing the monolog it is important to recognize the rather provocative nature of this unsolicited offer to a very prim, proper, and professional English secretary. What are the social implications? What are the — horrors! — potential consequences? These are the intriguing implications that need to be considered as the unpleasant incident is later cautiously shared with an office colleague; and there may be some indication to suggest that the offer may have some appeal. In playing the monolog, the actor may need to suggest the potential relationship between "risk" and "need" that might give this apparently colorless character a sense of vulnerability as well as a meaningful sense of Pinter's subtle shuffling of on- and off-stage absurdities that may masquerade for realities. Remember, also, that the anticipated comic response will be more of a wry smile than a belly laugh; so be simple and sincere in your performance blueprint to transform the "unfamiliar" events of the monolog into the more "familiar" character actions that express common truths recognized by all. Finally, the actor may wish to review the basic principles of the "mimetic instinct," discussed in some detail in Chapter 1, to suggest that the monolog is a "picture" of the reality experienced, interpreted, and related to others by the character — it may not be reality at all.

1 SECRETARY: *(At a desk in an office)* **Yes, I was in the rest**
2 **room at Swan and Edgars, having a little rest. Just**
3 **sitting there, interfering with nobody, when this old**
4 **crone suddenly came right up to me and sat beside**
5 **me. You're on the staff of the BBC, she said, aren't**
6 **you? I've got just the thing for you, she said, and put a**
7 **little card into my hand. Do you know what was**
8 **written on it? MEN FOR SALE! What on earth do you**
9 **mean? I said. Men, she said, all sorts, shapes and**
10 **sizes, for sale. What on earth could you *possibly***
11 ***mean?* I said. It's an international congress, she said,**
12 **got up for the entertainment and relief of lady**
13 **members of the civil service. You can hear some of**
14 **the boys we've got speak through a microphone, espe-**
15 **cially for your pleasure, singing little folk tunes we're**
16 **sure you've never heard before. Tea is on the house**
17 **and every day we have the very best pastries. For the**
18 **cabaret at tea time the boys do a rare dance imported**
19 **all the way from Buenos Aires, dressed in nothing but**
20 **a pair of cricket pads. Every single one of them is**
21 **tried and tested, very best quality, and at very reason-**
22 **able rates. If you like one of them by any of his**
23 **individual characteristics you can buy him, but for**
24 **you not at retail price. As you work for the BBC we'll**
25 **be glad to make a special reduction. If you're at all**
26 **dissatisfied you can send him back within seven days**
27 **and have your money refunded. That's very *kind* of**
28 **you, I said, but, as a matter of fact, I've just been on**
29 **leave, I start work tomorrow and am perfectly**
30 **refreshed. And I left her where she was. Men for Sale!**
31 **What an extraordinary idea! I've never heard of**
32 **anything so outrageous, have you? Look – here's the**
33 **card. *(Pause)* Do you think it's a joke...or serious?**
34

from *Scene of Shipwreck* ©
by Pamela Mills

A brutally powerful and incisive description of an incestuous family relationship, *Scene of Shipwreck* is set in the early 1980s in the desolate "bushveld" of South Africa. Daphne, the young adult woman featured in the narrative monolog that follows, and her sister were both violated by their callous and calculating father, John, when they were younger. The "unspeakable" acts are surely known by family members on some level of recognition or repression — but there is a conspiracy of silence to keep past events a buried secret. In this monolog, Daphne — now in her thirties — describes an argument with her abusive ex-husband Robert to her younger sister Ruth, who is now in her late twenties.

The exchange is chilling and yet beautifully illustrates the apparent resilience of Daphne's indomitable spirit at odds with the Pandora's box of a troubled past. "Robert," however, is a fiction — a desperate, escapist game that Daphne now plays to keep herself sane, and to dull the painful memories of her childhood. Her role models are the *femme fatales* of "True Confessions" magazines that now provide the diversions needed to exorcise the guilt and remorse which has plagued her, it seems, *all* her life. Unfortunately her father's control over her remains so complete that even her private fantasies cannot escape his intruding influence.

In playing the monolog the actor should use careful vocal and physical pacing of the character's dialog to clearly indicate shifting moods and attitudes that build to a climax; and there should be some attention paid to the degree to which the actor may personally relate to this character's past history and current given circumstances. However, it is more important to initially explore the character's feelings, thoughts, and emotions in the rehearsal period, and to discover an honest and authentic performance blueprint that suggests the "inner truth" of the character's secret dreams and private nightmares. Remember that your primary performance goal in playing the monolog is to give the "appearance" of action, character, and situation rather than the actual events themselves. So strive for an inventive performance approach that emphasizes honest emotional intensity and intimacy as well. The actor should also feel comfortable relating any appropriate or significant "emotional memories" that might give depth and dimension to an interpretation of the character and the subsequent performance.

1   DAPHNE: When we first met, Robert was so sweet. He
2   used to bring me flowers every time. He was always so
3   considerate. Once I was wearing a dress and he said,
4   "I don't think you should be wearing that." I said,
5   "But it's the fashion – everyone's wearing this kind of
6   thing this summer." And he put his arms around me,
7   and kissed my neck and said, "You're not everyone.
8   You're my special girl. Do it just for me." And he was
9   so sweet and gentle, I did it. Just to please him.
10   One time we were going somewhere. And just as we
11   were leaving, I remembered I had to phone a friend –
12   Irene – to make an arrangement with her. She wasn't
13   at home. She was at her boyfriend Jonathan's, so I
14   called her there, and he answered the phone. We
15   spoke a little while, then Irene came on the phone. I'd
16   been out with Jonathan a few times and Robert hated
17   him and that whole crowd. "Full of nonsense," he
18   said. "They think they're a cut above the rest of us."
19   When I got off the phone he was in such a temper.
20   "Just get in the car," he yelled and slammed the door.
21   As he drove, he got more and more worked up. "All I
22   hear these days is Jonathan Jonathan Jonathan," he
23   screamed. I just sat there. I didn't know what to do,
24   what to say. He was being so unreasonable. Then he
25   hit me. With the back of his hand across the face.
26   While he was driving. I was so...I'd never seen him
27   like that before. I mean he'd been jealous, but never
28   like that. So I just sat there. I didn't say a word, I was
29   so shocked, and the tears began to roll down my face,
30   and I couldn't stop them, and the more I couldn't
31   make them stop, the angrier I got. I was sobbing and
32   sobbing and I couldn't look at him...I felt so...humili-
33   ated. And then he pulled the car over and stopped. I
34   turned to look at him – I wasn't sure what he was

1   going to do. He had tears in his eyes, he was crying
2   himself. He said he was sorry, would I forgive him,
3   he'd never do it again. He looked so pathetic. I
4   believed him.
5
6
7
8
9
10
11
12
13
14
15
16
17
18
19
20
21
22
23
24
25
26
27
28
29
30
31
32
33
34

from *Fires in the Mirror* ©
"Anonymous Girl: Look in the Mirror"
by Anna Deavere Smith

A "poetic" retelling of the simmering tensions in the racially polarized events that revolve around several days in the 1991 riots in the Crown Heights section of Brooklyn — after a young African-American child was killed by a car in a rabbi's motorcade and a Jewish student was slain in retaliation — this monolog is a sensitive and plaintive look at the ethnic turmoil as seen through the eyes of a young African-American girl torn between the different cultures living in the community at the time of the social upheaval. It is a compelling view of racial and class conflict in the contemporary "urban jungle," and reveals the innermost feelings and intimate views of the victims themselves. Drawing verbatim accounts from interviews with gangs, social activists, street people, residents, and religious leaders, the author weaves a spirited tapestry of fear, mistrust, frustration, and rancor that should touch every citizen regardless of race, color, or creed.

The young African-American girl's point of view is fearless, proud, matter-of-fact, without surrendering either her personal integrity or sense of humor. Her observations crackle with biting social commentary and reflect clear-cut, no-nonsense assessments of herself as well as her Hispanic school classmates. Her's is a voice of the troubled times: sometimes irreverent, but always direct and spontaneous. She is, quite simply, an anonymous girl looking in the mirror — and reflecting the life she lives *every* day of the year.

In an interpretation of this monolog the actor needs to cultivate an intimate and introspective performance blueprint that avoids exaggeration of superficiality in dialect, vocal quality, or attitude. The "documentary" nature of the monolog suggests that the point of view of the character should reveal itself naturally, as if a camera snapshot "negative" were being developed and enlarged in a candid interpretation and performance. It may be appropriate to feature greater awareness of the tempo and the emphasis upon the "poetic" dialog and to distinguish the character's natural, rhythmic patterns of voicing thoughts and emotions from the everyday speech patterns of more traditional stage figures. Any personal performance additions like distinctive habits, mannerisms, or personality traits should be included *only* if they are complementary in helping to complete the already well-documented, well-drawn character portrait revealed in the monolog.

1   When I look in the mirror...
2   I don't know.
3   How did I find out I was Black...
4   *(Tongue sound)*
5   When I grew up and I look in the mirror and saw I was
6   Black.
7   When I look at my parents,
8   That's how I knew I was Black.
9   Look at my skin.
10 You Black?
11 Black is beautiful.
12 I don't know.
13 That's what I always say.
14 I think White is beautiful too.
15 But I think Black is beautiful too.
16 In my class nobody is White, everybody's Black,
17 and some of them is Hispanic.
18 In my class
19 you can't call any of them Puerto Ricans.
20 They despise Puerto Ricans, I don't know why.
21 They think that Puerto Ricans are stuck up and
22   everything.
23 They say, Oh My Gosh my nail broke, look at that cute
24   guy and everything.
25 But they act like that themselves.
26 They act just like White girls.
27 Black girls is not like that.
28 Please, you should be in my class.
29 Like they say that Puerto Ricans act like that
30 and they don't see that they act like that themselves.
31 Black girls, they do bite off the Spanish girls,
32 they bite off of your clothes.
33 You don't know what that means? biting off?
34 Like biting off somebody's clothes

1   Like cop, following,
2   and last year they used to have a lot of girls like that.
3   They come to school with a style, right?
4   And if they see another girl with that style?
5   Oh my gosh look at her.
6   What she think she is,
7   she tryin' to bite off of me in some way
8   no don't be bitin' off my sneakers
9   or like that.
10 Or doin' a hair style
11 I mean Black people are into hair styles.
12 So they come to school, see somebody with a certain style,
13 they say uh-huh I'm gonna get me one just like that un-huh,
14 that's the way Black people are
15 Yea-ah!
16 They don't like people doing that to them
17 and they do that to other people,
18 so the Black girls will follow the Spanish girls.
19 The Spanish girls don't bite off of us.
20 Some of the Black girls follow them.
21 But they don't mind
22 They don't care.
23 They follow each other.
24 Like there's three girls in my class,
25 they from the Dominican Republic.
26 They all stick together like glue.
27 They all three best friends.
28 They don't follow nobody,
29 like there's none of them lead or anything.
30 They don't hang around us either.
31 They're
32 by themselves.
33
34

from **K 2** ©

by Patrick Meyers

One of the most thought-provoking and widely debated Broadway dramas in recent history, this brilliant and perceptive playscript seizes on the metaphor of "mountain climbing" to explore the more profound theme of an individual's right to choose life or death in any given circumstance; and to do so calmly, with a touching sense of personal satisfaction and ultimate moral satisfaction. The setting for the monolog is an icy, precipitous mountain ledge high above the clouds on K 2, the world's second highest mountain in Pakistan. Two adult male climbers, Taylor and Harold, are stranded and trapped at 27,000 feet. They are desperately short of life-saving equipment and supplies, and there is no hope of a speedy rescue. Now, as they begin to confront the elements as well as themselves, they each make a "situation assessment" to deal with the reality of the predicament as well as the inevitability of their death.

Harold, the physicist who has an almost spiritual, selfless love for his wife and young son, has suffered a broken leg and cannot possibly climb down the mountain; Taylor, the brash assistant district attorney and Harold's best friend, has climbed back up the mountain to recover a rope so he can try and lower

Harold to the next level of the mountain. All of the heroic efforts of the climbers fail, however, when an avalanche claims the rest of their equipment and further injures Harold. Taylor — after having firmly ordered Harold to "save" himself and to salvage the only life worth saving — quietly slips over the edge of the mountain to lower himself to the next level...and is gone. Left alone, Harold continues to fight valiantly to "...hold on...hold on" to the fleeting moments and to his fading memories.

With intelligence and ingenuity, the actor playing this monolog needs to achieve a greater intensity of the "now" experience than in any other selection in the scene sourcebook. A simplified, abstract mountain setting and the predominantly prone or reclining position of the character in the monolog are *not* the primary performance obstacles here. It is the actor's creative ability to visualize his own "self" and his own "life" in the character's given circumstances, and to use every imaginative impulse to discover a *belief*, a *form*, and a *shape* that will give perceptive meaning and heightened focus to an interpretation of this monolog. The actor may wish to review the discussion of "self-image" and "body-image," in Chapter 3, to refine and refresh an effective performance blueprint that maintains the honesty and the validity of the characterization in the monolog as well.

1	*(TAYLOR slips over the edge in one easy motion and is*
2	*gone. HAROLD sits for a long moment looking down the*
3	*cliff after him. HAROLD is breathing more and more*
4	*spasmodically, his chest rising and falling rapidly. He*
5	*leans back and closes his eyes and eventually his*
6	*breathing slows, calms.)*
7	**HAROLD: Oh, baby. Sweet baby...hey. Hey. I was gonna**
8	**write you a letter. Yeah...you know me, Al. Better late**
9	**than never...right? I heard something real sad, but I**
10	**knew you'd wanna hear it...There's this little guy**
11	**called the Japanese glacier fox...this little guy is really**
12	**pretty...really special...long fine silky hair...the purest**
13	**white...you can spot him for miles when he's below**
14	**the timberline...You look so nice. You look so warm. I**
15	**got you now.** *(HAROLD feels the rope.)* **Tension. Great.**
16	**Go, Taylor...go, go, go...so apparently, darling...some**
17	**of these little nippers are born albinos, but it's in the**
18	**summer, so that's all right 'cause the snows are**
19	**melted, and they spend a lot of time in their burrows**
20	**when they're young, and in the fall and winter they**
21	**kind of quasi-hibernate...but when the spring comes,**
22	**the young albino foxes go out with the other foxes to**
23	**romp and run and play...the glare of the sun off the**
24	**spring glacier snow...burns their albino retinas to a**
25	**crisp within a couple of days...and they are**
26	**blind...sad, baby. I know...I know. It's all right...**
27	*(HAROLD strokes the rope)* **...and for a while they live in**
28	**the burrow, and the other foxes feed them...bring**
29	**back food for them...that's nice that's real nice...but a**
30	**day comes when they feel their way out of the burrow,**
31	**into the light...and start down, letting the earth pull**
32	**them, just going down, to where they have to go.**
33	*(HAROLD feels the rope again.)* **Go home, Taylor, go**
34	**home...and if nothing takes advantage of them, stops**

1	them, kills them, they make it to the base of those
2	purple Japanese mountains – out – onto a brown
3	sandy Japanese beach. I love you. I love you...And they
4	sit there and curl their plume-white tails around
5	their feet and wait, staring blindly at the rolling
6	Japanese sea...and they never move a muscle – not a
7	muscle – once they face the sea...they sit...and let the
8	waves rise around them...till they're gone, till they're
9	gone...the Japanese fishermen see one sometimes –
10	once in a great while...at dawn...sitting...waiting...on
11	the beach. *(The rope snaps sharply twice.)* **Taylor found**
12	**a crack. Taylor's got a crack, baby...I love you.**
13	*(HAROLD unties the rope and holds it closely to him.)*
14	**Taylor's goin' home...Taylor's gonna see your pretty**
15	**smile. Taylor's gonna be warm again.** *(HAROLD's*
16	*breathing starts to become violent again. He closes his*
17	*eyes. It calms.)* **Hold on...hold on...I have to hold on.**
18	**Help me hold on, honey. I want to stay with you now.**
19	**I want to be calm like the little fox...and stay with**
20	**you...I love you forever...forever.** *(The rope snaps*
21	*sharply in HAROLD's hands.)* ...**You know what I know?**
22	**I know why the little fox sits so still...My one...It's**
23	**because he knows he'll be back...and he'll have eyes**
24	**next time.** *(HAROLD throws the rope into space, and it*
25	*disappears.)* ...**He knows he'll have eyes next time.** *(We*
26	*hear HAROLD softly, very softly, as the lights dim out in*
27	*blues.)* ...**hold on...hold on...hold on...hold on...**
28	
29	
30	
31	
32	
33	
34	

from **The Search for Signs of Intelligent Life in the Universe** ©
by Jane Wagner

Originally written as a one-woman *tour de force* for the comedienne Lily Tomlin — who played all of the roles — this series of topical and satirical narratives features Trudy, an eccentric and "visionary" adult New York bag lady who freely offers her personal views on the meaning of life, the values of tofu consciousness, Astroturf neckties, or aura goggles, as well as her "sharing-for-the-sharing-impaired" philosophy of interpersonal communication. The slightly, but delightfully, deranged Manhattan bag lady dissects American society and values with her piercing, often dark and frightening, critical commentary — all the while nervously awaiting the arrival of her "friends" from outer space, anticipated radiophonically...on an umbrella-hat satellite dish!

The playscript is a delicately crafted and structured series of often casually related characters who voice their individual stories almost like the retelling of a modern morality play. The primary focus, however, is the narrator figure of Trudy and her stinging, satirical insight, wizened intelligence, and provocative call to arms to recognize the healing powers of love, the women's consciousness-raising movement, and female comradeship to address the mean-spiritedness and hypocrisy of society's contemporary virtues and values.

In approaching this monolog the actor needs to capture the character's power of compassion and refreshing honesty — in addition to the always witty implied subtext that lurks beneath the lines of dialog. Some attention should be paid to the character's bag lady costume and the performance opportunities presented for inventive stage business, complementary props, and movement as well. Of particular concern for the actor should be discipline and control of the character's suggested bodily actions and the vocal/physical reactions so that the fanciful characterization that results does not appear to be "larger than life." Finally, the actor needs a vivid self-image of the character to promote a more perceptive understanding of individual intention(s) or motivation(s) that are an integral part of the monolog. It might be a good performance idea to review the exercise "Star Search," in Chapter 9, when pursuing interesting personalities in all walks of life who may provide the gesture, attitude, voice, mood, walk, or distinguishing mannerisms most appropriate for this truly unique bag lady character.

1   I was not always a bag lady, you know.

2   I used to be a designer and creative consultant. For big

3   companies!

4   Who do you think thought up the color scheme

5   for Howard Johnson's?

6   At the time, nobody was using

7   orange and aqua

8   in the same room together.

9   With fried clams.

10 Laugh tracks:

11 *I* gave TV sitcoms the idea for canned laughter.

12 I got the idea, one day I heard voices

13 and no one was there.

14

15 Who do you think had the idea to package pantyhose

16 in a plastic goose egg?

17 One thing I personally don't like about pantyhose:

18 When you roll 'em down to the ankles the way I like 'em,

19   you

20 can't walk too good. People seem amused, so what's a little

21 loss of dignity? You got to admit:

22 It's a look!

23

24 The only idea I'm proud of –

25

26 my umbrella hat. Protects against sunstroke, rain and

27 muggers. For *some* reason, muggers steer clear of people

28 wearing umbrella hats.

29

30 So it should come as no shock...I am now creative consul-

31   tant

32 to these aliens from outer space. They're a kinda cosmic

33 fact-finding committee. Amongst other projects, they've been

34 searching all over for Signs of Intelligent Life.

1   It's a lot trickier than it sounds.

2

3   We're collecting all kinds of data

4   about life here on Earth. We're determined to figure out,

5   once and for all, just what the hell it all means.

6   I write the data on these Post-its and then we study it.

7   Don't worry, before I took the consulting job, I gave 'em my

8   whole

9   psychohistory.

10

11   I tole 'em what drove *me* crazy was my *last* creative consul-

12   tant job,

13   with the Ritz Cracker mogul, Mr. Nabisco. It was my job to

14   come

15   up with snack inspirations to increase sales. I got this idea

16   to give

17   Cracker consciousness to the entire planet.

18   I said, "Mr. Nabisco, sir! You could be the first to sell the

19   concept

20   of munching to the Third World. We got an untapped

21   market here!

22   These countries got millions and millions of people don't

23   even know

24   where their next *meal* is *coming* from.

25   So the idea of eatin' *between* meals is somethin' just never

26   occurred to 'em!"

27   I heard myself sayin' *this*!

28

29   Must've been when I went off the deep end.

30   I woke up in the nut house. They were hookin' me up.

31   One thing they don't tell you about shock treatments, for

32   months afterward you got

33   flyaway hair. And it used to *be* my best feature.

34

1   See, those shock treatments gave me new electrical circuitry
2   (frankly, I think one of the doctors' hands must've been wet).
3   I started having these time-space continuum shifts, I guess
4   you'd call it. Suddenly, it was like my central nervous system
5   had a patio addition out back.
6   Not only do I have a linkup to extraterrestrial
7   channels, I also got a hookup with humanity as a whole.
8   Animals and plants, too. I used to talk to plants all the
9   time;
10 then, one day, they started talking back. They said,
11 "Trudy, shut up!"
12
13 I got like this...
14
15 built-in Betamax in my head. Records anything.
16 It's like somebody's using my brain to dial-switch
17 through humanity. I pick up signals that seem to transmit
18 snatches of people's lives.
19 My umbrella hat works as a satellite dish. I hear this
20 sizzling sound like white noise. Then I know it's
21 trance time.
22 That's how I met my space chums. I was in one of my
23   trances,
24 watching a scene from someone's life, and I suddenly
25   sense
26 others were there
27 watching with me.
28
29 Uh-oh.
30 I see this skinny
31 punk kid.
32 Got hair the color of
33 Froot Loops and she's wearin' a T-shirt says "Leave Me
34   Alone."

1   There's a terrible family squabble going on.
2   If they're listening to each other,
3   they're all gonna get their feelings hurt.
4
5
6
7
8
9
10
11
12
13
14
15
16
17
18
19
20
21
22
23
24
25
26
27
28
29
30
31
32
33
34

from *How It Is* ©
by Samuel Beckett

Here is a rare monolog from Nobel Prize-winning absurdist playwright Samuel Beckett's book *How It Is* that provides a graphic description of contemporary society that the author envisions as an "existential wasteland." The excerpt is a fine performance example of nondramatic literature — short story, novel, poem, or diary for example — that is explored in the Chapter 9 exercise " 'Book Club' Monolgs" as a potential audition material. This eloquent and haunting character portrait relies on a "stream of consciousness" literary technique to fuse seemingly unrelated, isolated thoughts or disjointed fragments of memory into a rich and revealing mosaic of probing universal truths and underlying human frailties that give voice to the author's point of view on the human condition. The excerpt is also a clever and complex potential audition monolog that encourages "character transformation" as the actor re-creates the crucial attitudes and moods described in the selected narrative.

In playing the monolog the actor — male *or* female — will need to engage in careful, critical analysis of the narrative to clearly identify a pattern of thoughts and emotions that might reveal the character's apparent intention or motivation; and to phrase the thoughts and emotions in a performance blueprint that accurately conveys the inherent meaning of the monolog. A good performance approach may include dividing the narrative into "mental" and "physical" units of action that capture a tempo for the monolog, and establishing a specific "time" and "place" context in which the action being described might occur. It might also be a good performance approach to determine an appropriate "age range" and a *visual* as well as *oral* character portrait that will focus attention on the absurdist theme of "meaninglessness" in a contemporary world of distorted dreams and fantasies. In addition, the actor in performance of an absurd monolog is reminded to appear sensible and believable no matter what the apparent situation or character behavior might appear to be at first glance. Allow the incongruity of the dialog to encourage the audience to think; and avoid the initial temptation to appear merely outrageous or bizarre. Finally, the actor should pay special attention to gestures and facial expressions that might help to mirror the "interior" thoughts and feelings of the character or provide fresh, inventive insight into the dialog being spoken in the narrative monolog.

1   I learn it natural order more or less before Pim with Pim
2   vast
3   tracts of time how it was my vanished life then after then
4   now
5   after Pim how it is my life bits and scraps
6
7   I say it my life as it comes natural order my lips move I can
8   feel them it comes out in the mud my life what remains ill
9   – said
10 ill-recaptured when the panting stops ill-murmured to the
11 mud in the present all that things so ancient natural
12   order the
13 journey the couple the abandon all that in the present barely
14 audible bits and scraps
15
16 I have journeyed found Pim lost Pim it's over that life those
17 periods of that life first second now third pant pant the
18   pant –
19 ing stops and I hear barely audible how I journey with my
20 sack my tins in the dark the mud crawl in an amble towards
21 Pim unwitting bits and scraps in the present things so
22   ancient
23 hear them murmur them as they come barely audible to the
24 mud
25
26 part one before Pim the journey it can't last it lasts I'm calm
27 calmer you think you're calm and you're not in the lowest
28 depths and you're on the edge I say it as I hear it and that
29 death death if it ever comes that's all it dies
30
31 it dies and I see a crocus in a pot in an area in a basement a
32 saffron the sun creeps up the wall a hand keeps it in the sun
33 this yellow flower with a string I see the hand long image
34 hours long the sun goes to the pot goes down lights on the

1 ground the hand goes the wall goes
2
3 rags of life in the light I hear and don't deny don't believe
4 don't say any more who is speaking that's not said only
5   mine my words mine alone
6 one or two soundless brief movements all the lower no
7   sound
8 when I can that's the difference great confusion
9 I see all sizes life included If that's mine the light goes on in
10 the mud the prayer the head on the table the crocus the old
11 man in tears the tears behind the hands skies all sorts
12   differ –
13 ent sorts on land and sea blue of a sudden gold and green
14 of the earth of a sudden in the mud
15
16 but words like now words not mine before Pim no no that's
17 not said that's the difference I hear it between then and now
18 one of the differences among the similarities
19
20 the words of Pim his extorted voice he stops I step in all the
21 needful he starts again I could listen to him for ever but
22   mine
23 have done with mine natural order before Pim the little I say
24 no sound the little I see of a life I don't deny don't believe
25 but what believe the sack perhaps the dark the mud death
26 perhaps to wind up with after so much life there are
27   moments
28
29
30
31
32
33
34

CHAPTER NINE

REHEARSAL EXERCISES AND IMPROVISATIONS

"Any beginner is apt to have 'buck fever' the first time. What you need is not courage, but nerve control, cool headedness. This you can get only by actual practice. It is very largely a matter of habit, in the sense of repeated exercises of will power. If you have the right stuff, you will grow stronger and stronger with each exercise of it."

— Theodore Roosevelt

Although no simple rehearsal formula exists for predicting the degree of success an actor might anticipate in playing the role, playing the scene, or auditioning, the exercises and improvisations included in this chapter should lay an excellent foundation to support and reinforce further creative development. The actor should approach the exercises and improvisations in a manner that is comfortable and compatible with an individual style of critical review and disciplined study; and is encouraged to take the creative liberty of adjusting, modifying, or extending the basic techniques suggested to meet the special needs presented by scene performance or the audition process. Each exercise and improvisation is framed as a "participatory" exploration to stimulate awareness of the basic principles of character development based upon observation, the basic ingredients of vocal and physical development based upon imagery, and the basic elements of theatrical "gamesmanship" based upon mental symbols and visualization. All of these exercises and improvisations — especially " 'Book Club' Monologs" and "Star Search!" — are intended to promote an atmosphere of relaxed inquiry and "risk-free" experimentation so that the actor may define and enrich a more individual style of performance.

One of the special features of this sourcebook is that the exercises and improvisations are arranged in a sequence to assist the actor in constructing a "performance routine" that builds on increasingly complex techniques to cultivate the development of believable characterization. For example, the first exercise, "Extra! Extra! Read All About It!," asks the actor to begin role-playing by simply scanning the headlines of a daily newspaper and making note of specific references in the story to potential stage characters. As random characteristics emerge from the reading — age, attitude, actions, or circumstances — the actor integrates the general characteristics of the newspaper account with an interpretation of selected literature that is provided to explore the basic principles of using everyday, common events as "building blocks" to fashion a three-dimensional characterization for stage performance. Continued use of this particular exercise in the rehearsal period for a traditional theatre production should assist the actor to more easily identify performance "clues" found in a formal playscript and enhance a well-disciplined, imaginative approach to scene study as well.

Rehearsal exercises and improvisations are intended to promote an atmosphere of relaxed inquiry and "risk-free" experimentation so that the actor may define and enrich a more individual style of performance.

The carefully sequenced exercises and improvisations also address familiar problem areas related to the realistic portrayal of contemporary characters. There is a conscious attempt made here to translate selected performance study theories into meaningful, distinctly personal, rehearsal games that reveal the actor's natural ability to convey the thoughts and emotions of stage characters in honest, spontaneous responses that advance a relaxed and conversational tone of vocal delivery, as well as a heightened degree of sensitivity in characterization as part of an individual performance technique. The exercises "The Matchmaker" and "Zoo Story," for example, ask the actor to explore improvisation as a creative tool for amplifying and enlarging limited character descriptions provided in sample scenario; to seek "alternative" sources — in this case the zoo! — for character development by being alert and responsive to the many potential performance inspirations that may be found to exist in the natural world.

The potential role of rehearsal exercises and improvisations is, of course, dependent upon a willingness to explore as many newly acquired techniques as possible. There should also be a willing abandon to engage in experimentation that can lead to self-discovery and self-improvement. These exercises and improvisations have the added dimension of being designed to reveal the actor's ability to grasp difficult theoretical concepts like "beats" or "physicalization" and incorporate them into easily understood performance practices that are not only appropriate in imaginative role-playing but also appropriate for artistic conception in character-building as part of the initial rehearsal process.

One of the most challenging features of this sourcebook of exercises and improvisations is the demand for the actor to always strive to do better, and to constantly refresh and refine creative skills in line-reading, interpretation, movement, and vocal/physical characterization. It is never enough to prepare for the performance only — there must be a continuous enthusiasm and dedication to generate rigorous but inventive rehearsal schedules, training sessions, or exercise routines that "tune" the voice, the body, and the mind to meet the demands and expectations of any audition or performance situation. To guide the actor's exercise and improvisation potential further, set aside at least one hour each day to practice and polish the techniques explored in this chapter and there should be a marked improvement in the poise and self-confidence needed to engage in competitive auditions. Continued practice and polish in the vocal and physical techniques suggested in this chapter should promote those performance techniques needed to fashion authentic, honest character portraits that have intellectual as well as emotional integrity!

As part of the rehearsal schedule, the complete playscript of Eugene Ionesco's *The Gap* is included in this chapter to guide the actor's active participation in the individual exercises as well as in the improvisations. This brief, absurd playscript is referred to in a number of the exercises or improvisations and is intended to serve as an additional inventive exploration of the basic performance principles discussed in the scenebook. The actors are encouraged to continue — and, hopefully, to extend — their role-playing exploration and experimentation with repeated reference to the Ionesco playscript as a foundation for translating the "theory" discussed into the "practice" of performing scenes from the playscript in a number of different styles. The appended playscript may also serve as an additional source for scene study or a scene performance for adult men and women.

As you leave these exercises and improvisations, you should decide which particular rehearsal strategies work best in translating the theories of the sourcebook into practices that work well in performance. Remember, "You are not on trial — *you* are your only judge!" in the rehearsal process of self-exploration and self-expression. What ultimately accounts for your performance success, to paraphrase the title song in the musical *Fiddler on the Roof*, is the "tradition" of *preparation*; the "tradition" of *application*; the "tradition" of *expectation*; the "tradition" of *concentration*; and the "tradition" of *execution* that is fueled by the warm fires of your own imagination in a rehearsal period filled with inventive exercises and improvisations.

The more you learn about the tradition of rehearsal exercises and improvisations the easier it will be to execute swiftly and securely *any* performance assignment with creative and professional role-playing skills. The more experience you gain in the tradition of rehearsal exercises and improvisations that are challenging and complex, the easier it will be to gain the self-confidence and the self-respect that emerges in audition and performance situations as a dynamic and versatile *Actor*. The journey may be hazardous...but it begins with the first step; and you have taken that first step in turning to this sourcebook for assistance in your performance pursuits. Happy Trails to *you*!

EXTRA! EXTRA! READ ALL ABOUT IT!

One of the most important tasks of the actor is to develop three-dimensional characterization, and to present interpretations that are crisp and fresh. The most memorable characters, of course, are those rooted in reality — flesh-and-blood men and women who exhibit attitudes and moods that are unique as well as universal. In terms of their temperament, behavior and physical appearance, these "ideal" characters may actually resemble personalities quite literally ripped from the front page of a daily newspaper. They are the average, undistinguished men and women we witness in our daily lives; and it is only when they are exposed to personal catastrophes or traumas that their true capacity for dramatic character is clearly revealed.

In approaching "documentary" character development based on daily news events, it is important to remain unbiased and objective; dealing only with the vital information provided by the potential character you are seeking to discover. Begin this exercise by a random selection of one page of the daily newspaper. Scan the headlines of each section of the newspaper, making sure to include a review of the editorials, sports, business, and entertainment sections as well as the more obvious front page headlines. Select a story that has immediate appeal in terms of its dramatic plot, interesting character(s), unusual setting, theme, and potential for conflict.

Once you have made your selection of a potential headline for character development, carefully begin to read the storyline with attention to detail. Isolate the basic ingredients of the story that help to define the character(s). Make note of specific references in the story to ages, occupations, circumstances, attitudes, and actions that are exhibited by the potential characters. Extract any direct quotations or descriptive references made by the character(s), and note if others in the story provide additional information that helps to crystallize your initial portrait of the potential character being described.

312

The most memorable characters are those rooted firmly in reality — flesh-and-blood men and women who exhibit attitudes and moods that are unique as well as universal, and who may actually resemble personalities quite literally ripped from the front page of a daily newspaper.

Review all of the material you have extracted from the newspaper story. What are the specific characteristics emerging from your review in terms of physical and vocal qualities of the character(s) being described? The portrait that you initially draw should reveal a well-developed, three-dimensional character with specific goals and objectives. What now remains is your creative imagination in giving this "documentary" character a vitality and a vision that is memorable. Take further creative license and imagine how your potential character might dress, speak, or move in relationship to the circumstances described in the newspaper storyline.

When you are comfortable with the portrait you have drawn from the given circumstances of the newspaper headline and storyline — including physical, vocal, and visual elements — use the following selection from Fyodor Dostoevsky's *Notes From Underground* to give voice to your documentary character. Integrate the general performance characteristics you have

313

isolated in the newspaper storyline and the specific narrative situation being described by the author Dostoevsky. This exercise should encourage you to apply the basic principles of daily observation and contemporary events in visualization of character that is distinctive and robust. The primary approach to understanding the "building blocks" of characterization will also be of value when you later engage in more detailed playscript interpretation and scene analysis to determine potential performance ingredients essential to give your character dimension and diversity.

from *Notes From Underground*
Fyodor Dostoevsky

The frightened and wounded expression on her face was followed first by a look of sorrowful perplexity. When I began calling myself a scoundrel and a thief and my tears flowed (the tirade was accomplished throughout by tears) her whole face worked convulsively. She was on the point of getting up and stopping me; when I finished she took no notice of my shouting: 'Why are you here, why don't you go away?' Nut realized only that it must have been very bitter of me to say all this. Besides, she was so crushed, poor girl; she considered herself infinitely beneath me; how could she feel anger or resentment? She suddenly leapt up from her chair with an irresistible impulse and held out her hands, yearning towards me, though still timid and not daring to stir...At this point there was a revulsion in my heart, too. Then she suddenly rushed to me, threw her arms 'round me and burst into tears. I, too, could not restrain myself, and sobbed as I never had before.

Additional Dimensions

When you have the basic principles of "documentary" character development clearly in mind, approach the following excerpts from classical Greek tragedy and carefully review the actions and circumstances to present a more contemporary character interpretation that is fresh and crisp. First, review the speech by Sophocles' Antigone, who has just been condemned to death by her uncle, Creon, for disobeying his royal edict; and pay particular attention to the defiant mood suggested in Antigone's reasoned defense of her actions. Isolate the primary ingredients in the dialog that help to define the character and the storyline. Use your "documentary" analysis of the passage — and creative imagination — to voice a vocal and physical portrait of the character.

from *Antigone*
Sophocles

> Your edict, King, was strong,
> But all your strength is weakness itself against
> The immortal unrecorded laws of God.
> They are not merely now: they were, and shall be,
> Operative forever, beyond man utterly.
>
> I knew I must die, even without your decree:
> I am only mortal. And if I must die
> Now, before it is my time to die
> Surely this is no hardship; can anyone
> Living as I live, with evil all about me,
> Think Death less than a friend? This death of mine
> Is of no importance; but if I had left my brother
> Lying in death unburied, I should have suffered.
> Now I do not.
>
> You smile at me. Ah, Creon,
> Think me a fool, if you like; but it may well be
> That a fool convicts me of folly.

Now, conclude the exercise by approaching the following speech from Euripides' Medea to present a more contemporary character interpretation that is universal as well as unique. Review the speech by Medea, who has just been abandoned by her husband, Jason, so that he can make a more profitable, political marriage with the younger daughter of the King of Corinth. Pay particular attention to the jealousy that consumes Medea as she contemplates slaying her own children to render Jason desolate and alone in the world. Again, isolate the primary ingredients in the dialog that help to define the character and the storyline.

from *Medea*
Euripides

    O, do not do this deed! Let the children go,
Unhappy one, spare the babes! For if they live, they
will cheer thee in our exile there. Nay, by the friends of
Hell's abyss, never will I hand my children over to their
Foes to mock and flout. Die they must in any case, and
Since 'tis so, why I, the mother who bore them, will give
The fatal blow. O my babes, my babes, let your Mother kiss
Your hands. Ah! Hands I love so well, O lips most dear to me!
O the sweet embrace, the soft young cheek, the fragrant
      breath!
My children! Go, leave me! I cannot bear to look longer upon
You; my sorrow wins the day. At last, I understand the awful
Deed I am to do; But passion, that cause of direst woes to
Mortal man, hath triumphed o'er my sober thoughts.

    My friends, I am resolved upon the deed; at once will
I slay my children and then leave this land, without delaying
Long enough to hand them over to some more savage
      hand to
Butcher. Needs must they die in any case; and since they must,
I will slay them — I, the mother that bore them. O heart
      of mine,
Steel thyself! Come, take the sword, thou wretched hand
      of mine!
Away with the cowardice! This one brief day forget thy
      children
Dear, and after that lament; for though thou wilt slay them yet
They were thy darlings still, and I am a lady of sorrows.
*(MEDEA slowly moves toward the house with sword held
high.)*

THE MATCHMAKER

Improvisation plays a very important preliminary role in the initial development of three-dimensional characterization. The creative imagination necessary for inspired improvisation is limited only by the actor's own inhibition in exploring the emotional, vocal, and physical demands of responding intuitively to given circumstances like age, mood, attitude, situation, and objective. Once the actor has gained experience — and self-confidence — in improvisation, however, there is a noticeable spark of freshness and ingenuity in subsequent scene study and role-playing that often gives the immediate impression that the performance is marked by an energy and innovation that gives the illusion of spontaneous and imaginative creativity.

The basic ingredient of the improvisation is the *scenario*, a rather bare-bones outline of the action(s) and the objective(s) of the character in a given situation. The simple outline may include specific details related to the setting, the mood, or the attitude of the character — including the relationship to other characters in the scenario — but the primary role of the improvisation is to promote a "risk-free" environment for the actor to explore individual creative gifts and dramatic, imaginative talents in "fleshing out" the simple plot line; and in amplifying the limited character descriptions provided by adding those personal elements of individuality and personality that might enrich the character portrait being drawn and enhance the vitality of the scene being performed. In this creative approach to improvisation, the actor is a "matchmaker," integrating individual and personal traits, creative inventions, and imaginative performance additions and extensions that give infinite variety to the basic outline provided by the scenario.

Begin the exercise by marking note cards in the following categories: age, mood, attitude, and personal objective. For each category indicate five difference responses so that your selections will have challenging variety. For example, "age" choices might include young man, old woman, or middle-age man; "mood" and "attitude" choices might include happy, solitary, angry, depressed, anxious, or giddy; and possible "personal objective" choices might include to escape the crowd, join the

317

group, remain impartial and objective, or be the leader. When you have made your choices and completed your note cards for each category, shuffle the note cards by category and place them in individual stacks.

Now, draw one note card from *each* category and approach the following improvisation. Using the age, mood, attitude, and personal objective which you have chosen at random from your individual category stack of note cards, try to capture the simple plot outline of the sample scenario that follows using only the basic information provided by your own category note cards. When you are comfortable — and confident — with your initial improvisation, repeat the exercise using the same category note cards but extend the improvisation with your own addition of personal creative gifts and dramatic, imaginative talents that help to give additional dimension to the scenario. Remember to react and take whatever action(s) seem most appropriate given your selection of category note cards.

Improvisation plays a very important role in the initial development of three-dimensional characterization, and is limited only by the actor's own inhibition in exploring the emotional, vocal, and physical demands of responding intuitively to given circumstances like age, mood, attitude, situation, and objective.

Sample Scenario

On turning the corner of a narrow street, you find yourself in a spacious, walled-in plaza with an unbroken line of lofty apartment houses on each side, and a steepled building at the upper end with a watch-tower on top that has a faint light spilling onto the street below. It is late evening, the air is damp and cold. You hear strange sounds coming from the apartment houses and are about to turn and leave the plaza when a small band of youths — clothed in embroidered robes, gold-laced hats, and carrying silver-hilted swords — enter from behind and block your exit.

Shuffle your category cards again and draw a new set of age, mood, attitude, and personal objective information to approach a character improvisation and interpretation of one character based upon Eugene Ionesco's sample script *The Gap*. The rich narrative description provided by the playwright should present ample opportunities for character improvisation using your selected category note card information; and use the given circumstances described by the playwright to extend the storyline with your own imaginative talents. You may also wish to repeat this part of the exercise by shuffling your category note cards several times to draw a number of interesting "matchmaker" combinations of age, mood, attitude, or personal objective that will give each performance of this improvisation variety and vitality. It might also be a good performance idea to begin to add theatrical complementaries like hand props, suggestive costume fragments, and small set pieces to the rehearsal period as potential extensions of character action(s) and reaction(s).

Additional Dimensions

Here are some additional scenarios to explore as you continue to experiment with improvisation. Use your remaining category note cards to give substance and form to the descriptions provided below. An additional dimension in this part of the "matchmaker" exercise is to include a *partner* in the performance. With two actors now involved in the improvisational action, it will be necessary to take into account the elements of "reaction" and "interaction." In addition, improvisations involving two or more characters require an "interplay" and "exchange" of actions and intentions that are *not* easily predictable; and which are subject to the individual wishes or whims of the solo actor. The scenarios that follow also include obvious potential for the conflict of character goals and objectives that will need to be compromised if the storyline is to be advanced to a level of active, creative resolution. It is important, therefore, that each actor have *different* category note cards to indicate age, mood, attitude, and personal objective.

Sample Scenario

Two solitary figures are standing silently by the open grave of a magnificent tomb of gilt and gold. They gaze upon the elegant black Egyptian marble on which rests the last remains of a valiant soldier, who still clutches a gleaming sword in his solemn hand. The night air is cool and foreboding — there is a pale cast of doom hovering over the burial ground that is reflected in the blood-red glow of the moon. The tongueless silence of the moment is shattered by a wild blast of wind that scatters the winter's withered leaves like dried ashes above the sarcophagus. Leaning over the ancient balustrade railing that frames this sad and frightful scene, the solitary figures are startled to hear strange, muffled sounds rising from the tomb and to see the cold, white hand clutching the gleaming sword beginning to twitch ever so lightly.

* * *

Flasher Doright, a dashing space cadet on assignment in the Jupiter Fleet of the terrestrial medium Quad IV, and Smiley Smoot, his trusted lieutenant, are seated in front of the control board of the miniship "The Antheum." They adjust the air pressure, the star-watch needle, the ventilation gauge, the plutonium arch-screen, and the bi-arch light shield in speedy preparation for an emergency landing on the satellite station Icca-CP 2. Suddenly, the blinking red "abort" alert signals impending disintegration, the miniship begins to rotate and spin out of control, and the whirl of the helium ejector cylinders grinds to an abrupt halt that leaves Flasher Doright and Smiley Smoot suspended in space, floating aimlessly above the landing site.

Now, complete the exercise by writing and performing your own scenario for improvisation. Make sure that your bare-bones outline of the action(s) and the objective(s) of the character in the given situation includes the setting, mood, and attitude of the character — and indicate a specific age range to enrich the individuality or personality of the character portrait being sketched. Don't forget to add your own personal creative gifts and inventive talents to give depth and dimension to the scenario. Here are some potential "topics" for your imaginative exploration.

- A minister whose laughter masks a fear of crying.
- A teacher whose memory plays tricks in a lecture.
- A friend whose "babble" conceals a secret.
- A child whose noise signals a crime.
- A jogger whose running follows a parade.

ZOO STORY

It has often been said, perhaps as an apology rather than as a statement of fact, that it is easier to develop a believable character portrait by *not* thinking to much; and that the most effective exploration of character — vocal as well as physical — is to be found in the improvisational or spontaneous responses to the actions and the situations detailed in the playscript. Although there is certainly much truth in these perceptions, the more traditional approaches of "observation" and "objectivity" continue to play the major role in the initial development of realistic, honest characterization. Like Hamlet's wise advice to his merry band of Players, the actor of contemporary scenes is still reminded that the primary goal of meaningful character portraits is to "hold the mirror up to nature," and to consciously avoid any suggestion of distortion or deception in depicting characters collected from observed human nature.

Although contemporary drama itself is primarily concerned with commonplace, nonheroic characters usually engaged in day-to-day struggles and rather ordinary actions, the actor's primary concern in performance is to provide a frank and honest treatment of the "inner truths" of the character, and to depict everyday life and routine actions with a sense of dignity and importance that gives the character a measure of self-dignity and a certain spirit of nobility. There is also a concern that contemporary drama — with its interest in accurate and detailed observation — convey the basic thoughts and emotions of the character in a more direct, distinctly personal and individual, manner that bears witness to the resemblance of "real-life" role models.

A good exercise that doesn't involve a considerable amount of thinking *or* improvisation, but is directly related to observation, to acquaint the actor with alternative sources for character development is "zoo story." Begin the exercise with an extended visit to a park, natural habitat, zoo, "petting farm," or any other nature preserve location that might house a variety of animals for public viewing. Observe the animals in their natural environment, noting the peculiar mannerisms and individual traits that distinguish one animal from another. The detailed observation might, for example, reveal the animal's eating habits, movement patterns, vocal characteristics, and interpersonal relationships with other animals; or the observation might include specific notations related to personality traits, temperament, sensory awareness, and apparent level of intelligence. Collect your initial observations in a "Jungle Book" of notes, sketches, and impressions that easily identify and categorize each animal.

It is important to be as economical and as believable as possible in the subtle use of animal characteristics to depict parallel human behavior; and all subsequent actions should appear natural and spontaneous in both rehearsal and performance.

When you have completed your observations and memory book of distinct animal characteristics, begin to reduce the animal studies to an analogous portrait of human beings; translating individual animal traits into a comparative study of potential human behavior. Be acutely aware of observed animal characteristics like physique, peculiar vocal qualities, posture, and movement patterns; and don't forget to make mention of unique features like comic flair, spatial relationships, and communication techniques. Your compilation of animal observations and human comparisons should capture distinct individuality in voice, body, and movement that is easily applicable to imaginative character definition and subsequent development.

When you are confident that your animal studies are clearly drawn and that the human comparisons are fine-tuned and detailed, respond in *movement* to the following characterizations using your animal traits as a performance blueprint to express the comparable human behavior suggested in the examples provided. Your movement responses should be subtle, however, to avoid the impression of caricature or gross exaggeration; and special attention should be paid to avoid overly precise imitation or highly theatrical posing. Approach each suggested characterization with a sensitivity and objectivity that conveys a "natural" sense of movement influenced by a highly selective use of observed animal characteristics.

- Move like a witch doctor (animal) exorcising evil spirits from a possessed tribesman.

- Move like an infantryman (animal) approaching the outskirts of an enemy post.

- Move like a postman (animal) delivering mail and packages on an icy winter's day.

- Move like a waitress (animal) carefully balancing a tray of food in a crowded restaurant.

- Move like a long-distance runner (animal) slowly crossing the finish line of a marathon race.

- Move like a policeman (animal) directing rush-hour traffic during an apparent bank hold-up.

Now that you have explored the role of movement directly related to alternative sources of character development like animal studies, turn your attention to Eugene Ionesco's sample playscript *The Gap*. Refer to your "Jungle Book" notations again as you perform the scene, adding the basic ingredients of animal/human *vocal* qualities as well as appropriate actions, attitudes, and moods suggested by the storyline. Again, it is important to be as economical and as believable as possible in your subtle use of animal characteristics to depict parallel human behavior, especially in terms of vocal variety and character actions that should appear natural and spontaneous in performance. Remember that vivid, incisive character portraits drawn from alternative sources like animal studies must still exhibit the basic, fundamental performance principles of depth, dimension, and integrity as reflected in traditional stage figures drawn from the current reality of contemporary life.

Additional Dimensions

Detailed and objective observation of nature — and its implications for understanding human nature — can play a valuable role in creating truthful and honest character portraits. The imaginative performance blueprint that includes alternative sources to inspire character development, like animals, machines, slogans, events, or technologies, is encouraged for the actor who is alert and sensitive to the many inspirations that may be bound to exist in the natural world. The "here and now" point of view that sees all persons, things, and objects as fit material to develop and integrate into three-dimensional character portraits should encourage you to be more daring and adventurous in nontraditional approaches to characterization in future rehearsal and performance settings. It should also encourage you to search for the bodily actions, gestures, vocal qualities, and movement patterns of your future characters in the most unlikely location: *all around you!*

With these inventive approaches to characterization in mind, "visualize" the following improvisations and give voice and body to the characters that appear in your imagination. In addition to your use of observed and detailed animal characteristics, you may wish to use suggestive costume fragments — baggy pants, colorful vest, striped shirt, cape — or meaningful and descriptive hand props that reflect the influence of your animal studies and also enhance the character portrait being drawn. Your personal "zoo story" should also include a complete expression of the animal/human attitude or mood suggested in the following improvisations.

- A foreign spy (animal), who intends to steal the secret ingredient for a major Army defense weapon, breaks into a nuclear reactor laboratory and is in the act of opening a "top secret" vault when confronted by a janitor.

- A kindly old man (animal), who is threatened with eviction from his home unless he can pay his overdue taxes, barricades himself in a backyard garage and is in the act of loading a rifle when confronted by a "Jehovah Witness" evangelist.

- A frightened librarian (animal), who is alone in the "Special Collections Room" late at night, is in the act of replacing a rare volume of poetry on the top shelf of a bookcase when confronted by a homeless vagrant.

- A romantic young girl (animal), who spends her time reading *True Confession* magazines and watching afternoon soap operas, is in the act of washing her hair when confronted by a handsome, shy stranger asking for directions to a local sports event.

- A studious college freshman (animal), who is cramming for final examinations to earn "Dean's List" status, is in the act of an important review of psychology notes when confronted by a petty criminal escaped from prison and looking for a safe place to hide.

"BOOK CLUB" MONOLOGS

One of the most demanding challenges an actor must confront is the "open" audition and the selection of audition material that is both appropriate and suitable in terms of personal self-image and professional range of performance skill. It is very important to approach the audition in a calm, relaxed manner that exhibits your acting "personality" as well as showcases your performance talents in character analysis, scene study, and playscript interpretation. Remember that the audition is a performance in which a number of talents — voice, body, movement, interpretation, sensitivity, and intelligence — are on public display *simultaneously.* It is essential, therefore, that you radiate a "life spirit" in the audition so that what is "seen" and "heard" is natural, honest, and spontaneous.

Your initial choices of audition material should establish your age, vocal range, movement potential, and physical type; and you should avoid those audition choices that demand an overly precise use of the voice, exaggerated movement, or theatrical posturing. Remember that the audition setting is an intimate, fleeting glance at an individual character in a brief moment of time in the selected playscript; and that you must strive to *focus* that moment directly forward to the listening audience for the most immediate, meaningful impact. Choosing audition material with a decidedly "dramatic" framework — three-dimensional character, internal or psychological conflict, interesting point of view, and climactic resolution — is also essential in creating an initially favorable audition impression.

As valuable as all of these preliminary recommendations are, however, the actor's most important remaining performance resource material may be original, imaginative monologs adapted from nondramatic works like poems, short stories, novels, essays, or diary journals. In comparison to the "shopworn," familiar monologs that feature famous or favorite playwrights that quite figuratively litter the audition stage, original adaptations from less well-known nondramatic works — like those of *A Woman Called Truth* or *Anonymous Girl: Look in the Mirror* included in Chapter 8 — frequently provide refreshing, innovative material that more easily reveals your own individual, personal performance skills in an audition. Original adaptations also allow you to place a more "personal stamp" on the audition material because of your intensive and perceptive work of adapting and editing nondramatic literature for performance.

The scripting of nondramatic literature for the audition monolog involves careful editing to isolate the dramatic elements necessary for character development in a limited time frame; detailed cutting and timely transitions that help to visualize dramatic action in terms of an isolated moment that has a beginning, a middle, and an end, as well as a basic theatricality that highlights a dramatic conflict and a three-dimensional character relationship in a sustained progression from the initial episode to the climactic conclusion. The creative blueprint for audition scripting also includes the ability to conceptualize nondramatic literature as vocal and physical material that expresses authentic actions and honest emotions in simple, inherently dramatic, situations written specifically for performance. In adapting Thomas Mann's short story *Mario and the Magician*, for example, you are immediately aware of the author's colorful use of descriptive language and vivid dialog expressed by the magician character and the more restrained, reflective verbal exchanges written for the Mario character. The detailed character descriptions in the short story have such vivid, direct, and immediate appeal in terms of dramatic action, universal language, and vivid personality that they almost demand an inspired performance aloud!

Novels, as well as short stories and poems, are particularly effective when adapted for the audition performance because of the "thread of action" that appears to give each its basic unity. Each separate episode, adventure, or image of the primary and secondary characters is easily extracted from the longer text for dramatization without sacrificing meaning, form, or character development. The isolation of individual episodes, adventures, or images may be extremely valuable in revealing a character's insight or point of view in a given situation, and may also highlight fundamental character traits related to physicality, interior psychological state of mind, or self-image. An edited scripting of Helen Keller's autobiographical description of self-image in *Three Days to See*, for example, provides a compelling portrait of the blind humanitarian and also suggests a dynamic audition monolog for performance.

All of us have read thrilling stories in which the hero had only a limited or specified time to live. Such stories set us thinking, wondering what we should do under those similar circumstances. Most of us, however, take life for granted. We know that we must die, but usually we picture that day as far in the future. I have often thought it would be a blessing if each human being were stricken blind and deaf for a few days at sometime during their early adult life. Darkness would make them more appreciative of sight; silence would teach them the joys of sound.

Once you have explored the traditional pattern of scripting nondramatic literature for the audition performance, you will discover that your "theatrical mind" can actually enhance your reading, comprehension, and interpretation of "book club" characters discovered in the public library, local bookstores, or in your own personal collection of novels, short stories, and poems. The only remaining challenge is to move beyond the conventional playscripts conveniently used in auditions and visualize *any* form of literature as potential audition material by giving it the dramatic characteristics associated with theatrical performance and production. Just remember in scripting and editing your "book club" characters for audition monologs to (1) have a beginning, middle, and an end for the scene; (2) reveal character insight and purpose in your cutting; (3) sustain the episode with energetic movement toward a climax; (4) include appropriate introductions and transitions that "set the scene" and clarify the actions that follow; (5) have a strong sense of the "theatrical moment" being captured; (6) promote movement opportunities for creative staging; (7) remain faithful to the theme and author's point of view in the character descriptions and actions; (8) meet the time requirements of the audition; (9) display the range of your vocal and physical talents; and (10) reveal your *self* in a performance of authentic, honest emotion and intelligence.

The actor's most important performance resource material may be original, imaginative monologs adapted from nondramatic works like poems, short stories, novels, essays, or diary journals; and the detailed character descriptions have such vivid, direct, and immediate appeal in terms of dramatic action, universal language, and distinct personality that they almost demand an inspired performance aloud!

Here is a sample of nondramatic literature to help plant the seeds of your creative scripting for audition performance. Review the selection to determine potential for characterization, movement, voice, and body. Edit the selection as appropriate to meet a *three-minute* monolog audition time limit, including an appropriate introduction and any transitions. Remember that what is primarily "descriptive" in nondramatic literature must become "active" in audition performance. You may also wish to include a simple, suggestive costume fragment or hand prop which best suggests the character being described in the nondramatic literature. When you are confident that your scripting of nondramatic literature achieves the ten primary goals and objectives outlined previously, review your own personal collection of novels, short stories, poems, essays, letters, diaries, and song lyrics in search of potential "characters" for monolog audition performance. Exploring creative performance approaches to nondramatic literature should gain attention and win recognition, so bring a "book club" character friend to your next audition!

from *Please Hear What I'm Not Saying*
Anonymous

> Don't be fooled by me.
> Don't be fooled by the face I wear.
> For I wear a mask; I wear a thousand masks,
> masks that I'm afraid to take off,
> and none of them are me.
> Pretending is an art that's second nature with me,
> but don't be fooled, for God's sake don't be fooled.
> I give the impression that I'm secure,
> that all is sunny and unruffled with me,
> within as well as without,
> that confidence is my name and coolness my game,
> that the water's calm and I'm in command,
> and that I need no one.
>
> But don't believe me.
> Please.
> My surface may seem smooth, but my surface is my mask,
> my ever-varying and ever-concealing mask.
> Beneath lies no smugness, no complacence.
> Beneath dwells the real me in confusion, in loneliness.
> But I hide this.
> I don't want anybody to know it.
> I panic at the thought of my weakness and fear being
>   exposed.

That's why I frantically create a mask to hide behind,
a nonchalant, sophisticated facade to help me pretend,
to shield me from the glance that knows.

But such a glance is precisely my salvation. My only true
Salvation, and I know it.
That is if it's followed by acceptance, if it's followed by
Love. It's the only thing that can liberate me from myself,
from the barriers that I so painstakingly erect.
It's the only thing that will assure me of what I can't
    assure myself,
that I'm really worth something.
But I don't tell you this. I don't dare. I'm afraid to.
I'm afraid your glance will not be followed by acceptance
    and love.
I'm afraid you'll think less of me, that you'll laugh,
and your laugh would kill me.

I'm afraid that deep-down I'm nothing, that I'm just no
good, and that you will see this and reject me.
So I play my game, my desperate pretending game,
with a facade of assurance without, and a trembling child
    within.
And so begins the parade of masks,
the glittering but empty parade of masks.
And my life becomes a front.
I idly chatter to you in the suave tones of surface talk.
I tell you everything that's really nothing,
and nothing of what's everything, of what's crying within
    me.
So when I'm going through my routine do not be fooled by
what I'm saying.

Please listen carefully and try to hear what I'm *not* saying,
what I'd like to say, what for survival I need to say,
but what I can't say.
I dislike hiding, honestly.
I dislike the superficial game I'm playing, the superficial,
    phony game.
I'd like to be genuine and spontaneous, and me,
but you've got to help me.

You've got to hold out your hand
even when that's the last thing I seem to want, or need.
Only you can wipe away from my eyes the blank stare
of the breathing dead.
Only you can call me into aliveness.
Each time you're kind and gentle and encouraging,
each time you try to understand because you really care,
my heart begins to grow wings, very small wings, very
    feeble wings, but wings.

With your sensitivity and sympathy, and your power of
    understanding,
you can breathe life into me. I want you to know that.
I want you to know how important you are to me,
how you can be a creator of the person that is me if you
    choose to.
Please choose to.
You alone can break down the wall behind which I tremble,
You alone can remove my mask,
You alone can release me from my shadow-world of panic
    and uncertainty,
from my lonely prison.
So do not pass me by. Please do not pass me by.
It will not be easy for you.
A long conviction of worthlessness builds strong walls.
The nearer you approach me, the blinder I may strike back.
It's irrational, but despite what the books say about man,
    I am irrational.
I fight against the very thing that I cry out for, but I
am told that love is stronger than strong walls.
And in this lies my hope — my only hope.
Please try to beat down those walls with firm hands, but
    with gentle hands —
for a child is very sensitive.

Who am I, you may wonder? I am someone you know very
    well.
For I am every man you meet and I am every woman you
    meet.

333

AND THE "BEAT" GOES ON

One of the basic ingredients of a vivid characterization is the actor's creative ability to respond to the images suggested by words and phrases with a voice and a body that is both expressive and exciting. However, the actor must first conceptualize the images as a "mental symbol" before attempting to visualize the character and this requires a perceptive and sensitive analysis of the scene as well as an emphatic identification and genuine response to the suggestive words and phrases. Actor analysis and identification of character is a shared experience and a bond of mutual understanding that promotes the honest communication of actions and attitudes conveyed in the scene.

The first step in the process of conceptualizing images is to analyze the "beats" in a character's dialog. Beats are the "action maps" that chart the course of a character's alternating or changing points of view, mood, attitude, or objective in each section of the spoken text. Although beats are primarily a matter of individual interpretation and definition determined by the actor's analysis of the dialog, they are convenient performance road signs that signal significant character turns in action, thought, or mood which must also be addressed by corresponding vocal or physical changes that indicate a change of direction.

Using beats as "action maps" is a way of defining your character's motivation and objective in a selected scene and a convenient performance blueprint that outlines your character's specific goals in a selected moment of time in the playscript. Distinguishing character beats — which may vary in length and duration — may provide valuable insights and reveal the subtext of a character's thought or point of view. The pattern of thought, behavior, mood, or action suggested by an analysis of character beats may also present rich "mental symbols" for inspired interpretation and performance. Just remember, however, that beats do *not* exist in isolation; they are integral ingredients in the overall evolution of character development in the playscript and must be treated as a part of the whole dramatic mixture, not as independent or unrelated seasoning.

In order to respond to the images suggested by words and phrases, the actor must first conceptualize the images as a "mental symbol" before attempting to visualize the character.

Begin your preliminary exploration of beats by reviewing the following excerpt from William Shakespeare's *Romeo and Juliet*. In this scene, Juliet has just been informed by her Nurse that Tybalt, a cousin, has been killed in a sword fight with Romeo, to whom she has secretly been married. Juliet's concerns, fears, doubts, and regrets must all be voiced in different tones as she wavers from initial disbelief and self-pity to ultimate despair and shock at the reality of Tybalt's death and Romeo's banishment. The "action map" of her objectives in each segment of the speech that follows — suggested as key words — offers a vivid and compelling character interpretation for potential performance. There is powerful emotion, genuine compassion, and intense personal conflict revealed in the suggested objectives that should enrich the role-playing in this excerpt. As you voice the excerpt, concentrate on each objective in terms of the performance potential for voice and body responses. Give yourself freely to the character attitude and mood indicated, voicing the first objective clearly and distinctly until your understanding and expression of it is precise. Then voice the second objective so that it is as imaginative and vivid as the first. Continue to voice each objective with a precision and a clarity that gives significant vocal and physical contrast to the changes in attitude or mood experienced by the character in the dialog. This "vocal pacing" of the contrasting changes in the character's attitude or mood — that results from an analysis of the dialog and the suggested objectives — should provide a meaningful rhythm and tempo for the character's speech as well as for a dynamic and inspired interpretation of the dramatic situation. When each of the specific objectives has been voiced with clarity and distinction, modify your intensity and try to connect with the "mental images" suggested by the objectives listed below into a coherent pattern of behavior, action, and movement that best represents the character's point of view in this particular speech. Then repeat the selection with appropriate phrasing that highlights and underscores the apparent changes in character thought and point of view.

Dialog	Objectives
	Key Words
Shall I speak ill of him that is my husband?	*(Doubt)*
Ah, poor my lord, what tongue shall smooth thy name, When I, thy three-hours wife, have mangled it?	*(Self-pity)*
But, wherefore, villain, dist thou kill my cousin?	*(Command)*
That villain cousin would have kill'd my husband: Back, foolish tears, back to your native spring; Your tributary drops belong to woe, Which you, mistaking, offer up to joy.	*(Regret)*
My husband lives, that Tybalt would have slain;	*(Rejoice)*

> And Tybalt's dead, that would have slain my husband:
>
> All this is comfort; wherefore weep I then?
>
> Some word there was, worser than Tybalt's death,
>
> That murder'd me: I would forget it fain;　　　　*(Despair)*
>
> But, O, it presses to my memory,
>
> Like damned guilt deeds to sinners' minds:

> Tybalt is dead, and Romeo — banished!　　　　*(Shook)*

When you are confident that you understand the role of analysis, beats, and objectives in giving vivid dimension to character development, turn your attention to the following excerpt from John Dryden's *All for Love*. Based upon William Shakespeare's classic *Antony and Cleopatra*, here is the seductive, temptress Cleopatra at her most cunning and heroic. Surrounded by armed soldiers, she pleads in a rousing speech that alternates between a daring defense and an arrogant dismissal that Antony not leave her. This public presentation in an open forum provides an especially attractive setting to express Cleopatra's objectives. Review the speech, chart the actions, determine the objectives, indicate the "key words," and then unravel the ancient mystery of Cleopatra as the "beat" goes on!

　　　　　Yet may I speak?
How shall I plead my cause, when you, my judge,
Already have condemn'd me?
　　　　　Shall I bring
The love you bore me for my advocate?
That now is turn'd against me, that destroys me;
For love, once past, is, at the best forgotten;
But oft'ner sours to hate.

　　　　　'Twill please my lord
To ruin me, and therefore I'll be guilty.
But, could I once have thought it would have pleas'd you,
That you would pry, with narrow searching eyes,

Into my faults, severe to my destruction,
And watching all advantages with care,
That serve to make me wretched?

       You seem griev'd
(And therein you are kind) that Caesar first
Enjoy'd my love, though you deserv'd it better.
I grieve for that, my lord, much more than you;
For, had I first been yours, it would have sav'd
My second choice: I never have been his,
And ne'er had been but yours. But Caesar first,
You say, possess'd my person, you, my love:
Caesar lov'd me, but I lov'd Antony.
If I endur'd him after, 'twas because
I judg'd it due to the first name of men;
And, half constrain'd, I gave, as to a tyrant;
What he would take by force.
How often have I wish'd some other Caesar,
Great as the first, and as the second young,
Would court my love, to be refus'd for you!
You leave me Antony; and yet I love you,
Indeed I do: I have refus'd a kingdom —
That's a trifle:
For I could part with life, with anything,
But only you.

       Oh, let me die with you!
Is that a hard request?
No, you shall go; your int'rest calls you hence;
Yes, your dear int'rest pulls you strong, for these
Weak arms to hold you here.

       Go! Leave me, soldier
(For you're no more a lover); leave me dying.
Push me pale and panting from your bosom,
And, when your march begins, let one run after,
Breathless almost for joy, and cry, 'She's dead!'
The soldiers shout; you then, perhaps, may sigh
And muster all your Roman gravity:
Ventidius chides; and straight your brow clears up,
As I had never been.
Here let me breathe my last: envy me not
This minute; I'll die apace,
As fast as e'er I can, and end your trouble.

STAR SEARCH!

Contemporary scenes are very firmly rooted in the "here and now," and the actor generally includes personal observation, immediate experience, and creative invention in an imaginative interpretation of the character portrait being drawn. Alertness and attention to detail to events and interesting personalities in all walks of life may provide the gesture, attitude, voice, mood, walk, hand prop, costume, or distinguishing mannerism that gives vitality — and individuality — to a character interpretation. If you are sensitive and acutely aware of your immediate surroundings it may be possible to discover the creative impulse of transferring what has been overheard or witnessed from everyday life situations into a viable, believable character portrait that is as honest and authentic as it might have been found to exist in your initial observation.

Like the "cub reporter," the actor of contemporary scenes may enrich the performance potential in a scene by cultivating a journalistic attitude that explores the *who, what, where, when,* and *why* of the persons, things, and objects that surround daily activities and everyday happenings. This approach to objective observation also promotes a more personal, three-dimensional characterization that has depth, integrity, and believability because it is based upon a "flesh-and-blood" role model. Such a vivid, incisive character portrait mirrors current reality and contemporary life in a more direct and immediate reflection of characterization drawn from the common, instantly recognized walks of life familiar to all of us.

To promote your appreciation and understanding of the role that observation and the immediate experience of daily activities and everyday happenings might play in imaginative character development, set aside a period of two weeks for your own "star search." Observe closely — and with a critical eye — the actions of *three* of those with whom you come in contact for the two-week period. Those ripe for your observation may include parents, teachers, friends, strangers, or casual acquaintances. Following the period of detailed observation — and supplemented with a written "character diary" — review the mannerisms, gestures, movements, vocal qualities, and distinguishing personal habits of those observed. Based upon your diary notations and personal recollections, sketch an initial character portrait for each person observed. Your initial character sketch should also include basic physical characteristics like age, height, and weight as well as more subtle emotional or intellectual characteristics like attitude, mood, and point of view.

When you are confident that your initial character sketches are an accurate, precise reflection of those observed, give "voice" and "body" to the following selection, transferring what has been overheard or witnessed in your observation period of everyday life situations into a realistic character portrait. It may also be of value to the initial character sketch and the subsequent performance if you are able to discover in your observations a *metaphor*, or implied comparison, between the person observed and something inventive — and to incorporate such complementary features or distinguishing characteristics into your performance. For example, your detailed observation of the vocal quality of the casual acquaintance may suggest the performance metaphor of "ostrich"; the personal mannerisms of the friend may suggest the performance metaphor of "an unbridled horse"; or the movement patterns of the stranger may suggest the performance metaphor of a "dance of death."

from *The Major-General's Song*
W. S. Gilbert

I am the very model of a modern Major-General,
I've information vegetable, animal and mineral,
I know the kings of England, and I quote the fights historical,
From Marathon to Waterloo, in order categorical;
I'm very well acquainted too with matters mathematical,
I understand equations, both the simple and quadratical,
About binomial theorem I'm teeming with a lot o'news —
With many cheerful facts about the square of the hypotenuse.
I'm very good at integral and differential calculus,
I know the scientific names of beings animalculous;
In short, in matters of vegetable, animal, and mineral,
I am the very model of a modern Major-General.

I know our mythic history, King Arthur's and Sir Caradoc's,
I answer hard acrostics, I've a pretty taste for paradox,
I quote in elegiacs all the crimes of Heliogabalus,
In comics I can floor peculiarities parabolous.
I can tell undoubted Raphaels from Gerard Dows and
    Zoffanies,
I know the croaking chorus from the *Frogs* of Aristophanes,
Then I can hum a fugue of which I've heard the music's
    dinafore,
And whistle all the airs from that infernal nonsense
    Pinafore.
Then I can write a washing bill in Babylonic cuneiform,
And tell you every detail of Caractacu's uniform;
In short, in matters vegetable, animal, and mineral,
I am the very model of a modern Major-General.

In fact, when I know what is meant by "mamelon" and
    "ravelin,"
When I can tell at sight a chassepot rifle from a javelin,
When such affairs as sorties and surprises I'm more wary
    at,
And when I know precisely what is meant by "commissariat,"
When I have learnt what progress has been made in
    modern gunnery,
When I know more of tactics than a novice in a nunnery:
In short, when I've a smattering of elemental strategy,
You'll say a better Major-General has never *sat* a gee —
For my military knowledge, though I'm plucky and
    adventury,
Has only been brought down to the beginning of the century;
But still in matters vegetable, animal, and mineral,
I am the very model of a modern Major-General.

Additional Dimensions

Now that you have a clear understanding of the role that
personal observation, immediate experience, and creative invention might play in character development, conclude the exercise
by selecting three "star personalities" of your choice. Possible
role models might include famous actors, lawyers, rock stars,
politicians, notorious newspaper headliners, actresses, television newscasters, cartoon heroes, sports figures, novelists,

playwrights, radio announcers, or other public celebrities who exhibit distinguishing mannerisms — vocal as well as physical — that are unique, distinctive personality traits. Explore the new and original performance impulses that now surface as you abandon your own habitual patterns of voice and movement in a "star search" interpretation of Eugene Ionesco's sample playscript *The Gap*. Don't forget to focus attention on an expressive, explicit *visual* as well as *vocal* portrait of the famous personalities as well!

SAMPLE REHEARSAL PLAYSCRIPT

from *The Gap*©

Eugene Ionesco

This brief, but complete, playscript by Eugene Ionesco is an excellent example of the "early" absurdist vision of a world in which mankind is hopelessly adrift with no apparent meaning or purpose in life. It is typical of those absurdist comedies that call attention to solitary figures, focus attention on the struggle to regain a sense of personal identity, and direct attention to the mysterious truth of existing and existence itself. As a sample rehearsal playscript, it is a fun example of a simple story that is capable of a number of inventive interpretations depending upon the point of view of the performer or the specific goals and objectives spelled out in the selected exercises and improvisations. Repeated reference to the characters, the setting, and the given circumstances described in this brief playscript should provide the actors with a solid, consistent reference point to evaluate their own progress and achievements in the rehearsal period. When used effectively and efficiently, this sample rehearsal playscript is capable of enriching the actors' ability to translate specific performance goals and objectives into unmistakably stimulating character interpretations that reveal distinctive technique and distinguished style.

1   ***THE SCENE:*** A rich, bourgeois living room with artistic
2   pretensions. One or two sofas, a number of armchairs,
3   among which, a green, Regency style one, right in the
4   middle of the room. The walls are covered with framed
5   diplomas. One can make out, written in heavy script at
6   the top of a particularly large one, "Doctor Honoris
7   causa." This is followed by an almost illegible Latin
8   inscription. Another equally impressive diploma states:
9   "Doctorat honoris causa," again followed by a long, illeg-
10 ible text. There is an abundance of smaller diplomas,
11 each of which bears a clearly written "doctorate." A door
12 to the right of the audience.
13   As the curtain rises, one can see the Academician's
14 Wife dressed in a rather crumpled robe. She has obvi-
15 ously just gotten out of bed, and has not had time to
16 dress. The Friend faces her. He is well-dressed: hat,
17 umbrella in hand, stiff collar, black jacket and striped
18 trousers, with shiny black shoes.
19
20 WIFE: **Dear friend, tell me all.**
21 FRIEND: **I don't know what to say.**
22 WIFE: **I know.**
23 FRIEND: **I heard the news last night. I did not want to call**
24 **you. At the same time I couldn't wait any longer.**
25 **Please forgive me for coming so early with such**
26 **terrible news.**
27 WIFE: **He didn't make it! How terrible! We were still**
28 **hoping...**
29 FRIEND: **It's hard, I know. He still had a chance. Not much**
30 **of one. We had to expect it.**
31 WIFE: **I didn't expect it. He was always so successful. He**
32 **could always manage somehow, at the last moment.**
33 FRIEND: **In that state of exhaustion. You shouldn't have**
34 **let him!**

1   WIFE: What can we do, what can we do! How awful!

2   FRIEND: Come on, dear friend, be brave. That's life.

3   WIFE: I feel faint: I'm going to faint. *(She falls in one of the*

4   *armchairs.)*

5   FRIEND: *(Holding her, gently slapping her cheeks and hands)*

6   I shouldn't have blurted it out like that. I'm sorry.

7   WIFE: No, you were right to do so. I had to find out

8   somehow or other.

9   FRIEND: I should have prepared you, carefully.

10   WIFE: I've got to be strong. I can't help thinking of him,

11   the wretched man. I hope they won't put it in the

12   papers. Can we count on the journalists' discretion?

13   FRIEND: Close your door. Don't answer the telephone. It

14   will still get around. You could go to the country. In a

15   couple of months, when you are better, you'll come

16   back, you'll go on with your life. People forget such

17   things.

18   WIFE: People won't forget so fast. That's what they're all

19   waiting for. Some friends will feel sorry, but the

20   others, the others... *(The ACADEMICIAN comes in, fully*

21   *dressed: uniform, chest covered with decorations, his*

22   *sword at his side.)*

23   ACADEMICIAN: Up so early, my dear? *(To the FRIEND)*

24   You've come early too. What's happening? Do you

25   have the final results?

26   WIFE: What a disgrace!

27   FRIEND: You mustn't crush him like this, dear friend. *(To*

28   *the ACADEMICIAN)* You have failed.

29   ACADEMICIAN: Are you quite sure?

30   FRIEND: You should never have tried to pass the

31   baccalaureate examination.

32   ACADEMICIAN: They failed me. The rats! How dare they

33   do this to me!

34   FRIEND: The marks were posted late in the evening.

1   ACADEMICIAN: Perhaps it was difficult to make them out
2   in the dark. How could you read them?
3   FRIEND: They had set up spotlights.
4   ACADEMICIAN: They're doing everything to ruin me.
5   FRIEND: I passed by in the morning; the marks were still
6   up.
7   ACADEMICIAN: You could have bribed the concierge into
8   pulling them down.
9   FRIEND: That's exactly what I did. Unfortunately, the
10   police were there. Your name heads the list of those
11   who failed. Everyone's standing in line to get a look.
12   There's an awful crush.
13   ACADEMICIAN: Who's there? The parents of the candi-
14   dates?
15   FRIEND: Not only they.
16   WIFE: All your rivals, all your colleagues must be there.
17   All those you attacked in the press for ignorance: your
18   undergraduates, your graduate students, all those
19   you failed when you were chairman of the board of
20   examiners.
21   ACADEMICIAN: I am discredited! But I won't let them.
22   There must be some mistake.
23   FRIEND: I saw the examiners. I spoke with them. They
24   gave me your marks. Zero in mathematics.
25   ACADEMICIAN: I had no scientific training.
26   FRIEND: Zero in Greek, zero in Latin.
27   WIFE: *(To her husband)* You, a humanist, the spokesman
28   for humanism, the author of that famous treatise
29   "The Defense of Poesy and Humanism."
30   ACADEMICIAN: I beg your pardon, but my book concerns
31   itself with twentieth-century humanism. *(To the*
32   *FRIEND)* What about composition? What grade did I
33   get in composition?
34   FRIEND: Nine hundred. You have nine hundred points.

1   ACADEMICIAN: That's perfect. My average must be all the
2   way up.
3   FRIEND: Unfortunately not. They're marking on the basis
4   of two thousand. The passing grade is one thousand.
5   ACADEMICIAN: They must have changed the regulations.
6   WIFE: They didn't change them just for you. You have a
7   frightful persecution complex.
8   ACADEMICIAN: I tell you, they changed them.
9   FRIEND: They went back to the old ones, back to the time
10   of Napoleon.
11   ACADEMICIAN: Utterly outmoded. Besides, when did they
12   make those changes? It isn't legal. I'm chairman of
13   the Baccalaureate Commission of the Ministry of
14   Public Education. They didn't consult me, and they
15   cannot make any changes without my approval. I'm
16   going to expose them. I'm going to bring government
17   charges against them.
18   WIFE: Darling, you don't know what you're doing. You're
19   in your dotage. Don't you recall handing in your
20   resignation just before taking the examinations so
21   that no one could doubt the complete objectivity of
22   the board of examiners?
23   ACADEMICIAN: I'll take it back.
24   WIFE: You should never have taken that test. I warned
25   you. After all, it's not as if you needed it. But you have
26   to collect all the honors, don't you? You're never satis-
27   fied. What did you need this diploma for? Now all is
28   lost. You have your Doctorate, your Master's, your
29   high school diploma, your elementary school certifi-
30   cate, and even the first part of the baccalaureate.
31   ACADEMICIAN: There was a gap.
32   WIFE: No one suspected it.
33   ACADEMICIAN: But *I* knew it. Others might have found
34   out. I went to the office of the Registrar and asked for

1   a transcript of my record. They said to me: Certainly,
2   Professor, Mr. President, Your Excellency...". Then
3   they looked up my file, and the Chief Registrar came
4   back looking embarrassed indeed. He said: "There's
5   something peculiar, very peculiar. You have your
6   Master's, certainly, but it's no longer valid." I asked
7   him why, of course. He answered: "There's a gap
8   behind your Master's. I don't know how it happened.
9   You must have registered and been accepted at the
10   University without having passed the second part of
11   the baccalaureate examination."
12 FRIEND: And then?
13 WIFE: Your Master's degree is no longer valid?
14 ACADEMICIAN: No, not quite. It's suspended. "The dupli
15   cate you are asking for will be delivered to you upon
16   completion of the baccalaureate. Of course you will
17   pass the examination with no trouble." That's what I
18   was told, so you see now that I had to take it.
19 FRIEND: Your husband, dear friend, wanted to fill the
20   gap. He's a conscientious person.
21 WIFE: It's clear you don't know him as I do. That's not it at
22   all. He wants fame, honors. He never has enough.
23   What does one diploma more or less matter? No one
24   notices them anyway, but he sneaks in at night, on
25   tiptoe, into the living room, just to look at them, and
26   count them.
27 ACADEMICIAN: What else can I do when I have insomnia?
28 FRIEND: The questions asked at the baccalaureate are
29   usually known in advance. You were admirably situ-
30   ated to get this particular information. You could also
31   have sent in a replacement to take the test for you.
32   One of your students, perhaps. Or if you wanted to
33   take the test without people realizing that you
34   already knew the questions, you could have sent your

1   maid to the black market, where one can buy them.

2   ACADEMICIAN: I don't understand how I could have

3   failed in my composition. I filled three sheets of

4   paper. I treated the subject fully, taking into account

5   the historical background. I interpreted the situation

6   accurately...at least plausibly. I didn't deserve a bad

7   grade.

8   FRIEND: Do you recall the subject?

9   ACADEMICIAN: Hum...let's see...

10   WIFE: He doesn't even remember what he discussed.

11   ACADEMICIAN: I do...wait...hum.

12   FRIEND: The subject to be treated was the following:

13   "Discuss the influence of Renaissance painters on

14   novelists of the Third Republic." I have here a photo-

15   static copy of your examination paper. Here is what

16   you wrote.

17   ACADEMICIAN: *(Grabbing the photostat and reading)* "The

18   trial of Benjamin: After Benjamin was tried and

19   acquitted, the assessors holding a different opinion

20   from that of the President murdered him, and

21   condemned Benjamin to the suspension of his civic

22   rights, imposing on him a fine of nine hundred

23   francs..."

24   FRIEND: That's where the nine hundred points come

25   from.

26   ACADEMICIAN: "Benjamin appealed his case...Benjamin

27   appealed his case..." I can't make out the rest. I've

28   always had bad handwriting. I ought to have taken a

29   typewriter along with me.

30   WIFE: Horrible handwriting, scribbling and crossing out;

31   ink spots didn't help you much.

32   ACADEMICIAN: *(Goes on with his reading after having*

33   *retrieved the text his wife had pulled out of his hand.)*

34   "Benjamin appealed his case. Flanked by policemen

1   dressed in zouave uniforms...in zouave uniforms..."
2   It's getting dark. I can't see the rest...I don't have my
3   glasses.
4 WIFE: What you've written has nothing to do with the
5   subject.
6 FRIEND: Your wife's quite right, friend. It has nothing to
7   do with the subject.
8 ACADEMICIAN: Yes, it has. Indirectly.
9 FRIEND: Not even indirectly.
10 ACADEMICIAN: Perhaps I chose the second question.
11 FRIEND: There was only one.
12 ACADEMICIAN: Even if there was only that one, I treated
13   another quite adequately. I went to the end of the
14   story. I stressed the important points, explaining the
15   motivations of the characters, highlighting their
16   behavior. I explained the mystery, making it plain and
17   clear. There was even a conclusion at the end. I can't
18   make out the rest. *(To the FRIEND)* Can you read it?
19 FRIEND: It's illegible. I don't have any glasses either.
20 WIFE: *(Taking the text)* It's illegible and I have excellent
21   eyes. You pretended to write. Mere scribbling.
22 ACADEMICIAN: That's not true. I've even provided a
23   conclusion. It's clearly marked here in heavy print.
24   "Conclusion or sanction...Conclusion or sanction..."
25   They can't get away with it. I'll have this examination
26   rendered null and void.
27 WIFE: Since you treated the wrong subject, and treated it
28   badly, setting down only titles, and writing in
29   between, the mark you received is justified. You'd
30   lose your case.
31 FRIEND: You'd most certainly lose. Drop it. Take a
32   vacation.
33 ACADEMICIAN: You're always on the side of the others.
34 WIFE: After all, these professors know what they're doing.

1   They haven't been granted their rank for nothing.
2   They passed examinations, received serious training.
3   They know the rules of composition.
4 ACADEMICIAN: Who was on the board of examiners?
5 FRIEND: For mathematics, a movie star. For Greek, one of
6   the Beatles. For Latin, the champion of the automo-
7   bile race, and many others.
8 ACADEMICIAN: But these people aren't any more quali-
9   fied than I am. And for composition?
10 FRIEND: A woman, a secretary in the editorial division of
11   the review *Yesterday, the Day Before, and Today.*
12 ACADEMICIAN: Now I know. This wretch gave me a poor
13   grade out of spite because I never joined her political
14   party. It's an act of vengeance. But I have ways and
15   means of rendering the examination null and void.
16   I'm going to call the President.
17 WIFE: Don't! You'll make yourself look even more ridicu-
18   lous. *(To the FRIEND)* Please try to restrain him. He
19   listens to you more than to me. *(The FRIEND shrugs his*
20   *shoulders, unable to cope with the situation. The WIFE*
21   *turns to her HUSBAND, who has just lifted the receiver*
22   *off the hook.)* Don't call!
23 ACADEMICIAN: *(On the telephone)* Hello, John? It is
24   I...What? What did you say? But listen, my dear
25   friend...but listen to me. Hello! Hello! *(Puts down the*
26   *receiver.)*
27 FRIEND: What did he say?
28 ACADEMICIAN: He said...He said..."I don't want to talk to
29   you. My mummy won't let me make friends with boys
30   at the bottom of the class." Then he hung up on me.
31 WIFE: You should have expected it. All is lost. How could
32   you do this to me? How could you do this to me?
33 ACADEMICIAN: Think of it! I lectured at the Sorbonne, at
34   Oxford, at American universities. Ten thousand

1   theses have been written on my work; hundreds of
2   critics have analyzed it. I hold an *honoris causa*
3   doctorate from Amsterdam as well as a secret univer-
4   sity Chair with the Duchy of Luxembourg. I received
5   the Nobel Prize three times. The King of Sweden
6   himself was amazed by my erudition. A doctorate
7   *honoris causa, honoris causa*...and I failed the
8   baccalaureate examination!
9   **WIFE:** Everyone will laugh at us! *(The ACADEMICIAN takes*
10   *off his sword and breaks it on his knee.)*
11   **FRIEND:** *(Picking up the two pieces)* **I wish to preserve**
12   **these in memory of our ancient glory.** *(The ACADEMI*
13   *CIAN, meanwhile in a fit of rage, is tearing down his*
14   *decorations, throwing them on the floor, stepping on*
15   *them.)*
16   **WIFE:** *(Trying to salvage the remains)* **Don't do this! Don't!**
17   **That's all we've got left!**
18
19
20
21
22
23
24
25
26
27
28
29
30
31
32
33
34

ABOUT THE AUTHOR

Gerald Lee Ratliff has been an active member of the academic and artistic community at both the state and national levels for more than twenty years. An author of numerous books and articles in performance studies, literature, and dramatic theory, he has served as President of the Eastern Communication Association and Theta Alpha Phi, the national theatre honorary fraternity. National board memberships have included the Association for Communication Administration, American Council of Academic Deans, Society of Educators and Scholars, and the International Arts Association.

He was awarded the "Distinguished Service Award" from both the Eastern Communication Association and Theta Alpha Phi. In 1990, he was a Fulbright scholar to China and in 1991 was a delegate of the John F. Kennedy Center for the Performing Arts to the Soviet Union.

In addition to writing textbooks, position papers, and study guides in a wide range of liberal arts subjects, he teaches Readers Theatre, dramatic criticism, theatre history, and interdisciplinary approaches to the arts.

Order Form

Meriwether Publishing Ltd.
P. O. Box 7710
Colorado Springs, CO 80933
Telephone: (719) 594-4422
Website: www.meriwetherpublishing.com

Please send me the following books:

_____ **Playing Contemporary Scenes #BK-B100** $16.95
edited by Gerald Lee Ratliff
Thirty-one famous scenes and how to play them

_____ **The Theatre Audition Book #BK-B224** $14.95
by Gerald Lee Ratliff
*Playing monologs from contemporary, modern,
period and classical plays*

_____ **Playing Scenes — A Sourcebook for** $14.95
Performers #BK-B109
by Gerald Lee Ratliff
How to play great scenes from modern and classical theatre

_____ **Theatre Alive #BK-B178** $29.95
by Dr. Norman A. Bert
An introductory anthology of world drama

_____ **The Scenebook for Actors #BK-B177** $15.95
by Dr. Norman A. Bert
Collection of great monologs and dialogs for auditions

_____ **Theatre Games and Beyond #BK-B217** $15.95
by Amiel Schotz
A creative approach for performers

_____ **One-Act Plays for Acting Students #BK-B159** $16.95
by Dr. Norman A. Bert
An anthology of complete one-act plays

These and other fine Meriwether Publishing books are available at
your local bookstore or direct from the publisher. Use the handy
order form on this page.

Name: _____

Organization name: _____

Address: _____

City:_____ State:_____

Zip: _____ Phone: _____

❑ **Check Enclosed**
❑ **Visa or MasterCard #** _____

Signature: _____ *Expiration
Date:* _____
(required for Visa/MasterCard orders)

COLORADO RESIDENTS: Please add 3% sales tax.
SHIPPING: Include $2.75 for the first book and 50¢ for each additional book ordered.

❑ *Please send me a copy of your complete catalog of books and plays.*